**THE PREACHING LIBRARY
VOLUME ONE**

**PREACHING THROUGH THE YEAR**

by Steve May

## ALSO BY STEVE MAY

### BOOKS
*Sermons for Seekers*
*The Story File*
*Preaching Through the Year*
*Preaching Matthew*
*Preaching Peter and Paul*
*Preaching in Series*
*Sermons for Growing Christians*
*Sixty Sermons*

### COMPACT DISCS
*The Preaching Library Complete Collection*

### WEBSITES
*AboutSunday.com*
*ProjectBrasil.com*
*SteveMay.com*

**PREACHING THROUGH THE YEAR**

Preaching Through the Year

First Printing 2006

© 2006 by Steve May

ISBN : 9780615444420

Unless otherwise noted, scripture quotations from each message are taken from the *Holy Bible New International Version*, NIV. Copyright © 1973, 1978, 1984 by International Bible Society. Used by permission of Zondervan Publishing House. All rights reserved.

Scripture quotations identified NASV are from the *New American Standard Bible*, ©The Lockman Foundation, 1960, 1962, 1963, 1968, 1971, 1972, 1973, 1975, 1977. Used by permission.

Scripture quotations identified NLT are from the Holy Bible, New Living Translation, copyright © 1996. Used by permission of Tyndale House Publishers, Inc., Wheaton, Illinois 60189. All rights reserved.

Scripture quotations identified NRSV are taken from the New Revised Standard Version of the Bible, copyright © 1989, Division of Christian Education of the National Council of Churches of Christ in the United States of America. Used by permission. All rights reserved.

Scripture quotations identified KJV are from the *King James Version* of the Bible.

All rights reserved. No part of this publication may be reproduced, stored in a retrieval system or transmitted in any form or by any means — electronic, mechanical, photocopy, recording, or any other — without the prior written permission of the publisher. The only exception is brief quotations in printed reviews, or for use in a local church setting.

For more information on the teaching ministry of Steve May, visit www.stevemay.com

Published by Alderson Press
212 Harts Bridge Road
Jackson TN 38301

Printed in the United States of America

**SERIES: MAKE YOUR LIFE A MASTERPIECE**

1. What Do You Think Of Yourself?...................................................................5
Ephesians 3:1-12

2. What To Do When There's Nothing You Can Do.................................11
Isaiah 43:1-7

3. Life In The Spirit............................................................................................17
1 Corinthians 12:1-7

4. The Power To Change Your Life ...............................................................23
Psalm 19

**SERIES: 24/7 — ROUND THE CLOCK CHRISTIANITY**

5. Taking God As Your Partner......................................................................31
Psalm 127

6. Getting Your Day Off To A Great Start ...................................................35
Psalm 5

7. Dealing With The Distractions Of Day-To-Day Life ............................41
Psalm 55

8. What To Do When God Seems Far Away .............................................47
Psalm 13

**SERIES: HOW CAN I BE GOOD?**

9. Winning The War On Sin: .........................................................................53
Romans 6:1-23

10. Make Up Your Mind To Be Holy .............................................................61
Romans 8:1-17

11. We're More Than Conquerors ................................................................67
Romans 8:26-39

**GENERAL MESSAGES**

12. What To Do When You've Blown It.......................................................73
Psalm 51

13. The Significance Of Easter .....................................................................79
Mark 16:1-8

14. It Doesn't Matter Who You Used To Be
1 Timothy 1:12-14................................................................................................85

**SERIES: THE FAMILY CIRCLE**

15. How To Develop A Tight-Knit Family .................................................................. 91
John 10:22-30

16. How To Rear Excruciatingly Perfect Children ..................................................... 97
John 14:23-24

17. How To Influence Your Family .......................................................................... 103
Acts 16:16-34

18. Treat Your Mate To A Better Marriage............................................................... 109
Genesis 2:18-24

19. A Mother's Faith.................................................................................................. 117
John 2:1-11

20. A Father's Love................................................................................................... 125
Luke 15:11-24

21. What Does God Want Me To Do? ..................................................................... 133
2 Thessalonians 1:11-12

**SERIES: SOUL SURVIVOR**

22. Jesus Loves Me This I Know ............................................................................. 141
1 John 5:9-13

23. Come Holy Spirit ................................................................................................ 149
Ezekiel 37:1-14

24. The Heart Of Worship ........................................................................................ 157
Isaiah 6:1-8

25. When The Storms Of Life Are Raging............................................................... 165
Psalm 107:23-32

**GENERAL MESSAGES**

26. A Lesson In Forgiveness .................................................................................... 173
Luke 7:36-50

27. Dealing With Difficult People............................................................................ 181
Luke 12:57-59

28. How To Treat A Mistreater ................................................................................ 187
Genesis 45:1-15

29. Eliminating Envy ................................................................................................ 197
Psalm 37

30. Peace For A Troubled Heart ........................................................... 205
Psalm 4

31. The Answer To Worry .................................................................. 211
Philippians 4:4-7

32. How To Attack Panic .................................................................. 217
Psalm 31

33. Getting A Handle On Happiness ................................................. 223
Isaiah 55:1-5

34. Becoming A Team Player ........................................................... 231
Ephesians 4:2

35. Living In The Zone ...................................................................... 239
John 15:1-8

36. Six Things Every Leader Must Forget ........................................ 245
Numbers 11:4-34

37. The Search For Significance ...................................................... 253
1 Corinthians 9:24-27

38. Dealing With Doubts .................................................................. 257
John 20:19-31

39. Living In A Material World .......................................................... 265
Luke 12:13-21

40. The State Of The Heart .............................................................. 273
Jeremiah 17:9-10

**SERIES: PRAYER: THE ULTIMATE LIFESTYLE**

41. How To Develop a Prayer Lifestyle ............................................ 281
1 Thessalonians 5:17

42. Guidelines to Answered Prayer .................................................. 289
Various Texts

43. How To Pray For Yourself .......................................................... 297
Various Texts

44. How To Pray For Anyone and Everyone .................................... 305
Philippians 1:3-11

45. Learning How To Ask In Faith .................................................... 313
Mark 10:46-52

46. The Key To Praying With Power ............................................................. 319
Luke 18:1-8

**SERIES: HANGING ON THROUGH HARD TIMES**

47. It's A Good Thing You've Got Problems ............................................... 323
Joshua 3:7-17

48. How To Avoid Burnout ......................................................................... 327
Exodus 20:9-11

49. Dealing With Discouragement ............................................................. 332
John 20:1-18

50. Crisis Management .............................................................................. 337
1 Samuel 17

51. When You've Got Problems That Can't Be Solved ............................. 345
1 Peter 1:3-9

**THANKSGIVING SERMON**

52. Becoming A Giver ................................................................................ 351
2 Corinthians 9:6-15

**SERIES: A SIMPLE CHRISTMAS**

53. A Christmas List For Family And Friends ............................................ 359
1 Thessalonians 3:9-13

54. How To Beat The Holiday Blues .......................................................... 365
Luke 1:68-79

55. How To Give Christmas Gifts All Year Long ........................................ 371
Matthew 2:1-12

56. What Christmas Is All About ................................................................ 375
Micah 5:4-5

*Don't you know, young man, that from every town and every village and every hamlet in England, wherever it may be, there is a road that leads to London?*

*So from every text in scripture there is a road towards the great metropolis, Christ. And my dear brother, your business is, when you get to a text, to say, now what is the road that leads to Christ?*

*The sermon cannot do any good unless there is a savor of Christ in it.*

—Charles Spurgeon

SERIES: MAKE YOUR LIFE A MASTERPIECE
# WHAT DO YOU THINK OF YOURSELF?
EPHESIANS 3:1-12

Today is the first Sunday of the New Year, and if you listen carefully, you can hear the sound of resolutions breaking as we speak. That's what happens to the majority of resolutions the first week of January. Some, however, are being kept even today; and for some of you, your presence here proves that. Congratulations. It's a great way to start the New Year—with a commitment to come to church.

New Year's Resolutions are a great idea. We should make them every year, every month, every week, or as often as we need. One of God's greatest gifts is the gift of the second chance. He gives us a fresh start when we need one—and without exception we all need a fresh start from time to time.

The Apostle Paul needed a second chance, too. When we look at him from this side of history we often see only the good that he did. He wrote most of the New Testament, he started churches throughout the world, and he helped shape human history. Today he's called *Saint* Paul—and many churches are named after him—but the fact is that there was a time in his life when he was anything but a saint. In those days his name was Saul, and he was, in fact, quite a rascal. By his own admission he was an enemy of God and an enemy of the Christian faith. He persecuted Christians and did all he could to stop the growth of the church. Then suddenly his life changed.

He was walking on the road to Damascus one day when a bright light from heaven overtook him and a voice spoke to him, saying *"Saul, why are you persecuting me?"* He asked *"Who are you?"* The voice responded, *"I am Jesus of Nazareth, the one you are persecuting."* From that day on, Paul was a new man. He wasn't perfect—he still struggled with sin—but his life took on a new direction, and the world hasn't been the same since.

Today we are beginning a new series called *Make Your Life a Masterpiece*. Over the next four weeks we'll look at several things we can do to make the process of living more beautiful, more enjoyable, and more rewarding. The first message focuses on our reason for living. We make New Year's Resolutions because we want this year to be better than last year. Too often though, our resolutions are surface level and don't address the real source of the problem. Today I will challenge you all to make a resolution that will start a revolution in the world you live in. The resolution is to adopt the same attitude as Paul: *I am not an important person, but I have an important job to do.* If any phrase could sum up Paul's life, this is it. There are three things we need to keep in mind as we strive to live according to this resolution. First of all...

- **Live with a sense of purpose.**

Have you ever seen Bruce Springsteen in concert? He's all but retired now, but in the 80's he was one of the hardest working people in the entertainment business. His concerts typically last 4 hours—and whether he is playing to 20,000 people in an outdoor arena, or just a few hundred people in a small room, he gives 100% of himself to every performance. The encore alone lasts 45 minutes. At one point in every performance the band dramatically stops playing and Springsteen shouts into the microphone, "I'm just a prisoner of rock and roll!"

You know what? He *is* a prisoner of rock and roll. All his life he's been obsessed with playing music. Nothing could stand in his way. Once in the early days he attended the wedding of a fellow struggling musician. Bruce said to his friend, "I'm happy for you, but I'm sad—you'll never be able to make it now that you're married."

Springsteen pursued his career in music with unbridled enthusiasm, and ultimately became the biggest name in rock music. Only then did he decide to settle down, get married, and start a family. Till that moment, he gave his life to rock and roll. In the very same way, Paul gave his life to preaching the gospel.

In Romans Paul referred to himself as the *bondservant* or *slave* of Christ. In Ephesians he called himself *the prisoner of the Lord*. In verse 7: *I became a servant of this gospel...*

Paul was consumed with a mission. And I want you to understand that it was a radical mission. His purpose in life wasn't just to be a religious person and preach in church on Sunday. His purpose was much more innovative, much more dangerous, much more revolutionary than that. His purpose was save souls, change lives, and bring about worldwide racial equality through the ministry of the church. Look at verse 6...*through the gospel the Gentiles are heirs together with Israel, members together of one body, and sharers together in the promise of Jesus Christ.*

Paul was Jewish. Like most Jewish men of his time, he was raised to believe there are two types of people in the world: Jews, who are God's chosen people, and everyone else. In the early days of the church, many Jewish Christians would have been content to let Christianity remain exclusively Jewish. Paul couldn't do it, though. After his face-to-face meeting with Jesus, he recognized that he had a purpose in life: to bring Gentiles into the Christian faith. This made Paul unpopular in certain circles, but he never lost sight of his mission.

What about you? What's your mission? God has given you a purpose. Your purpose wasn't created to serve you—you were created to serve your purpose. The greatest resolution you can make this year is to decide "I will be a slave to the purpose God has for my life." We need to get past the idea that we need—or deserve—an easy life. Instead, our attitude must be: *I am not an important person, but I have an important job to do.* In order for us to do this, it requires that we...

- **Live with a sense of humility.**

Paul says some surprising things about himself. Undoubtedly one of the greatest men this world has seen, yet he spoke of himself in rather harsh terms. In 1 Timothy he called himself *the chief of all sinners*. In Romans 7 he referred to himself as a *wretched, sinful man*. And in today's passage he says...*(v. 8) I am less than the least of all God's people.* .Now the fact is, theologically speaking, Paul knew this statement was inaccurate. He knew that everyone is equal in God's eyes. Equality was the heart of his message. He knew that God shows no partiality and he knew that he himself was no worse than anyone else. Yet, he chose to view himself from this perspective because it was necessary for him to keep his ego in check. He would not allow himself to become too important in his own eyes.

Paul was like us. Our tendency is to act as if the alphabet begins with the letter "I". Our tendency is to act as if we're the center of the universe. So Paul challenges us to see ourselves a different way. *I'm not an important person, but I have an important job to do.*

A few years ago a religious magazine published an issue on the subject of racism. To give readers an idea of what it's like to be the object of discrimination, they sent photocopies to each subscriber, with a letter explaining that they had inadvertently printed too few magazines this issue. The letter said that the limited quantity of printed copies went to top priority subscribers, so the recipient would have to accept this lesser-quality photocopy. Of course, all readers got the photocopied issue, but many of them didn't get the point. The magazine's office was flooded with complaints. One pastor wrote a letter saying, "I have never been treated with such disrespect. I demand a written apology." Sometimes we forget to live with a sense of humility.

In his book *The Winner Within*, Pat Riley, former coach of the Los Angeles Lakers, talks about the danger of the "Disease of Me." He tells how the Lakers' out-of-control egos brought about one of the quickest falls in the history of the NBA. They won the Championship in 1980 and they were predicted to do it again the following season. Then resentment set in among the players. Some thought Magic Johnson got too much attention from the media. Kareem Abdul Jabbar believed that he was being snubbed by other players. Some players believed they weren't getting the recognition they deserved. As a result, the Lakers shifted their focus from winning to whining. And the following season they got beat in the first playoff round. This is the ultimate humiliation for a reigning champ; it had happened only twice before in NBA history. Riley summed it up by saying, "The Disease of Me leads to the Defeat of Us." When we put our egos ahead of our responsibilities we lose—and lose big. This is why we must adopt Paul's attitude: *I am not an important person, but I have an important job to do.* This is living with a sense of humility. The third principle...

- **Live with a sense of wonder.**

In 1982 Kenneth Blanchard co-wrote a little book called *The One Minute Manager*. The book was a huge success, ending up on the New York Times best-seller list and selling millions of copies. Overnight, Blanchard became a celebrity in the business world. Later, he said that during this time he realized that he had two choices. One was to take all the credit for his success and assume that he was a better writer and more insightful thinker than anyone else. The other was to take the path of wonderment. He asked himself "Why has this happened to me, and what can I learn from it?" As an observer of his own success, he was better able to manage the pitfalls and challenges that came with it.

Paul lived his life with a sense of wonder. He said...*(v. 2) Surely you have heard about the administration of God's grace that was given to me for you...(v. 7) I became a servant of this gospel by the gift of God's grace given me through the working of his power.*

Paul repeatedly used a certain word to describe God's work in his life. Grace. Grace means, literally, an undeserved gift. Paul didn't fool himself into thinking that he was doing God a favor by being his servant. He had a sense of wonder about the calling God had placed on his life.

There are two temptations we must learn to resist. The first is *smugness*—thinking that God is lucky to have us on his team. The second is *self-pity*—complaining about our lot in life and the limitations we must face. In many ways life seems to be unfair.

Some are born rich, some are born poor. Some have talent, some don't. Some are born handsome, some look like me. As we examine our lives, we need to maintain a sense of wonder about us. We need to ask, "Why did God place me in this time, this place, this situation? What can I learn from it and what does he expect me to do about it?"

We can expect some big wins and big losses throughout life. That's part of being human. Dean Smith, the legendary basketball coach, once said, "If you make every game a life and death situation, you'll be dead a lot." Our challenge is to accept the events in our lives with a sense of wonder—and seek to learn what God is teaching us in each one.

## CONCLUSION

God has put you here for a purpose. If you're willing, God can use you for his glory. It requires taking yourself off the throne and giving him his rightful place. It requires focusing your attention on doing the work he has called you to do. This can be your best year ever. It can be the year that your life becomes a masterpiece—if you adopt the attitude that says, *I'm not an important person, but I have an important job to do—and by God's grace I will do it.*

*SERIES: MAKE YOUR LIFE A MASTERPIECE*
**WHAT TO DO WHEN THERE'S NOTHING YOU CAN DO**
ISAIAH 43:1-7

Have you ever watched PBS's *The Joy of Painting* with Bob Ross? Bob was the textbook definition of laid back. He had a favorite saying: "There are no mistakes in painting—only happy accidents." If you accidentally splatter a big blob of orange paint across the middle of a mountain scene he would tell you not to throw away the canvas. Instead, he would advise you to incorporate that "happy accident" into your painting, work around it, and keep on creating your "masterpiece".

In the same way, as you strive to make your life a masterpiece, you experience many accidents—but if you're like me, "happy" isn't how you want to describe them. There are times when you lose someone close to you, or when you struggle with your health, or when you have problems at work. Blobs end up on your canvas that you never intended to be there. When this happens, what should you do? Throw away the canvas? Give up? Forget about having a great life? That may sound tempting, but there's a better way.

Psychiatrist Victor Frankl knows from experience how desperate you feel when circumstances beyond your control take over. During World War II he was arrested and placed in a German concentration camp. He was separated from his wife, his possessions were seized, and he was tossed in a cell. In the process of enduring unspeakable horror in this death camp, he developed an approach to life that has helped many who are facing tragedy.

After the war Frankl wrote a book called *Man's Search for Meaning*. He tells the story of an elderly man who had struggled with severe depression since the death of his wife. He had loved her above all else, and he missed her terribly. Frankl asked the man, "What would have happened if you had died first, and your wife would have had to survive you?" The man said, "Oh, for her this would have been terrible; how she would have suffered!" Frankl then said, "Such suffering has been spared her, and it was you who spared her this suffering—at the price that you now have to mourn her death." The man left Frankl's office that day changed. His situation wasn't changed—he was still alone and his wife was still gone—but his attitude toward his situation had changed.

Your attitude is your most powerful weapon. There may be times when it is the only resource you have, but it can get you through anything life sends your way. From the book of Isaiah, here are three promises that will strengthen your attitude when circumstances overwhelm you. First of all, remember that...

- **You belong to God.**

Isaiah 43:1-2 states that it was God who created you, it was God who formed you, it was God who redeemed you, and it is God who calls you by name. Then, in verse 2 God speaks directly through Isaiah, saying..."*You are mine.*"

You belong to God. Jesus Christ came into this world and died on the cross for your sins. The Bible teaches that through his death you were bought and paid for, and you now belong to him. [Acts 20:28; Revelation 5:9] You belong to God, and he takes it seriously. He gave his Son so you could be his. Don't make the mistake of thinking that God's commitment to you is only as strong as your commitment to him.

You may fail from time to time, you may have a hard time keeping your promises, some days your heart may be cold and your faith may be weak. But God doesn't change his mind about us as often as we change our minds about him. As far as he is concerned, you belong to him and that will never change. [see 2 Timothy 2:13]

Sometimes when we go through hard times, we're tempted to think "I'm not a good Christian, I'm not a good person, I don't have great faith—why should God help me?" At these times you must remember what he said: *"You are mine...you belong to me."*

Each football season the Texas Longhorns play the Oklahoma Sooners in the neutral city of Dallas, and thousands of fans from each team invade the city to witness the clash between these two arch rivals. Sometimes the clash extends beyond the playing field. One year a scuffle broke out in the stands and a handful of men were arrested, taken downtown, and required to pay $250 bail. One fan didn't have bail money. All he had was his Neiman Marcus credit card. The judge said, "You can't pay bail with that. You're spending the weekend in jail." When the man made his one phone call, he called the Neiman Marcus store and told them his story. The request made its way up the company ladder until finally a Neiman vice-president said, "This man is one of our customers, we'll help him out." They paid his bail and charged it to his account.

Do you see the loyalty this retailer has for their customers? God's loyalty to you is even greater. You belong to him. When things get out of control, he doesn't turn his back on you.

Do you remember back in 1994 when that young man was arrested for vandalism in Singapore? He was found guilty and sentenced to punishment by "caning" — being whipped with a cane. I won't speculate on whether or not he was guilty, or whether or not the punishment was appropriate — that's not the point. His story made front page news in America — and our president appealed to Singapore authorities for leniency — for one reason: the kid was an American citizen. He belongs to us, and our country went to bat for him.

Remember that you belong to God. He doesn't turn his back on his own. When circumstances are beyond your control, he doesn't say "You're finally getting what you deserve." Instead, he says, "You belong to me." Remember that. Secondly...

- **He protects you every step of the way.**

In August 1955, over a period of just a few days, twelve inches of rain was dumped on Putnam, Connecticut. Nearby runs the Quinebaug River, which was contained at the time by old earth and stone dams. The rain was too much for the dams;

one by one they burst and tons of water came crashing through the town at speeds of twenty five miles per hour. Bridges and roads were destroyed, along with one fourth of the town's businesses and homes. The water poured into a warehouse stocked with barrels of magnesium. As the magnesium came into contact with water, it ignited. The fire department and the rest of the town watched helplessly as barrels exploded, shooting fire 200 feet into the air. The flaming bombs landed on buildings throughout the community and fire spread throughout the town.

It was truly a disaster—the cost of the damage ran into the tens of millions, and it took years to rebuild. In spite of all the damage done to this tiny New England town, not one single person died during the storm. Putnam, Connecticut was consumed with fire and flood, yet everyone was saved. Notice what God promises us through the prophet Isaiah...*(v. 2) When you pass through the waters I will be with you; and when you pass through the rivers they will not sweep over you. When you walk through the fire, you will not be burned; the flames will not set you ablaze...(v. 5) Do not be afraid, for I am with you.*

Isaiah doesn't promise that you will be saved from the fire or the flood. He promises that you'll be protected in the midst of it. He is saying, "You'll face circumstances beyond your control, but God will get you through them."

Some people interpret the fires and the floods as evidence that God has deserted them. Don't believe it. The fires and the floods are evidence only that you are human. Everyone has problems. Jesus said, *"The rain falls on the just and the unjust." (Matthew 5:45)* We all experience tragedy at some time in life. But remember: God is not the source of your problems, he's the solution. He doesn't create misery, he helps you through it. Sometimes we forget that.

Victor Frankl's six year old daughter asked him once why he always referred to God as "the good Lord." He said to her, "Because he is good to us. Remember when you had measles a few weeks ago? He helped you get over them." His daughter said, "Yes, but Daddy, don't forget that he was the one who gave me the measles in the first place." That's a child's perspective; we have the capacity to know better. God doesn't send the crisis, he helps you through it. Thirdly, remember that...

- **Nothing can keep you from reaching your potential.**

Do you know why God created you? *(v. 7) ...everyone who is called by my name, whom I created for my glory.* This is your potential: to glorify God. Too often we often set our sites too low. We see our potential in terms of income and career position. We work for a promotion, a little recognition, a little money, a little comfort—and God has so much more in store for us! His plan is that we live the kind of life that shines a positive light on Jesus Christ for all the world to see.

Dennis Byrd was a man with great potential. He was a professional football player: a defensive end for the New York Jets, an up-and-coming superstar predicted to help turn the Jets organization around. Then tragedy struck. On November 29, 1992, the Jets were playing the Kansas City Chiefs. Dennis was about to sack the quarterback when he collided with a teammate and his spinal cord was snapped. In a split-second his football career ended. He was paralyzed from the neck down. All his hopes and dreams came to a screeching halt. Later he wrote about waking up in the middle of the night at Lenox Hospital in a halo brace, not knowing where he was, not knowing why he couldn't move, not knowing what was happening. Suddenly he went from dreaming of making it to the Pro Bowl to hoping he could someday hold his daughter in his arms again.

From the world's perspective, Dennis was no longer able to reach his potential. But in God's eyes, this man is capable of more than sacking quarterbacks. In God's eyes, Dennis Byrd is capable of giving Him glory. And Dennis has done that in a tremendous way. The world watched and listened as he told the media that Christ was his source of comfort in his time of tragedy. The doctors announced publicly that Dennis may never walk again, and it would be years before they would know. Dennis announced publicly that with God's help, he would walk soon.

On opening day of the 1993 football season, less than a year after the tragic collision, millions of television viewers watched Dennis Byrd walk out to the middle of the Meadowlands Stadium while 75,000 fans stood cheering in ovation. It was, without question, the highlight of the entire season.

The miracle in Dennis Byrd's life is not that he broke his neck and walked again. The miracle is that the injury that destroyed his career didn't destroy his life. God protected him through the fire and flood. Even though he no longer plays sports he is able to reach his full potential of glorifying God.

A financial setback may prevent you from becoming rich, an illness may prevent you from doing work you love, a tragedy may prevent you from reaching some of your goals—but nothing can prevent you from reaching your true potential. You have the potential to glorify God. That means, simply, that you can show the world how great God is.

There's a difference in the way a nonbeliever and a believer experience tragedy. The nonbeliever is sidelined, his hopes are dashed, and his purpose in may dwindle to nothing. But the believer can keep going, knowing it's not the hand you're dealt that determines your ability to reach your potential—it's your attitude in the process. No matter what happens, you can glorify God. And that's what makes your life a masterpiece.

## CONCLUSION

*In this you greatly rejoice, though now for a little while you may have had to suffer grief in all kinds of trials. These have come so that your faith...may be proved genuine and may result in praise, glory and honor when Jesus Christ is revealed. (1 Peter 1:6-7)*

There are circumstances you can't control, but you are always able to control the most important thing: your attitude. When you get knocked down, your attitude determines how long you stay down and how soon you get back up. So when tough times come your way, let this be your attitude: *No matter what happens, I belong to God.* He will see you through, so that through you, the world may see his glory.

SERIES: *MAKE YOUR LIFE A MASTERPIECE*
**LIFE IN THE SPIRIT**
1 CORINTHIANS 12:1-7

If you want to be overcome with the notion that life is just a hollow series of meaningless events leading toward a miserable conclusion, it isn't hard to do. I'll tell you how. Focus only on the tangible aspect of your existence. Think only about the natural world. Tell yourself that this life is all there is and despair will overtake you before you can say "Carl Sagan."

You are made in such a way that you cannot be satisfied with only the material world. You have a built-in spiritual vacuum that must be filled. This is why all cultures—no matter how remote or primitive—have developed some system of theology. It's in our nature to yearn for something more, something spiritual. Otherwise, what is our purpose for being here?

Paul argued this point. He said if this world is all there is, then Christians are fools and should be pitied above all others. [1 Corinthians 15] If, however, there is more to our existence than the eye can see and the hands can touch, then those who are most to be pitied are those who spend their lives obsessed exclusively with material things. In the end, all they have to show for themselves is a little land, a house, some money in the bank, a nice lawn, a photo album from a couple of good vacations, maybe a time-share, a car, a family portrait in the hall, and that's about it. Even as I read this list, some may nod their heads and say, "Sounds good to me." Although there is absolutely nothing wrong with any of these things, the tragedy is that so many people settle for this exclusively, overlooking the fact that life offers so much more.

Today, we'll consider how to find that "something more." The key is in living a Spirit-filled life. We come alive spiritually through the Holy Spirit. He is the difference that makes a difference in our lives. It's the Holy Spirit that transforms us from being merely religious to being truly spiritual.

Bill Bright, founder for Campus Crusade for Christ, once said "If there were only one truth I could share with the Christian world, it would be 'how to be filled with the Holy Spirit,' for there is no single truth that is more important to the believer." It is impossible to make your life a masterpiece without experiencing the fullness of the Holy Spirit. If your life is being lived in black and white, the Holy Spirit can transform it into living color. Today, we'll talk about how to experience the fullness of the Spirit-filled life. First of all, Paul commands us...

- **Learn more about the Holy Spirit.**

*(v. 1) Now about spiritual gifts, brothers, I do not want you to be ignorant.* The word translated "spiritual gifts" is *pneumatikon*, which can also be translated "things of a spiritual nature" or "things belonging to the Spirit." Paul is saying, "Don't overlook the spiritual side of life. Don't be ignorant of the role the Holy Spirit plays."

There are two mistakes when it comes to spiritual things. The first mistake is to disregard spiritual things altogether with the attitude "If I can't see it, I don't believe it." This person is focused only on the material world and rejects (or is at least uncomfortable with) any reference to the supernatural. This person is likely to say, "Why pray for God to help me? I can get more done by rolling up my sleeves and working hard." This type of person is a "practical atheist." He or she may claim to believe in God, but there is nothing in their personal life that would show any sign of a spiritual pulse.

The other mistake is to embrace everything related to spirituality without any sense of discernment or spiritual perception. There are countless pseudo-spiritual self-help speakers who talk about God and quote scripture in the context of their "success message" — yet there's no real Biblical substance to what they're saying. Those who gulp down this ankle-deep theology often wonder why their spiritual lives seem so empty.

When it comes to living the Spirit-filled life there are a variety of opinions out there, and you can find fanatics on both ends of the spectrum. You need to reach an informed level of balance in your spiritual life so that you aren't tossed around by everyone else's view. This is why Paul says, "Do not be ignorant."

How is balance achieved? The Bible tells everything we need to know about the nature and work of the Holy Spirit. Through the Bible that we learn that the Holy Spirit is not just some Star Wars type of "force"; the Holy Spirit is personal and should be referred to as "he" not "it." Through the Bible we learn how the Holy Spirit speaks to us and gives us direction from day to day. Through the Bible we learn how not to grieve the Spirit, and how to pray through the Spirit. Through the Bible we learn how to experience the fullness of the Holy Spirit. So take Paul's advice. Do not be ignorant about spiritual things. If you want to make your life into a masterpiece—if you want to live in the fullness of the Spirit—begin with a commitment to learn more about the Holy Spirit's work. Be aware of spiritual things. Secondly...

- **Be filled with the Holy Spirit.**

*(v. 13) For we were all baptized by one Spirit into one body...and were all given on Spirit to drink.* We are saved by the blood of Christ. His death on the cross bought our salvation. The Holy Spirit is involved in every aspect of conversion. He convicts us of sin [John 16:9], he calls us to repentance, he leads us to Christ [John 16:13], he regenerates us [Titus 3:5], he gives us assurance of salvation [Romans 8:16].

Now, let's split a theological hair. When you are saved you receive the Holy Spirit—all of the Holy Spirit. When you are filled with the Holy Spirit, that doesn't mean you get more of the Spirit. It means that the Spirit gets more of you. "Being filled" with the Holy Spirit means "being led by" or "controlled by" the Holy Spirit. This is the key to victorious living. Paul said...*So I say, live by the Spirit, and you will not gratify the desires of the sinful nature. (Galatians 5:16)*

The obvious question, then, is "How do I get filled with the Holy Spirit?" Let me warn you: It's difficult. You've got to know the right things, you've got to do the right things, you've got to say the right things. There's a specific process you go through to be filled with the Holy Spirit, and it has to be done exactly right or it won't work at all. Are you ready for me to tell you what it is? Here goes...

*Ask.*

That's it. If you want to be filled with the Holy Spirit, you must ask God to fill you with the Holy Spirit. That's what it takes. You receive the Holy Spirit the same way you receive salvation—through asking. Paul said, *Did you receive the Spirit by observing the law, or by believing what you heard?* (Galatians 3:2)

Making your life a masterpiece is a matter of living in the fullness of the Spirit. Being filled with the Spirit is a matter of asking to be filled and making yourself available to him. Be filled with the Spirit. Thirdly...

- **Discover your spiritual gift and use it.**

*(v. 7) Now to each one the manifestation of the Spirit is given for the common good.* In this section of Corinthians Paul talks at length about spiritual gifts. He mentions several gifts of the Spirit, including a message of wisdom, a message of knowledge, faith, gifts of healing, miraculous powers, prophecy, discernment of spirits, speaking in tongues, interpreting tongues. Many times we get distracted by the "sign gifts" and start arguing until we miss the point Paul is making: everyone has been given a spiritual gift that can be used to serve others.

By the way, this list of spiritual gifts is not exhaustive. Your gift may not be one of the ones mentioned here. In Romans 12 Paul mentions more spiritual gifts, and he adds a few more in Ephesians. Your spiritual gift could be giving, or service, or prophecy, or wisdom, or encouragement, or teaching, or helping, or any number of possibilities. The common characteristic of all spiritual gifts is they build up others. Paul said in verse 7, *...the manifestation of the Spirit is given for the common good.*

Ask yourself "What gift (or gifts) has God given me that I can use to help others?" Gifts are defined by the benefit they give. That's why there's a difference between a talent and a spiritual gift. For example, piano playing isn't a spiritual gift. Lots of people can play the piano. However, the piano player at our church sacrifices two nights a week and every single weekend in order to play in each service. She works very hard for very little money and not nearly enough recognition. She could make more playing at weddings, funerals, or at the piano bar in the Marriott Lounge. But she's more than a piano player. She's a servant. Her spiritual gift is service, and her musical ability gives her the opportunity to practice her spiritual gift. If she were suddenly unable to play the piano, she would find another way to serve.

You don't need talent to be gifted. The Spirit has given you a gift that you can use to build up others. Maybe it is giving. Maybe it is teaching. Maybe it leadership. What do you think it could be?

Using your spiritual gift puts purpose into everything you do. It becomes an act of obedience to God. It goes from being a hobby to being a ministry. You're not just playing the piano, or working in the nursery, or leading a committee, or dropping a few bucks in the plate—you're ministering to others. You are doing the work of God. The result is that the seemingly mundane details take on new meaning—suddenly they are rife with eternal significance. Discover your spiritual gift and put it to use. It will make your life a masterpiece.

## CONCLUSION

Before Jesus ascended into heaven he promised to send the Holy Spirit. He told about the work that the Spirit would perform in our lives. The Spirit is our comforter, our counselor, our teacher. He convicts us of sin and righteousness. He directs us to a closer walk with Jesus and helps us glorify God with our lives. And he gives us power to live holy, to witness, and do what God has called to do.

The Holy Spirit does all of these things, but only if we let him. He will not invade your life. Like Jesus, he waits for an invitation. Ask God today to fill you with the Holy Spirit so that you can use the gifts he has given you to build up others and glorify the name of Jesus. This is living in the fullness of the Spirit. This is what makes your life a masterpiece.

SERIES: MAKE YOUR LIFE A MASTERPIECE
**THE POWER TO CHANGE YOUR LIFE**
PSALM 19

Recently I began a home Bible study with this question: "If you were stranded on a desert island and could choose five books to take with you, which books would you choose?" The answers were interesting. C.S. Lewis made the list, of course. So did Tolkien. The *Book of Virtues* by William Bennett was mentioned. And *People* Magazine. Others said they would take their scrapbook or high-school year book. Of course, the Bible was at the top of the list; this was, after all, a home Bible study.

The most unique answer came from a man named Pink. Pink is 50 years old, works as a carpenter, and is still holding fast to the sixties. He has long blonde hair (with hints of gray) that he wears in a ponytail. I have never seen him in anything but shorts, sandals and a tee-shirt, including Sunday morning. He somehow manages to maintain three days worth of beard stubble at all times. Pink has a way of looking at life that cuts through the dross and gets to the heart of the matter.

When it was his turn, he said in his raspy voice, "If I was stranded on an island I would take only one book." Of course, everyone assumed he meant the Bible. Then he said, "The only book I would need would be *The Time Life Do-It-Yourself Guide to Basic Ship Building*. (I have since heard that same answer from others, so the idea might not have been original with Pink. Still, it was a good answer.)

If I had to choose just one book, there is no question which book it would be. The Bible. It is undeniably the most important book in my library. I have read from it nearly every day for the last 20 years, and still it continues to challenge, motivate and inspire me.

From a literary point of view, the Bible is an amazing book. Written by more than 40 authors over a period of two thousand years, it is remarkably consistent from beginning to end, in spite of the fact that most of the writers didn't know each other. They came from almost every conceivable background: Some were educated, some were illiterate; some were young, some were older; some were male, some were female; some were Jewish, some were Gentile; some were preachers, some were laypeople. It was a mixed bag of individuals who combined efforts to produce this "great work of literature."

Of course, as far as Christians are concerned, the Bible is more than just great literature. It is a book with the power to change people for better and forever. It is a book whose message is to be not just read, but lived. It contains the wisdom of the ages. When you apply the teachings of the Bible, you will never be the same. The best advice anyone can take is to start reading the Bible regularly. It will benefit you in many ways. Today we'll look at Psalm 19, which shows four ways you benefit from reading the Bible. First of all, the Bible is a source of...

- **Spiritual renewal**

*(v. 7) The law of the Lord is perfect, reviving the soul.* There's an example in an Old Testament story. The wall surrounding the city of Jerusalem had fallen into disrepair, bringing shame to the city and making it vulnerable to enemy attack. A Babylonian slave name Nehemiah organized the people of the city into work parties and together they rebuilt the wall in record time. As they completed their work, they realized something else: not only had the wall of their city fallen into disrepair, so had their lives. They had forsaken the God of their ancestors. People from all over the nation gathered together and asked Ezra to read from the law. He spent the entire morning reading from the Bible. When the Israelites heard the word of God, they turned their hearts toward him and committed themselves to live according to his law. This happens when the Bible is read; it is a source of spiritual renewal.

This is true in my own life. I became a Christian by reading the Bible. At 15 I became interested in Christianity, and though I had gone to church most of my life, I wasn't clear on exactly what it meant to be a Christian. I assumed salvation meant: "Try to live a good life. When you die, God will weigh your good deeds against your bad, and which ever way the scales tip will determine where you spend eternity." I thought being a Christian was like balancing a check book—if you debit the account with bad behavior, you better deposit some good behavior before the check gets cashed!

One evening I was reading the book of Romans from *The Living Bible*. Now, I know some people don't like the Living Bible because they believe it's too "fluffy." But I was young and had not yet studied Koine Greek, so I didn't know better. Besides, we were Methodists; the only other Bible reference materials we had in the house were a Noah's Ark pop-up book, a copy of Guideposts, and a recording of Burl Ives reciting the Christmas Story, so my choices were rather limited. As I read from the book of Romans, I encountered Paul's words that changed my life forever. He said...

*But now God has shown us a different way to heaven – not by being "good enough" and trying to keep his laws, but by a new way (though not new, really, for the Scriptures told about it long ago.) Now God says he will accept and acquit us – declare us "not guilty" – if we trust Jesus Christ to take away our sins. And we all can be saved in this same way, by coming to Christ, no matter who we are or what we have been like. (Romans 3:21-22)*

It was like scales were removed from my eyes. Suddenly I understood salvation is not something you earn—it is a gift that can only be received. As much as a 15 year old can understand grace, I understood grace. I decided then to accept this promise to be declared "not guilty" and I put my faith in Jesus Christ. It wasn't a sermon, it wasn't a song, it wasn't a play, it wasn't a movie, it wasn't a tract—it was the Bible that showed me how to be saved.

The Bible is a source of spiritual renewal. This is one way it will benefit you. Another way is to recognize that the Bible is a source of...

### • Practical wisdom

*(v. 7) The statutes of the Lord are trustworthy, making wise the simple.* Wisdom has nothing to do with intelligence. It's more like common sense. Wisdom gives you the ability to solve problems and get results. Herbert Hoover defined wisdom as "knowing what to do next." A wise person sees through the haze of the problem to the solution on the other side—like my friend Pink and his shipbuilding book.

There are times when the choice between right and wrong may not always be clear. There are times when the choice between good and best aren't clear, either. You need wisdom. You get it from reading the Bible.

For example, if you're single, the Bible offers a great deal of wisdom about the kind of person you should marry. If you're self-employed, the Bible tells you the kind of person you should do business with, and the kind of person you should avoid like the plague. The Bible instructs parents in how to relate to their children, and it shows friends how to treat friends. The Bible is full of wisdom on the subjects of parenting, finances, friendships, health, business, sex, marriage, spirituality, success, and on and on. It covers all areas of life. That's why David said...*(v. 7) The commands of the Lord are radiant, giving light to the eyes.*

The Bible is a source of practical wisdom. It helps you know what to do next. Third, the Bible is a source of...

### • Confident living

*(v. 9) The ordinances of the Lord are sure and altogether righteous.* Overall, the Christian life is a life of certainty. The uncertainties that many accept as a fact of life, believers simply do not have to worry about. A few years ago I was leading a home Bible study designed for people who wanted to learn more about the Christian faith. There were about a dozen in the group, some of them not yet believers. One evening I began with the question: "If you could ask God anything in the world, what would it be?" The overwhelming response was, "Am I on the right track? Are you satisfied with me? Am I going to heaven?" These are good

questions to ask; more people should be asking them. But the good news is that we don't have to wonder where we stand with God. We can be sure. John wrote... *I write these things to you who believe in the name of the Son of God so that you may know that you have eternal life. (1 John 5:13)* How can we know that we have eternal life? Because the Bible is full of promises offering this assurance.

- *(Romans 10:13) All who call upon the name of the Lord shall be saved.*
- *(Romans 10:9) If you confess with your mouth, "Jesus is Lord," and believe in your heart that God raised him from the dead, you will be saved.*
- *(1 John 1:9) If we confess our sins, he is faithful and just and will forgive us our sins and purify us from all unrighteousness.*
- *(Hebrews 10:10) We have been made holy through the sacrifice of the body of Jesus Christ once for all.*

We can be confident in our relationship to God. We can also be confident about the future. The Bible paints a picture of the future that is, ultimately, good. Yes, the world is going downhill and seems be getting worse with every passing minute, and yes, the Bible predicts there will be political and economic instability throughout the world. But when you read the rest of the story you see how it boldly asserts that finally Jesus Christ will establish justice for all, he will wipe away every tear, and "of his kingdom there will be no end."

I talk to people frequently who believe the future is the worst thing that could possibly happen. They don't mean in terms of the end of time. They mean typical day-to-day living. They approach every aspect of life with exaggerated caution: what if this job doesn't work, what if this relationship doesn't work, what if my children rebel, what if the economy goes bad? These aren't people who wisely hedge their investments; these are people who do not invest at all because they are afraid of the future. We don't have to live that way. We can face tomorrow with confidence because we have God's assurance that he is in control of every aspect of our lives, and he is working all things together for our good. We can face life with optimism and joy. David said...*(v. 8) The precepts of the Lord are right, giving joy to the heart.*

When you read the Bible you find yourself overcome with a sense of optimism—persistent optimism. When you fill your mind each day with scripture you are reminded that God loves you, God is in control, God takes care of you, God protects you, God will bring his kingdom to earth—and you won't be able to suppress your joy.

Some of you may be thinking, "Wait a minute! I know people who read the Bible all day long and they are anything but optimistic and joyful! What about those who use the Bible to preach gloom and doom?"

Fair question. The Bible is the Word of God. It is inspired, inerrant, and infallible. It is God's complete message for humanity. But the whole Bible is to be our guide—not just a few targeted passages. Sure, anyone can pull a few verses out of context to support some crazy notion. This has been done for slavery, racism, classism, socialism, oppression, and war. Some have even said that Jesus' statement "The poor you will have with you always," means that we shouldn't try to end poverty! An isolated verse here and there can be made to fit any idea, but when you examine the sum total of the Bible's message, these crazy notions fall apart.

For example, some people twist Paul's statement that "women should be silent in the church" to mean that the role of Christian women is subservient, and that they are less important than men. Some churches base their entire governmental structure on this single statement. However, when you look at all of scripture you see that Paul gives instruction to women about how to pray and prophesy in a church service.

In Romans he makes reference to the deaconess Phoebe. And Proverbs 31 gives a thorough description of a Godly woman, and she is anything but "subservient." The fact is that the Bible elevates the role and status of women in society. It places women and men on equal ground.

The purpose of scripture is not to give us ammunition for arguing. Its purpose is to transform lives. This happens only when we approach scripture with a teachable attitude of prayerful humility. The Bible will change your life when you allow it be a source of...

- **Daily guidance**

David said about the laws and statues and precepts and commands and ordinances of God...*(v. 11) By them is your servant warned; in keeping them there is great reward.* Again and again the Bible tells us the risks and rewards of our behavior. In one example, Proverbs says, *Plans fail for lack of counsel, but with many advisers they succeed. (Proverbs 15:22)*

This means if you consider a major decision without seeking good advice, you're likely to fail. That's the risk of making decisions without getting input from people who know what they're talking about. On the other hand, if you do get advice before making a decision, the Bible says your plans are more likely to succeed.

As you read scripture day after day, you'll be amazed at how often you receive plain and unmistakably clear direction for the problems and opportunities you face. It's not magic, it's miraculous. God speaks to you through the Bible. The Bible has the power to change your life. It will help you establish and maintain a life-long, life-changing connection with Jesus Christ.

## CONCLUSION

So, how do you begin? The best way is to start reading from the Bible daily. The best place to start is in the New Testament. I recommend beginning with Matthew, John, or James.

Read a few verses—four or five, maybe ten or eleven—and think about them. Read the passage again and ask God to speak to you. Search your heart. Is this passage challenging you to do something you've been putting off? Is it reminding you of a promise you need to keep? A sin you need to confess? Is it giving you an example you need to follow? As you meditate on scripture and direct your thoughts to God, he will speak to you.

And you will experience the benefits of reading the Bible: You grow spiritually, you develop wisdom, you experience joy, you receive daily guidance. The end result is that the word of God does the work God intends for it to do: it changes you—forever and for better.

**SERIES: 24/7: ROUND THE CLOCK CHRISTIANITY**
**TAKING GOD AS YOUR PARTNER**
PSALM 127

A little more than 300 years ago a middle aged man named Nicholas Herman entered a monastery in France and lived the remaining 30 years of his life as a cook. (He was, you might say, a French Friar.) Though his life was lived in obscurity, he accomplished one thing that destined him for greatness. He sought and eventually achieved the ability to walk continually in God's presence. As he approached the end of his life, he wrote about it in a book that came to be called *The Practice of the Presence of God*. This book, written under the penname Brother Lawrence, has influenced countless Christians through the centuries, helping them discover the joy of living day-in, day-out in God's presence. Brother Lawrence wrote:

*"If I were a preacher I would, above all other things, preach the practice of the presence of God. For there is nothing in the world sweeter or more delightful than continual conversation with God."*

For the next four weeks we'll consider how to practice the presence of God—how to experience God 24 hours a day, 7 days a week. Today, we're tackling the first step: Taking God as your partner.

Whatever you do with the majority of your time—whether you're a businessman, a student, a homemaker, or whatever else it may be—God wants to be part of it. Today, as we look at Psalm 127, we'll discover how we can include him in the totality of our lives. Listen to what the Psalmist says... *(v.1) Unless the Lord builds the house, its builders labor in vain. Unless the Lord watches over the city, the watchmen stand guard in vain.* There are three things I want you to notice here. First of all, this Psalm tells us...

• **God wants to be in charge of your responsibilities.**

This Psalm says that in whatever you do, God wants to be involved. If you've got a house to build, God wants to build it. If you've got a city to watch, God wants to guard it. If you've got a business to run, he wants to run it. If you've got a family to take care of, he wants to be the Lord of your home. Whatever you do, God wants to be involved; he wants to be in charge. There's nothing about your life that is unimportant to him.

Sometimes you may wonder, "Does God really care whether or not I make this sale? Whether or not I meet this deadline? Whether or not I pass this test?" The answer, always, is "Yes!" He wants to be involved in your responsibilities. And not merely involved—he wants to be in charge. In all that you do, God wants you to do it his way. There's a reason for this: His way is always the best way.

Surrender your responsibilities to God's control. Say, "God, I'm giving you control of my business; build it for your glory...God, I'm giving you control of my marriage and control of my family; build us together for your glory...God I'm giving you control of my future; build it for your glory."

When Herman Cain took over as CEO of Godfather's Pizza, the company was in the midst of a severe financial crisis. Within one year, he brought the company into profitability. When he was asked how he did it, he said, "The secret to my success is my faith in Christ and God almighty—and they are no secret! I have to give God the glory in everything I do and in every success I've achieved."

God wants to be in charge of the details. He wants to build the house. He wants to run the business. He wants to watch over the family. He wants to be in charge, because his way is the best way for you. The second thing this Psalm teaches us is...

- **Giving God responsibility doesn't end your responsibility.**

*(v.1) Unless the Lord builds the house, its builders labor in vain.* Notice what Solomon is implying here. The builders keep building, even though God is charge of the house. The watchmen keep watching, even though God is guarding the city. We keep doing our jobs, even though we've given control to God. You give your business to God, but you still show up for work. You

give your family to God, but you still spend time with your children. Giving God responsibility doesn't eliminate your responsibility. But it does empower you; though you're still working hard, the results are no longer up to you. You can trust God for the results.

Have you ever seen the bumper sticker that says, "God is my co-pilot"? I've seen a variation on that one that is probably more accurate. It says, "God is my pilot. I'm just the co-pilot." This is more than just a matter of semantics. It's a matter of defining who's the boss. Our attitude can't be "God, this is what I'm doing, please bless it." It must be, "God, show me what to do and how to do it, so that everything I do brings you honor." Giving God responsibility doesn't relieve you of responsibility, it just puts you in the position of co-pilot.

- **Giving God responsibility is the key to finding peace.**

*(v. 2) In vain you rise early and stay up late, toiling for food to eat – for he grants sleep to those he loves.* Responsibility is a heavy-handed word. People who are serious about their responsibilities tend to lose sleep over them. They're conscientious. They work hard. They get to the office early. They stay up late. They go the extra mile. They worry. And they frequently find themselves frazzled.

There's nothing wrong with getting up early and going to bed late – that comes with having high expectations for yourself – but you don't have to live in a constant state of tension. You don't have to lie awake at night, staring at the ceiling, wondering how you'll make it through another day...*if* you'll make it through another day. A wonderful by-product of giving God control is that you experience peace of mind. If you let him build the house, then "your problems" becomes his problem.

When you give God control, he takes it. He handles it. Then, does everything work out the way you want? Better than that. Everything works out the way he wants. Everything works out the way that he, in his sovereign mercy, knows is best for you.

When you give God responsibility for your life, you face every day with the assurance that he causes events to work together for good. As Paul said, *We know that God causes all things to work together for good to those who love God, to those who are called according to his purpose. (Romans 8:28)*

I'll make you a promise. Actually, it's not my promise, it's God promise. If you want to live in God's presence 24/7, you can. You can experience God's presence; you can experience God's protection; you can experience God's peace. It's yours for the asking. And there's more. You can have the assurance that everything that happens will work out for the best...for your best. This is God's promise. He'll take care of you. He'll take responsibility for your responsibilities. He'll lift the burden that you carry. He'll carry it for you. He'll give you peace.

What do you have to do? Open the door of your heart—and your life—to Jesus. Some of you have never done this before. You've never said, "Jesus, I give my entire life to you. Be the Boss. Take control." If you haven't made that choice, and you want to, you can do it right now.

Some here today have been following Christ for years, but you stubbornly keep getting back in the driver's seat. You're trying to do everything on your own. You're attempting to build your own house and watch your own city—and you're discovering the truth of Solomon's words: *(v. 2) In vain you rise early and stay up late.* When you try to do it on your own, there's just no peace. You'll never find peace in your hard work, or in your accomplishments, or in your possessions, or in your relationships, or in anything else. There's only one place of peace in this world: living every day—day-in, day-out—in the presence of God.

The first step to a 24/7 Christian life is to take God as your partner. But understand: it's not a 50/50 arrangement. You're not equals. He's the senior partner; you're the junior partner. You follow his lead, and he'll take you to the best place you can possibly be.

SERIES: 24: AROUND THE CLOCK CHRISTIANITY
**GETTING YOUR DAY OFF TO A GREAT START**
PSALM 5

About 20 years ago a teacher told me, "The first hour of your day sets the tone for the entire day. How you spend that hour determines—more than anything else—how your day will end." When I gave it a try, I discovered that my teacher was right. Soon it became a habit that has stayed with me all my life. Starting every day the right way has made an enormous difference for me.

In the last 20 years I've survived more battles than I thought possible. I've endured setbacks, failures, disappointments, and heartaches. I've faced extended periods of financial stress, health problems, business problems, church problems, people problems—you name it. There were times when I woke up every day to face a new crisis, even before yesterday's crisis had been resolved. The only thing that got me through those tough times was a commitment I made 20 something years ago to greet every day brand new, to begin each day in the best possible way.

When you begin your day the right way, you have a better chance of ending it the right way. You're more likely to do the right thing throughout the day. So, today we'll take a closer look at how to get each and every day off to a great start.

This is, in many ways, the most personal sermon I have ever preached. I'm opening the door to a private part of my life because I want you to experience each day the same power that I have experienced for the past twenty years. It has worked for me, and it will work for you. There are three things I want to point out about getting your day off to a great start. First of all…

- **Get up earlier than you have to.**

*(v. 3) In the morning, O Lord, you hear my voice, in the morning I lay my requests before you.* Notice the phrase, *"in the morning."* Many people say they can't get alone with God in the morning

because they don't have time. Their mornings are too hectic. I understand that. Your morning will be hectic unless you make a commitment to get up earlier than you have to.

When I was in high school my first class began at 8:00 a.m. I knew that it took me at least five minutes to get from the school parking lot to the classroom; it took at least ten minutes to get from my house to the high school, and it took at most two minutes to roll out of bed, put on jeans, t-shirt, and tennis shoes, and run outside and jump in the car. So, that's five minutes, ten minutes, two minutes—seventeen minutes. I had to be there at 8:00, so, naturally, I set my alarm for…7:43. Now, I will say that I was rarely late for school, but I always felt a little frazzled during the first couple of classes. It was usually lunch time before I hit my stride.

Obviously, this is no way to start the day. It might work you're a kid, but in the *real world*, you have to make some adjustments. Getting up earlier prevents you from starting the day in crisis mode. You know about that, don't you? You wake up and the first thing you think is "Yikes! I'm already behind!" Each day doesn't have to begin so stressfully.

Before the day is over, you'll go through a number of stresses and anxieties and maybe even a crisis or two, but you don't have to start your day like that. Getting up earlier than you have to allows you to move a little slower, be a little more deliberate in the choices you make, and enjoy a little more the beauty of the morning.

Once I visited a computer programmer friend of mine in San Jose, California. His office was only 4 miles from my hotel, but it took me more than 30 minutes to get there during rush hour. I asked, "How can you stand fighting this traffic every day?" He said, "I rarely fight traffic. I come in at 6:00 a.m. and the interstate is practically empty. I read my Bible, pray, order breakfast, and then I'm ready to start writing code." His job is intense, and not without stress, but he faces the pressure by making sure he gets each day started right. He begins by getting up earlier than he has to.

It's probably the same where you work. By 9:15 you're in the thick of things. You're dealing with employees who didn't show up, or a boss that's on your back, or customers who are complaining, or a kid with a runny nose, or a car that's making a funny noise, or a computer that won't print, or any number of other things. By 9:15 you're in the middle of it—so why not give yourself an advantage? Give yourself some extra time in the morning so you can fuel up, so to speak. Get your day off to a great start; get up earlier than you have to.

Jesus did this very thing. Mark says, *Very early in the morning, while it was still dark, Jesus got up, left the house, and went off to a solitary place, where he prayed. (Mark 1:35)* There's something about getting up early that helps you keep your priorities straight. That's why Proverbs warns against sleeping too much. *How long will you lie there, you sluggard? When will you get up from your sleep? (Proverbs 6:9)* It also says, *Do not love sleep or you will grow poor. (Proverbs 20:13)* Last week we saw that one of the benefits of living in God's presence is that he gives you peaceful sleep, but that doesn't mean you can sleep all day! If you want to get your day off to a good start, get up a little earlier than you have to. Secondly...

- **Fill your mind with words and music of praise.**

I don't watch the news in the morning. I don't even turn on the TV. Neither do I listen to the radio or read the newspaper. Why? Because those things are rarely uplifting. Think about it: Do you really believe *Good Morning America* can get your day moving in the right direction? Do you really want to enter the battlefield of the workplace armed with depressing news and mindless chatter? I realize you need to know what's going on in the world. Believe me, you'll find out. You have the rest of the day to hear about it. To start the day, however, it's better to fill your mind with thoughts that will empower you. Listen to music that inspires you. Read something that uplifts you. Make sure that what goes in your mind in those early morning hours strengthens you to face the day.

I begin each day listening to worship music—quiet, peaceful, reverent, uplifting, worship music. I especially enjoy listening to scripture songs. The first sound I hear almost every morning is God's word.

When I'm ready to meet with God I turn off the stereo and get as quiet as I can. I begin each day with a prayer—the same one every day. It's an old prayer—dating back to the fifth century—but the words are still relevant.

> *This day I call to me:*
> *God's strength to direct me,*
> *God's power to sustain me,*
> *God's wisdom to guide me,*
> *God's vision to light me,*
> *God's ear to my hearing,*
> *God's word to my speaking,*
> *God's hand to uphold me,*
> *God's pathway before me,*
> *God's shield to protect me,*
> *God's legions to save me:*
> *from snares of the demons,*
> *from evil enticements,*
> *from failings of nature,*
> *from one man or many*
> *that seek to destroy me*
> *anear or afar.*

I also read the Bible each morning. I begin with a few Psalms. Psalm 95 is one of my favorites. So are Psalms 16 and 30. No doubt as you read through the Psalms, there will be some that speak especially to you. Next I read from the New Testament, usually a few verses as I work my way through a book. Right now, I'm in Philippians. As I read, I ask: What is this scripture telling me to do today? Is it pointing out a sin in my life? Is it challenging me to step out in faith? Is it telling me to take a certain action? It never fails: when I read the Bible God speaks to me. He tells me something I need to do, or something I need to know. As I close my Bible, I know there is something specific God wants me to do THAT DAY. Maybe it's spend time with my children, maybe it's call a friend, maybe it's apologize to someone I've offended. Every day, during this "quiet time" God speaks to me. This is so much more empowering than listening to a morning DJ laugh at his own jokes.

During the first hour of my day I don't see or talk to anyone. The first hour is spent entirely alone in the presence of God. That hour gets me through the rest of the day. We see this very same habit in King David, expressed in the Psalms.

- *(Psalm 5:3) In the morning, O Lord, you hear my voice.*
- *(Psalm 59:16) In the morning I will sing of your love*
- *(Psalm 88:13) O Lord, in the morning my prayer comes before you.*
- *(Psalm 143:8) Let the morning bring me word of your unfailing love.*
- *(Psalm 92:1-2) It is good to praise the Lord...to proclaim your love in the morning.*

Do you want to start the day right? Get in God's presence as early as possible. Fill your mind with him by reading his word, by listening to worship music, by offering a prayer of praise to him. This gives you the power to face the day.

- **Item by item, surrender each part of your day to him.**

Like many people, I carry a notebook containing my schedule. It tells me everything I have to do on a particular day. Items that get done are scratched out, the others are carried over to another day. On any given day I have anywhere from 10-20 items that *have* to be done. And usually there's time only to do about half of them!

Each morning I go over my schedule, presenting each entry to God: "Lord, help me to do today what needs to be done ." If a meeting is sure to be tense, I say, "Give me the wisdom to handle it the right way." If I'm speaking or performing somewhere, I say, "Help me to draw others into a closer relationship with you." As I go through my schedule, I lift each item to God, asking his blessing and his guidance. This helps me prioritize my to-do list. When there's more than can possibly be done in a day, he helps me determine the most important items on my schedule.

The best thing about knowing God is being able to talk to him about everything. No problem is too big or too small for him to handle. Each morning, as you begin your day, you can lay every item of your schedule at his feet. He will give you the guidance you seek. This is exactly what King David did. *(v. 3) In the morning I lay my requests before you, and wait in expectation.* I love the way King James translates this verse: *(v. 3) O Lord, in the morning will I direct my prayer unto you, and will look up.*

David says, "I'll wait in expectation. As I bring my requests to you in the morning, I'll look to you for answers." This gets your day off to a great start. Bringing every part of your day to him, in advance, gives you power throughout the day. Later in the day, when you're in the midst of the battle, you'll remember: "This is something I've already laid at God's feet. I can count on him to get me through".

## CONCLUSION

A key to being in God's presence 24/7 is to begin your day the right way. To start right, get in God's presence as early as possible. Let him be the first one you speak to. Let his be the first voice you hear. Let him be the one to influence how you think about the day ahead.

Every day is a fresh start. It doesn't matter what happened yesterday, or what might happen tomorrow. You've got today, and God is giving you the opportunity to make today great. Daniel said, *Because of the Lord's great love we are not consumed, for his compassions never fail. They are new every morning; great is your faithfulness. (Lamentations 3:23)*

This week I hope you choose to start every day the right way. Get into his presence as early as you can. It means getting up a little earlier than you have to. It means filling your mind first thing with his word, and filling your heart with praise. It means offering your entire day to him — giving him control of each event, allowing him to direct you each step of the way. This gets you moving in the right direction, and keeps you moving forward no matter what the day may bring.

SERIES: 24: AROUND THE CLOCK CHRISTIANITY
**DEALING WITH THE DISTRACTIONS OF DAY-TO-DAY LIFE**
PSALM 55

In dealing with daily distractions, the first two lessons of this series are crucial to successfully implementing today's lesson. Giving God control of your business and/or career will help you face the nagging distractions of day-to-day life, as will making the effort to start your day with a heart full of praise and worship. Assuming you're committed to doing these, today we'll look further at some ways to handle the frustrations and setbacks you face day in, day out.

In Psalm 55 David talks about this very thing. He was no stranger to frustration. He knew about the distractions of day-to-day life. As king of Israel, he had what you could call a high pressure job. In addition to being a political and military leader, he was a spiritual leader. Like any leader, his actions were scrutinized and, like any leader, his failures were magnified. When he failed, he failed big—and everyone knew about it. As David went about his typical day, he faced complications of all sorts. In Psalm 55 he lists some of them:

- **Destructive mental attitude**

    *(v. 2) My thoughts trouble me and I am distraught. (v. 4-5) My heart is in anguish within me; the terrors of death assail me, fear and trembling have beset me; horror has overwhelmed me.*

This is what Zig Ziglar (or Stuart Smalley, depending on your point of reference) refers to as "stinking thinking." It's thinking thoughts that only serve to immobilize you. It's thinking, "What's the use? This project will never get off the ground." or..."What's the use? I'll never get over this problem." or..."What's the use? I'm in over my head; I'm outmatched; I'm bound to lose." If you feel this way from time to time, you're not alone. David felt that way, too. Another complication David dealt with was...

- **Determined enemies**

*(v. 10-11) Day and night they prowl [the city's] walls; malice and abuse are within it. Destructive forces are at work in the city; threats and lies never leave its streets.*

It's a sad fact of life that some people in this world do not wish you well. If you're in business, they want you to fail. If you coach a team, they want you to lose. If you teach a class, they want your students to perform poorly. If you pastor a church, they want it to split down the middle. If you have a little money, they want to get their hands on it. Some days you don't see these people, but other days they get in your way. They distract you. They complicate things. David dealt with them, too. Next...

- **Disloyal friends**

At some point every leader gets stabbed in the back. It hurts when you're attacked by an enemy; it's devastating when it comes from a friend. At 18 I saw something I'll never forget. Some disgruntled members at church decided to break away and start their own congregation, led by the Associate Pastor. The church had 3000 members, and only about 100 people were leaving, so it wasn't a matter of the split causing irreparable damage—but the pastor and associate pastor had been best friends for many years.

I worked part time as church janitor. That evening, after everything had hit the fan, I walked by the pastor's office. Inside, behind his closed door, I could hear him sobbing. I couldn't believe it. Here was a man I had identified with King David—one of God's mighty warriors—and he was sitting at his desk crying like a baby.

If I had one ounce of discretion, I would have gone on my way. But, as I mentioned earlier, I was 18—so I knocked on the door. When the pastor let me in, I asked if he was all right. With resignation, he said, "Yeah...it's been a tough day. I guess you know about it." I admitted that I did. He said to me, with a breaking voice, "The worst part is that I have lost my best friend." I still don't know if the people who left had a good reason to be disgruntled, but the lesson I learned that day was that no amount of success can offset the pain of getting stabbed by a friend. David faced this, too. He said... *(v. 12-14) If an enemy were insulting me, I could endure it; if a foe were raising himself against me, I could hide from him. But it is you, a man like myself, my companion, my close friend, with whom I once enjoyed sweet fellowship as we walked with the throng at the house of God.* Disloyalty is one of the complications we'll have to deal with from time to time. Yet another distraction David faced was a....

- **Desire to escape**

*(v. 6-8) Oh that I had the wings of a dove! I would fly away and be at rest — I would flee far away and stay in the desert; I would hurry to my place of shelter, far from the tempest and the storm.*

Have you ever wanted to run away? I guess everyone has. Here's the problem. If you're focused on running, you're not focused on doing the job God has given you. The desire to escape can be a tremendous distraction in our daily life. It causes us to peruse the want-ads when we really have no intention of changing jobs. It causes us to daydream about being single, when we know that divorce isn't an option. It causes us to spend more time watching TV than we should; it causes us to spend more money than we should on empty diversions, it causes us to eat more than we should, or abuse alcohol, or abuse drugs.

I'm talking about more than merely looking forward to a much-needed vacation. I'm talking about a desire that causes us to compromise our values and avoid our responsibilities. If you're like everyone else, you'll probably have to deal with this from time to time.

These are some of the distractions of day-to-day life. Of course, there are others — employee problems, employer problems, computer problems, money problems, over-extended schedules, over-priced contractors, over-booked flights, and more items on your to-do list than can possibly be done in a single day. If you're not careful, you'll find yourself in a situation where you start every day with a bang and end every day with a whimper. You need God's power throughout the day. In Psalm 55, David shows us how to get it. *(v. 17) Evening, morning and noon, I cry out in distress, and he hears my voice.*

This principle is to follow, and it works. Return to God again and again throughout the day. Last week we talked about getting your day started right, and that's certainly a crucial part of experiencing God's power, but there's more to it. Think of it this way. When you take a journey, you stop along the way to refuel. For example, when I drive from Nashville to Dallas, I have to fill-up in Forest City, Arkansas, and then again in Texarkana, and then again about 30 miles outside the Dallas city limits. Our spiritual life works the same way, because each day is a long journey. If you want to experience God's presence all day then you need to return to him again and again throughout the day.

Monastic communities have practiced this for centuries. They begin their day with prayer. At mid-morning they stop working and pray. At noon they stop working to pray and eat lunch. In mid-afternoon they stop working to pray. In the evening, as they finish the work-day, they pray again. Before they retire for the night, they pray again. Some communities even get up in the middle of the night to pray!

The idea is to return to God again and again through out the day. This helps you remember that Christ is your constant companion—at work and at home. Jesus is available always; every moment of every day can be spent in his presence. Throughout the day, return to him again and again. As you do this, there are three promises in Psalm 55 that you need to keep in mind. Here they are...

- **Talk to God, and he will hear you.**

*(v. 17) Evening, morning and noon I cry out in distress, and he hears my voice.* It is wonderful to know that who to us when we pray. Of course, we all know that God is not our errand boy, and he doesn't do everything we ask him to do. Things don't always work the way we want. Prayers are not always answered on our terms. Even still, when we talk to God we know he will listen.

Here's a comparison. I once had a banker so unsympathetic to my company's objectives that I wondered sometimes if he was capable of human emotion. (The jury is still out on that one.) On those few occasions I went to him requesting a loan or a line of credit, it was obvious that my words were falling on deaf ears. Fortunately, he wasn't the only banker in town. I switched banks and I have a more cooperative relationship with the new one. My new banker is interested in what my company is trying to accomplish; she's been as supportive as possible. Though she hasn't always said "yes" to my requests, she has thoughtfully considered each one. When she says "no", she always suggests alternatives. In other words, when I talk to her, she listens. Even though we still goes through all the typical struggles of a small business, it helps to know that we have a sympathetic banker.

This is similar to our relationship with God. He listens, because he cares. You can return to him again and again through out the day, talking to him about your problems, and you can be sure that he will hear you. The second promise is...

- **Cast your cares on Him, and he will sustain you.**

*(v. 22) Cast your cares on the Lord, and he will sustain you.* Another verse you've probably heard before is, *Cast all your anxiety upon him, because he cares for you. (1 Peter 5:7)* When the complications of the day become too much for you to handle, you can turn them over to God. He will give you the strength to survive. One of the most empowering statements you'll ever make is "Lord, I don't have the strength to get through this on my own; I need your help." You don't have to deal with your worries and cares all alone. You can offer them up to God: "Lord, this is a problem that I don't know how to handle. I need your strength, I need your wisdom." This is a prayer that he always answers. When you ask for strength, or when you ask for wisdom, it is always available. James said, *If any of you lacks wisdom, he should ask God, who gives generously to all with finding fault, and it will be given to him. (James 1:5)*

Psalm 55 promises that if you return to God again and again

throughout the day, casting your cares upon him, he will hold you up. The third promise is...

- **Trust in God, and he will save you.**

*(v. 16) I call to God, and the Lord saves me. (v. 23) But as for me, I trust in you.* When it comes to salvation, we know that we can only be saved by trusting Christ to forgive our sins. We know there is nothing we can do to save ourselves. However, too often we consider our personal lives another matter. We think we can handle the problems that come our way. Our attitude is, "Never mind, Lord, I can handle today on my own." That attitude is a recipe for disaster, because life just doesn't work that way.

This is difficult to admit, but the fact is you can't handle the day-to-day complications of life any more than you can save your own soul. You need God's intervention; you need him to save you—from your sins, and from yourself. The good news is that he'll do it. He'll save you from your sins. All you need to do is call on him, ask him to come into your life, and he will. He'll also save you from the problems of day-to-day life. I don't mean he'll prevent you from experiencing problems, I mean he'll give you the power to face them one by one. This is why you want to return to him again and again throughout the day, because when you continually put your trust in him, he will save you.

## CONCLUSION

Every day comes with its own distractions, problems, and complications. These are inevitable, and unavoidable. Even Jesus said, *"Do not worry about tomorrow...Each day has enough trouble of its own"*. (Matthew 6:34) Troubles can rob you of experiencing the benefit of God's presence. He never leaves you, but if you look at your problems instead of Jesus, how can he help? If you want to experience God's presence 24/7, develop the habit of returning to him again and again throughout the day. Just like David. *(v. 17) Evening, morning and noon, I cry out in distress and he hears my voice.* God is waiting for you. Return to him again and again. Talk to him; he'll listen. Cast your cares on him; he'll sustain you. Trust in him; he'll save you. You can count on him, all day long.

SERIES: 24: AROUND THE CLOCK CHRISTIANITY
**WHAT TO DO WHEN GOD SEEMS FAR AWAY**
PSALM 13

When I became a Christian, I went through a radical transformation. Most profound was a sense of God's presence every where I went. Each morning I woke up with a "bubbly" feeling—feeling God's love, feeling right with him, feeling that I was in center of his will, and feeling that all was well in my world. Throughout the day I sensed his presence; I saw evidence of him in every detail.

At this point, my experience was consistent with everything I had heard about the Christian life. This was the early seventies, during the Jesus Movement, and it was common to hear things like, "Turn on to Jesus...Get high on Jesus...He is a natural high; he's an eternal high." Therefore, I thought that since I had given my life to Jesus, I would feel good all the time.

In a few months, however, things began to change. I came down from my high. The bubbles evaporated. I didn't sense God's presence as I had before. Suddenly there seemed to be a distance between us. Where before he had spoken to me so clearly, he now seemed to be silent. Where before I had felt wrapped up in his love, now my heart felt cold. There must be something wrong, I thought. There must be something wrong with me. God's feelings for me must have changed, or I wouldn't feel this way. I went to see my youth minister and told him what I was going through. I was relieved to discover he knew just what I was talking about, and he knew how to help me get past it. He wrote out some scriptures to memorize. At the bottom of the page he drew a picture of a train—an engine and a caboose. On the engine he wrote Faith. On the caboose he wrote Feelings. He gave me the paper and said, "In the Christian life, your feelings will go up and down, and will sometimes run hot or cold. You can't be driven by your feelings; faith has to be the engine of your Christian life. It is faith that drives you forward." The longer I've been a Christian, the more I've seen how common this experience is. You go through times when you experience the highs of the mountain top, then you go through times when you face the lows of the valley. And it doesn't happen just once—it happens again and again throughout the course of your life.

It is important to realize that even during the valley-lows, God's presence is just as real as during the mountain-top experiences. In fact, when you're going through the valley—when you don't feel God's presence—you have the opportunity for exponential growth in your Christian walk, because these are times you learn to walk by faith. Regardless of how you feel, it doesn't change the fact that God is always there, and you can live in his presence 24 hours a day, seven days week, 52 weeks a year. Practicing the presence of God is not a feeling you depend on, it is a faith you live by.

This is a lesson King David learned. He went through times when he couldn't feel the presence of God. One example is found in Psalm 13. He begins by saying, (v. 1-2) *How long, O Lord, will you forget me forever? How long will you hide your face from me? How long must I wrestle with my thoughts and every day have sorrow in my heart?* Have you ever felt that way? I hope you never do, but the fact is this: if you haven't, you probably will. There will be times when God seems to be far off, and the joy of feeling his presence will seem like a fading memory. When this happens, you have the opportunity to become closer to him than ever before, because this is when you learn to walk by faith, not by feelings.

Psalm 13 teaches us what to do when God seems far away. It was written when David was going through an emotional valley. Yet he continued to find strength in God. There are three things we can learn from David. First, regardless of how you feel...

- **Assume God's presence, and do what you know to do.**

After detailing his desperate situation in verses 1-4, David says, (v. 5) *But I trust in your unfailing love.* He's saying: I won't let despair get the best of me. I'll assume you are with me...watching over me...taking care of me...leading me along the way.

My friend who works for a struggling company hears rumors every day about he and his co-workers being transferred or being laid off. It's put him in a state of limbo, not knowing if he is staying, going, or even if he'll have a job next month. He not sure how to do his job. He's afraid to begin long-term projects and he finds himself floundering at a time when he can least afford to flounder. He finally said to me, "I'm going to assume that everything will work out for the best, and keep doing my job the way it's supposed to be done."

Regardless of how you feel, assume God's presence and do what you know you should do. This means you continue the habit of getting up early and spending time alone with God—regardless of how you feel. Come to church each week regardless of how you feel. Continue to serve regardless of how you feel. Include God in your work life regardless of how you feel. Even when you don't feel God's presence, he is there. Assume his presence and do what you know you should do. This is how you put your trust in his unfailing love. It's a matter of saying, "God, even when my feelings don't cooperate, I'll keep doing what I should do, because by faith I know you are right here with me." Secondly, this Psalm teaches that regardless of how you feel...

- **Cling to what you know is true.**

*(v. 5-6) My heart rejoices in your salvation...I will sing to the Lord, for he has been good to me.* When God seems far away, cling to what you know is true. Remember what God has done for you. Rejoice in it. Offer thanks to God. "Lord, you've made such a difference in my life. You've given me joy. You've provided for me. You've forgiven my sins. You've given me eternal life. You've answered my prayers." As you remember and rejoice in what God has done for you, you will find yourself strengthened in him.

There's no need to pretend feeling something you don't feel. God knows your feelings; you can be honest with him. Search your heart for what you know to be true, and cling to the truth. When I feel as if God is far away I sometimes think about where my life would be if I had never become a Christian. Based on where I was before I met Jesus, what would my life be like had it followed its logical progression? What kind of career would I have pursued? What kind of person would I have married? What kind of father would I have become?

Every time I think through this, I am overcome with gratitude for God's sovereign mercy. Even when he seems far away, I know beyond a shadow of a doubt that he has made a difference in my life. I cling to that. And I thank him for it. The third thing this Psalm teaches us is, regardless of how you feel...

- **Keep singing praise to God.**

Love isn't a feeling, it's something you do. Most of you already know that. What we sometimes forget, though, is that praise (or worship) isn't a feeling either; it's something you do. It's true that praise is often an emotional experience. Sometimes when your heart is "bubbling" you overflow with praise, and you can't help but sing to God what you're feeling in your heart. When that happens, it's wonderful. However, even during those times when your heart isn't bubbling, you should continue to worship him. Even when the feelings aren't there, you should lift your hands to him. Even when he seems far away, you should continue to sing praise to him. This is what David did. As I've already pointed out, he begins this Psalm by admitting that God seems very far away. And he ends it by saying, *(v. 6) I will sing to the Lord, for he has been good to me.*

David didn't say this because he suddenly experienced an emotional turn-around (in the time it took him to write these six verses) and was now back on top of the mountain. He said it because he understood that praise is an act of faith, not an act of feelings. He's saying, "I will sing to the Lord, regardless of how I feel." Some people ask, "Isn't it hypocritical to sing praise when you don't feel close to God?" I guess it would be hypocritical—if you believe that you should praise God only when you feel good.

But that's not what the Bible teaches. We are to praise him all during the day, regardless of how we feel. Our feelings will come and go; our praise to him should be consistent.

I'll take it a step further. God knows how you feel, and I think he is more pleased when you praise him during those times that you don't feel all bubbly inside. Think of it this way. If you gave your teenage son a car, he most likely would be overcome with joy, and say something along the lines of "Thank you, thank you, thank you! I love you, I love you, I love you!" And, no doubt, the words would be sincere. But suppose you woke him up at 6:00 on a Saturday morning to help you clean the garage, and in the midst of the groggy grumpiness that teenagers do so well, he was to say, "You know, Dad, I love you. And I want you to know that I am glad you are my father." Wouldn't those words, spoken in those circumstances, carry tremendous weight? It's easy to praise God when you're feeling giddy, but if you continue to praise him even when he seems to be far away, he is especially pleased.

## CONCLUSION

There are cycles to the Christian life. There will be times when you feel close to God, and there will be times when you feel like he is far, far away. That's inevitable. We don't have to be driven by our feelings. We can be driven by faith. Even during those times when God seems distant, we can experience the power of his presence. Regardless of how you feel, keep doing what you know you should do; regardless of how you feel, cling to what you know is true; regardless of how you feel, keep praising God. This is what David meant when he said, *(v. 5) But I trust in your unfailing love, My heart rejoices in your salvation. I will sing to the Lord, for he has been good to me.*

Practice the presence of God. It's the life he designed for us—living in his presence 24/7. This is how we get beyond surface level emotionalism into a life driven by faith. That's what "around the clock Christianity" really is. It's more than a feeling we hope for, it's a faith we live by.

SERIES: HOW CAN I BE GOOD?
**WINNING THE WAR ON SIN**
ROMANS 6:1-23

Today we're beginning a new series called *How Can I Be Good?* Now, if you were to ask that question, which word would you emphasize? Because the word you emphasize indicates your attitude toward to holiness. For example, is it "How can **I** be good?"—as if to say, "I'm such a sinner, how in the world can I ever become a good person?"

Or is it, "How can I be **good**?—as if I to say, "What does it mean to live a life of holiness; what does holiness look like?"

Or is it, "**How** can I be good?"—as if to say, "I want to live a holy life, but how do I get there?"

Or...do you say, **How** can **I** be **good**?—as if to say, "I feel like I'm such a sinner, and even if I knew what holiness is, I have no idea how to get there."

Some of you may have asked this question using slightly different terminology: How can I become a better person? How can I become a better Christian? How can I become holy? Regardless of how you phrase it, and regardless of which word you emphasize, if you have the desire to improve yourself, this series is for you. For the next three weeks we'll look at Paul's teaching from the book of Romans on how to become good—how to become holy. Today, it's how to win the war on sin. Some may think it's impossible to win this war, but it's not. In fact, there's a promise in the sixth chapter of Romans that we all need to claim. It's in verse 14: *Sin shall not have dominion over you (KJV)* God has promised us victory over sin. In Romans 6, Paul shows us how to claim that victory. To win the war against sin, there are three steps to take. Here they are...

- **Understand the meaning of salvation.**

Becoming a Christian isn't a matter of turning over a new leaf. It's a matter of beginning a new life. It's not just that we think differently, though we do. And it's not just that we act differently, though we will. It's that we ARE different. Our souls, which were empty and lifeless, have been made alive through the power of Christ. This is what Paul referred to when he said, *(v. 4) For we died and were buried with Christ by baptism. And just as Christ was raised from the dead by the glorious power of the Father, now we also may live new lives.*

When you accepted Jesus Christ as your Lord and Savior, God gave you a new life. He gave you a capacity for holiness you didn't have before. I want you to understand that Paul is not being allegorical, or metaphorical, or symbolic when he says *you've been made alive in Christ.* He's being as literal as he can be. Something supernatural happens at the moment of salvation. You are transferred from spiritual darkness to spiritual light, from spiritual death to spiritual life, and you now have potential to live a Godly life.

*How we praise God, the Father of our Lord Jesus Christ, who has blessed us with every spiritual blessing in the heavenly realms because we belong to Christ. (Ephesians 1:4) You were dead because of your sins...Then God made you alive with Christ. He forgave all our sins. (Colossians 2:13)*

Because of God's gift of salvation, we have power over sin. We are, quite literally, dead to sin. That's how Paul phrased it. *(v. 6-7) Our old sinful selves were crucified with Christ so that sin might lose its power in our lives. We are no longer slaves to sin. For when we died with Christ we were set free from the power of sin.* He went on to say, *(v. 11) So you should consider yourselves dead to sin and able to live for the glory of God through Jesus Christ.*

I remember the first teaching I heard about this. I was driving to school, listening to Chuck Smith (pastor of Calvary Chapel, Costa Mesa, CA) on the radio. He was teaching Romans 6:11, which in the King James says that we should "reckon" ourselves dead to sin. I thought: This doesn't make sense. How can I reckon (or consider) myself dead to sin when it is painfully obvious that I am anything but dead to sin? Sin was alive and well and living in just about every area of my life. Even though I had been a follower of Christ for less than 2 years, I had already learned that *when I want to do good, I don't. And when I try not to do wrong, I do it anyway. (Romans 7:19)* I could say about myself, as Paul said about himself, *Wretched man that I am! (Romans 7:24)*

I wondered, "How am I supposed to reckon myself dead when I don't feel dead or act dead?" Paul is not teaching a psychological trick. He's teaching a principle upon which we can build a life of holiness. Your spiritual standing isn't based on your feelings. It's based on the word of God.

The world's view of faith is often different than ours. The movie *Keeping The Faith* is about a Catholic priest and a Jewish Rabbi. As is typical for Hollywood, both characters are given lines that no one with a theological education would ever repeat. In trying to explain faith to his congregation, the priest says, "Faith is not about having the right answers. Faith is a feeling. Faith is a hunch that there is something bigger connecting us all together. And that feeling — that hunch — is God." Profound, isn't it?

The Christian life isn't based on a feeling or a hunch. It's based on facts — the fact of God's love for you, the fact of his Word, the fact of the resurrection. Regardless of your feelings or hunches, these facts don't change. So, when Paul tells us to "reckon" ourselves dead to sin, he's not suggesting we attempt to manufacture a certain feeling. He's telling us to *consider* it so, because God has already said it is so. You are dead to sin *whether you feel like it or not*.

Or, for that matter, whether you act like it or not. Your feelings and your actions will eventually catch up with your faith, but first of all you must accept what God has stated to be true: Jesus Christ has made you dead to sin and alive to righteousness. This gives you the *capacity* for holiness.

It's like this. You can get a fishing license in Tennessee by just filling out a form and paying a small fee. Does having a license make you a great fisherman? No, but it gives you the *potential* of becoming a great fisherman. Without the license, you can't fish at all (at least, not legally.) With the license, you have the right to become the best fisherman in the world. Some guys get good at it, others don't. It's a question of how seriously they take the privilege of fishing. In the same way, when you accepted Jesus Christ as your Savior, he gave you a license, so to speak, to experience power over sin. He gave you the capacity to become holy. The question is, how seriously will you take it?

God made you dead to sin and alive to Christ. Accept it. Consider it so. Don't wait for a feeling to confirm it. And don't doubt God's Word simply because your behavior hasn't caught up with your faith. Believing in the power of God is a prerequisite to experiencing the power of God. So, believe it. Understand the meaning of salvation. A second thing that will help you win the battle is...

• **Do the math on sin and righteousness.**

When you think about it, sin is really stupid. Nothing good can come of it. It only wreaks havoc for those who entertain it. You'll never hear someone say, "The smartest thing I ever did was embezzle from my employer...or cheat on my income taxes...or have an affair...or experiment with cocaine...or criticize my friend behind his back" and on and on. That's because sin does nothing but destroy. Paul reminds us of this when he says...

*(v. 16) You can choose sin, which leads to death, or you can choose to obey God and receive his approval. (v. 21) And what was the result [of committing sins]? It was not good, since now you are ashamed of the things you used to do, things that end in eternal doom. (v. 23) For the wages of sin is death.*

In these verses, Paul mentions three things we need to remember about sin.
- It leads to death
- It leads to shame
- It brings about its own punishment

Let's take a closer look at that last item: Sin brings about it's own punishment. Many people have a concept of God that involves him watching us, waiting for us to sin so that he can punish us. There's an old country song...

*God's gonna getcha for that, God's gonna getcha for that
There ain't no place to run and hide, he knows where you're at.*

That's not how it works. God doesn't "getcha." Sin brings about its own punishment. Sin pays its own wages—and they aren't good. Parents understand this. When your young child reaches out to touch a hot stove, what do you say? "Don't touch the stove, you'll burn yourself!" If the child touches the stove anyway, what happens? He gets burned. Parents, what do you say? "OK. You touched the stove and got burned, now I'm going to spank you!"? Of course not. You take the child in your arms. You comfort him, dry his tears, and spray some Bactine on the burn. And you say, "Do you see why I don't want you to touch the stove? I don't want you to hurt yourself."

It's the same with our heavenly Father. He wants you to avoid sin because sin hurts. It burns. It destroys. It brings about its own punishment. The best argument for avoiding sin is to do the math on sin. Nothing good can come of it. It leads only to misery.

On the other hand, what does righteousness lead to? Life. Joy. Peace. Holiness. Fellowship with God. Paul said, *(v. 16) You can choose sin, which leads to death, or you can choose to obey God and receive his approval.* He goes on to say, *(v. 22) Now you do those things that lead to holiness and result in eternal life.*

Sin can take you in only one direction. It leads to death, shame, and misery. Obedience to God, on the other hand, takes you in a different direction. It leads to life, joy, peace, holiness, and every good thing God wants to give you. It's a non-negotiable reality. So, get the right perspective on sin and righteousness. Do the math, then make your choice. A third thing that will help you win the battle against sin...

- **Choose the master you will obey.**

Paul said, *(v. 16) Don't you realize that whatever you choose to obey becomes your master? You can choose sin, which leads to death, or you can choose to obey God and receive his approval.* This goes against the grain of the American ideal—we like to think we're rugged individualists serving only ourselves, but it's not true. Paul says that every action is an act of obedience—an act of slavery, so to speak—either to sin or to righteousness. With every action you're becoming more holy or less holy. Do you remember that Bob Dylan song from the late 70's that said...

*You gotta serve somebody,*
*It may be the devil, or it may be the Lord,*
*But you still gotta serve somebody.*

We serve the one we obey. The question is, whose slave do you want to be? Paul said, *(v. 17-18) Once you were slaves of sin, but now you have obeyed with all your heart the new teaching God has given you. Now you are free from sin, your old master, and you have become slaves to your new master, righteousness.* Imagine that— being a slave to righteousness. Being so controlled by holiness that you can't help but do right. Have you ever seen a movie in which the hero is *such a hero* that he can't help but do good? Like *Star Wars*. Han Solo decides not to participate in the rebel attack because there's no money involved. He leaves Luke Skywalker to continue without him. But Solo can't stay away. At the last moment he re-joins the fight because it's the right thing to do, and being the hero, he can't help but do the right thing. In a Hollywood way of seeing it, he's a slave to doing what's right.

This is what God wants you to be. A slave to righteousness—so resolutely committed to him that you cannot help but do what's right. He's your master, you're his slave; you have chosen to obey him and him alone. You don't have to be a slave to sin. Sometimes you may feel as though you are, but you don't have to be one. You can live a holy life. God made a promise, *(v. 14) Sin is no longer your master, for you are no longer subject to the law, which enslaves you to sin. Instead, you are free by God's grace.*

This verse is translated differently in other versions because in Greek, the word "master" is a future tense verb. It means literally, *Sin shall not have dominion over you.* It's a promise. Paul is saying, "You don't have to be controlled by sin. You can have victory. But you have to decide which master you will obey."

When Greg Maddux pitched for the Chicago Cubs, he didn't take the mound any time he wanted—he pitched when the coach said he could pitch. And he pitched the way they told him to pitch. Now he plays for the Dodgers. Picture this: The Cubs are playing in Los Angeles. Before the game, Cubs manager Lou Piniella enters the Dodger dugout and says, "OK, Maddux, we've mapped out your pitching strategy for today's game. We want only fastballs, down the middle, waist-high. Got it?" What would Maddux say? Something to the effect of, "Sorry, you're not my boss anymore. I don't play for you, I play for the Dodgers." A player's former coach can't tell him how to play the game; he has a new coach—a new master to serve, so to speak.

It's the same with you. When you became a Christian, you switched teams. Your loyalties changed. You used to be a slave to sin, but you don't have to be any more. You now have a new master to serve. Paul said, *(v. 20,22) In those days, when you were slaves of sin, you weren't concerned with doing what was right....but now you are free from the power of sin and have become slaves of God.* Choose your master. Choose who you want to serve. It's either sin or righteousness; the devil or the Lord. The one you obey is your master. Who do you want your master to be?

**CONCLUSION**

God's grace sets you free from sin—from the penalty of sin, the power of sin, and the presence of sin. Because of God's grace, you can win the war on sin. Paul said, *(v. 6) Our old sinful selves were crucified with Christ so that sin might lose its power in our lives. We are no longer slaves to sin.*

You have the capacity for holiness. That's what salvation means. You've been forgiven; you have a new life and a new master. If you continue to serve your old master, you will only experience shame and misery. But your new master offers you freedom, joy, peace and holiness. Choose your master.

SERIES: HOW CAN I BE GOOD?
**MAKE UP YOUR MIND TO BE HOLY**
ROMAN 8:1-17

*(v. 5) Those who are controlled by the Spirit think about things that please the Spirit. (NLT)* This is a powerful verse, but for years I completely missed its point. I finally discovered I was reading it wrong. I didn't see that part "B" of this phrase was the key to accomplishing part "A". I thought it was saying, "When you're controlled by the Spirit, then you'll be able to think that which pleases the Spirit." That's not what Paul is saying. He's saying, "In order to be controlled by the Spirit, *first* think about things that please the Spirit." It's the same as saying, "Those who are physically fit are those who exercise." Part B is the cause, part A is the effect. Do you want to be good? Do you want to live a Spirit-controlled life? Then learn to think about things that please the Spirit. Another translation says it this way... *(v. 5) Those who live in accordance with the Spirit have their minds set on what the Spirit desires.*

A motivational speaker said, "Ask yourself continuously, 'Is this how I really want to feel?' Because if you don't feel the way you want to feel, you should do something to change your feelings." I recommend a different approach. Ask yourself continuously, "Is this what the Holy Spirit wants me to think about? Is my mind set on his desires? Am I focused on what he wants for my life?" Becoming good—becoming holy—is a matter of putting your mind where you want your life to be. It's a matter of taking charge of your thoughts and filtering out everything that is inconsistent with God's will. Paul calls this having *a mind controlled by the Spirit.* He mentions two benefits of this kind of thinking: *(v. 6) The mind controlled by the Spirit is <u>life</u> and <u>peace</u>.*

*Life.* Of course, he's talking about more than physical existence. He's talking about quality. Life with a capital L. Life with an exclamation point. In the 60's Sammy Davis Jr. sang a song (*I've Gotta Be Me*) that contained the line: "I want to live, not merely survive." That's what God offers: Living that goes far beyond surviving, living that can best be described as thriving. It's life to the fullest. Jesus called it the abundant life. You receive it by allowing your mind to be controlled by the Holy Spirit.

*Peace.* It's the opposite of stress, the opposite of turmoil. When you make up your mind to be holy—when you set your mind on what the Spirit desires and allow him to influence your thoughts—you experience peace, even in the midst of stressful situations.

So the question is: What does the Spirit desire? What pleases him? What exactly am I supposed to think about? Romans 8 shows us three things that the Spirit wants for us. If you think on these things, you'll experience transformation—God guarantees it. First of all...

- **He wants you to experience freedom from guilt.**

I'm referring to real guilt and imaginary guilt, because both are killers. God offers freedom from both. Paul said, *(v. 1) Therefore, there is now no condemnation for those who are in Christ Jesus.* Sin separates you from God. That's why you struggle with guilt. You've done things that are wrong. You knew it was wrong at the time, and you did it anyway. Welcome to the human race. Unfortunately, sin carries a huge price tag. Paul said, *The wages of sin is death... (Romans 6:23)*

Sin leads to guilt, shame and condemnation. But God doesn't want you to live the rest of your life with guilt, shame and condemnation. Contrary to what the world may think about Christianity, our goal is not to make people feel guilty. Our goal is to show people how they can be free from guilt forever. Though you've committed sins, the good news is that God will forgive your sins. Though you deserve judgment, the good news is that God has chosen not to condemn you. When you come to Christ, he sets you free from the law of judgment. You never have to fear his judgment again: *(v. 1) Therefore, there is now no condemnation for those who are in Christ Jesus.*

Many struggle with guilt long after their sins have been forgiven, hanging on to the memory of sins that God has long-since forgotten. They say, "I don't deserve to be happy; I don't deserve to be blessed; I don't deserve to be forgiven." Of course, it's true. *No one* deserves to be forgiven...but we have been. The judgment we deserve has been lifted by the grace of God.

To become holy, think about the things which please the Spirit. Think about how God has set you free from the law of sin and death. How he sent his Son Jesus Christ into the world to die on the cross for your sins and mine, so that we could experience the fullness of life. Everyday we should wake up singing...

*Free at last, Free at last*
*Thank God almighty I'm free at last!*

We have been set free from the law of sin and death. We need never live under condemnation again. Think about that; it pleases God. Secondly...

- **He wants you to experience power over sin.**

God created us to live with power. When Jesus told his disciples about the Holy Spirit, he said, *"You will receive power when the Holy Spirit comes on you..." (Acts 1:8)* This power isn't in ourselves, it's in him. It's his power, but it's available to you. Notice what Paul says, *(v. 11) And if the Spirit of him who raised Jesus from the dead is living in you, he who raised Christ from the dead will also give life to your mortal bodies through his Spirit, who lives in you.* He's saying "The same power that brought Jesus back from the dead can be yours." Think about it: if God's power can bring a dead man back to life, don't you think his power can help you overcome temptation? God wants you to experience power over sin, but you cannot do it on your own. You need his power to make it happen. Paul said, *(v. 13) If you live according to the sinful nature you will die; but if by the Spirit you put to death the misdeeds of the body, you will live.*

"*Misdeeds of the body*" refers to more than just physical, or sexual, sins. It refers to all sins, including anger, jealousy, selfishness, pride, dishonesty, hatred, discord, and the rest. Paul says that these misdeeds — these sins — need to be put to death by the Holy Spirit. How? When sin rears its ugly head — or even when the temptation to sin presents itself — we can say, "Father, by your power you raised Christ from the dead. By your power, help me overcome this sin. Take it away, and take away my desire to sin." But understand: this is not always a one-time event. Sometimes you have to "put to death the misdeeds of the body" again and again. Sin can be like a monster in a horror show — it keeps coming back and coming back and coming back.

You've seen it in the movies, haven't you? The villain gets thrown of the roof of a building, but he survives the fall and continues to torment the victim. He gets zapped with 10,000 volts of electricity, but it doesn't kill him. He gets thrown to the bottom of the river and he swims back to shore. He gets trapped in a burning building and somehow emerges from the blaze unscathed. That's the way bad guys are in the movies — they don't die easily.

Neither do our sins. They are deeply rooted in our habits, our desires, and our way of thinking. Try to put them to death, and they'll keep coming back for more. When you try to live holy, you quickly learn that sin is a powerful presence — a force to be reckoned with. But there's good news. Even greater than the power of sin is the power of God's Spirit. The Spirit that raised Jesus from the dead gives life to your mortal body. He will give you victory over sin, no matter how many times it comes back to haunt you. You can't expect it to be easy, but you can expect to win. God wants you to experience victory, so look forward to it. Think about it. Set your mind on it. It's what the Spirit wants for you. Next...

- **He wants you to experience the benefits of adoption.**

*(v. 15) For you did not receive a spirit that makes you a slave again to fear, but you received the spirit of sonship.* The word translated *sonship* is literally the word *adoption*. Most translations say it like this: *You have received the spirit of adoption.* Paul uses the term *adoption* because the term *child of God* doesn't accurately portray

the level of relationship God wants with you. Adoption was a serious and sacred rite in Roman times involving elaborate ceremonies filled with symbolic gestures. It was not uncommon for an adult man to be adopted into a certain family for business or political reasons. For example, the Emperor Claudius adopted the full-grown Nero so that Nero could legally succeed him on the throne.

Roman adoptions were irrevocable. Once adopted always adopted, you might say. The adopted child's old life was wiped out, including all debts and all rights as the child of the former father. The adopted child became, in every sense of the word, the full and complete heir of the adoptive father. There was no legal distinction between being a biological son and an adoptive son. A man's estate belonged equally to his biological children and his adopted children.

Those who have adopted children today understand this concept. The adopted child becomes your child with no strings attached. I have a friend whose adopted son is now grown. One of his relatives once commented, "You love that boy as if he is your own son." My friend said, "You don't get it. He *is* my own son."

A friend of mine who was adopted told me his parents used to say, "Of all the babies in the world to choose from, we chose you." That's what Paul is saying: God chose you. He adopted you. You are, in every sense of the word, God's son or God's daughter. You're not his slave or his hired hand, you're his child. Paul says, *(v. 16) By him we cry 'Abba, Father'*. Abba was an intimate term that only a son or daughter would use. The word "Father" is a title; the word "Abba" is a name. A comparison today is the name "Dad." My best friend is a father, and I may refer to him as *a* father, but I don't call him "Dad" because he's not *my* father. God says, "Call me Dad. You're my child, my chosen child. All that I have belongs to you." Notice what Paul says, *(v. 17)" Now if we are children, then we are heirs — heirs of God and co-heirs with Christ, if indeed we share in his sufferings in order that we may also share in his glory.*

God wants you to experience the benefits of being his son. He's not your taskmaster or your tyrant. He's your father. He chose you to be his child. This is what you need to think about.

Paul said, *(v. 16) The Spirit himself testifies with our spirit that we are God's children.* To be holy you must set your mind on what the Spirit desires; he desires for you to know that you are God's chosen child. He doesn't want you to have an attitude of fear and slavery, he wants you bask in knowing that he is your loving father, your "Dad."

## CONCLUSION

Being holy is a matter of making up your mind to be holy. I'm not referring to a process of determination, I'm referring to a process of *realization*—realization of who you are in Christ. In Christ, your sins are forgiven. You are free from guilt and condemnation. In Christ, you have the power of the Holy Spirit to give you power over sin. In Christ, you have been adopted into God's family and you are his child, specially chosen by him.

Think about these things. Think about you are in Christ. Without him, we are lost. With him, we are his children, free from guilt, who can claim as our birthright power over sin.

*SERIES: HOW CAN I BE GOOD?*
**WE'RE MORE THAN CONQUERORS**
ROMANS 8:26-39

I grew up in Oklahoma, where football is (for some) not just a way of life, but the very meaning of life. In the seventies the OU Sooners were a college football powerhouse who didn't just defeat their opponents, they obliterated them—often scoring 60 or 70 points in a game. And no one could accuse them of running up the score, because their offense wasn't pass oriented, it was run-oriented.

The only way the Sooners could have scored fewer points would have been to just take a knee for three downs and punt. In those days, OU won by large margins because they were so much better than most of the teams they played—it just wasn't a contest.

Just as Oklahoma won football games by a lopsided margin, we've been promised the ability to win at life by a lopsided margin. In the 8th chapter of Romans, Paul says, *In all these things we are more than conquerors through him who loved us. (Romans 8:37)*

I love that phrase: *More than conquerors.* It reminds me that God didn't create us to limp through life, getting knocked around by the devil, or our circumstances, or anything else. We're made to win—and not just by a narrow margin in the closing seconds of the game. We're made to win by a blowout. We're not more conquerors, we're *more than conquerors.* For those trying to become holy, this is great news. Too often the battle against sin seems to be one we're destined to lose. The truth is, we lose only when we choose to lose—when we don't take advantage of the weapons God has provided for each of us.

Holiness begins in your mind: it's the result of what you believe about God, yourself, salvation, sin, and God's power in your life. The key to holiness is also found (as we saw last week) in controlling your thought life—setting your mind on what the

Spirit desires. This week we'll see how the ability to overcome sin—to be more than a conqueror—is a matter of finding strength in God's goodness.

Suppose two lovers are separated by distance. The young lady has undying devotion to the young man, but he doesn't know it. For him, the separation is torture. He finds no strength, no joy, no comfort in their love. Instead, he spends his days wondering what her true feelings are. "I received no letter today," he thinks. "Maybe she doesn't love me anymore. Maybe she has forgotten me." No matter how much she loves him, if he doesn't believe in her love, he will feel restless and alone. It's the same with Christ. His promises guarantee a victorious life, but if we don't believe those promises, we'll never experience their benefits. If we don't trust in his goodness and power, then his goodness and power go to waste in our lives.

God said you can be more than a conqueror. You can find strength in him, if you're willing to put his promises to work in your life. Today we'll look at three way he helps you. These are things that you can't do for yourself—he does them for you. If you will rely on him, trusting in his goodness along the way, you will experience his power—you will be more than a conqueror in life. Here are the three things we need to keep in mind.

- **The Holy Spirit is your prayer partner.**

*(v. 26) ...the Spirit helps us in our weakness. We do not know what we ought to pray for, but the Spirit himself intercedes for us with groans that words cannot express.* Awhile back I developed the habit of writing out my prayers long-hand. I got the idea from Bill Hybels, who, I think, got the idea from King David. My purpose was to become more attentive, focused, and disciplined in my prayer life. It works; I recommend it giving it a try.

However, many times I haven't known what to pray for, or how to pray about a particular situation. There were days of discouragement when I didn't *have* the words to pray. During those times I could only yield to the Holy Spirit and allow him to pray for me.

This is what the Holy Spirit does. He talks to God the Father on your behalf. He prays for you. You may not know what to say, but he does. He always prays the right prayer for you; he always prays in accordance with God's will. As Paul said, *(v. 27) And he who searches our hearts knows the mind of the Spirit, because the Spirit intercedes for the saints in accordance with God's will.*

It's like this. When my kids were little, they would often come in the kitchen and say, "I'm hungry! I need a snack! Can I have a cookie?" Their mother would say, "Of course, you can have a snack. Here's a banana." My kids knew they had a "need", but they didn't always ask for the right thing. Their mom knew how to translate the request and give them what was best for them.

There were also times when my children didn't have any idea what to ask for. Their body had a fever, their stomach was too upset to hold down food, and all they could do was cry. During those times, their mother heard their cries, and she knew what they meant. (Isn't it amazing how moms know?)

When you pray, remember that the Holy Spirit is praying with you. We don't always know how we ought to pray, but he does. And he intercedes for us according to the will of God.

Have you heard the saying, "Be careful what you ask for, because you just might get it." The only way you can believe that statement is if you don't believe in the goodness of God. A cruel, apathetic God might not stand in the way of you receiving some of your foolish requests—like a bad parent might give their kids cupcakes every time—but our God isn't like that.

When you ask for things that aren't good for you, or aren't in accordance with God's will for your life—the Holy Spirit searches your heart and intercedes on your behalf. You have an all-powerful, all-knowing prayer partner. In fact, not just one prayer partner, but two. Paul said... *(v. 34) Christ Jesus who died—more than that, who was raised to life—is at the right hand of God and is also interceding for us.*

This is an example of God's goodness towards you. Jesus prays for you. The Holy Spirit prays for you. You're a member of an Almighty prayer team. Remember this when you pray; it will help you become more than a conqueror. Secondly, keep in mind...

- **God is in control of the events of your life.**

*(v. 28) And we know that in all things God works for the good of those who love him, who have been called according to his purpose.* If your heart is yielded to God, nothing bad can happen to you, ever. Period. Now, take note. I didn't say that nothing unpleasant can ever happen, or nothing irritating can ever happen, or nothing sad can ever happen. These things are a fact of life. But when they happen, God has promised to work them out for our good...for our benefit.

Don't you know someone who lost a job, only to find a better one? Don't you know someone (maybe yourself) whose heart was broken in a bad relationship, only later to find true love? I'm sure we've all seen the occasional negative experience turn into something positive. For believers, these experiences aren't just lucky coincidences. This is part and parcel of our everyday experience. God makes the events of your life work out for the best.

To benefit from this promise, you must trust in God's goodness. Otherwise, you'll fall apart every time things don't go according to plan. One minor setback will cause you to think that God has deserted you and the world is caving in on you. This isn't what God intended for you. He made you to live above your circumstances. He wants you to live with absolute, total, and complete confidence. That's why Paul said, *(v. 31) If God is for us, who can be against us?* No situation need get the best of you, because God is in control of the events in your life. Through him, you are more than a conqueror. But, to experience it, you must believe it. You must trust in God's goodness. Thirdly, keep in mind...

- **You are surrounded by God's inseparable love.**

*(v. 35) Who shall separate us from the love of Christ? Shall trouble or hardship or persecution or famine or nakedness or danger or*

*sword?... (v. 37) No, in all these things we are more than conquerors through him who loved us. (v. 38) For I am convinced that neither death nor life, neither angels nor demons, neither the present nor the future, nor any power, neither height nor depth, nor anything else in all creation, will be able to separate us from the love of God that is Christ Jesus our Lord.*

If you're tempted to think God no longer loves you, stop and ask yourself, "What caused me to think such a thing?" Was it a business failure or financial problems? Were you victimized by some cruel and hateful person? Was it a health problem, or the death of someone close to you? Was it the memory of a sin you committed long ago? Or a sin you committed yesterday? If it was a hardship, Paul says hardship can't separate you from God's love. If it was mistreatment, Paul says persecution can't separate you from God's love. Neither can sickness, poverty, crime or danger. Nothing in all creation — not even sin — can separate you from the love of God

A friend of mine was convinced that no one at work liked him — and he was probably right. Every day his co-workers gave him the cold shoulder. The more he tried to ingratiate himself to them, the more they seemed to despise him. Needless to say, this had a devastating effect on his self-confidence. He wanted to quit, but he was contractually bound to stay.

But then he experienced a profound change. He began to meditate on God's love. He realized that the one who matters most loves him most of all. He realized that the people at work — those whose affection he had tried so hard to win — were really insignificant in terms of the big picture. Each day at the office he reminded himself that he was surrounded by God's inseparable love. The more he basked in God's love, the less affected he was by his co-workers' cold shoulder.

There's strength in knowing God's love. When you focus on him, the fickleness of others becomes insignificant. He promised he'll always love you, but if you don't believe that promise, you'll miss out on the benefits. If you don't believe his promise, you'll be a slave to the opinions of others. But if you trust in

God's goodness, if you rely with all your heart on his promise to love you forever—you can approach challenges with strength and security. If you want to be more than a conqueror, remember that nothing in the world can separate you from God's love.

## CONCLUSION

Do you want to become holy? Do you want to become good? Paul says, *Be transformed the renewing of your mind. (Romans 12:2)* The battle for holiness is fought and won in the mind. It's all about what you think, what you believe. When you believe the right things about God, you experience his power—the power to become good.

To become more than a conqueror, you must learn to trust in God's goodness. Believe his promises. When you pray, he prays with you. When hard times come your way, he works them out for your good. And when others turn their back on you, his love remains eternally faithful. Relying on these promises—that's what makes you more than a conqueror.

## WHAT TO DO WHEN YOU'VE BLOWN IT
PSALM 51

Today we'll read about a man of God who "blew it" in a big way. He committed sins you wouldn't expect a good man to commit. And it wasn't one of those cases where he accidentally sinned before he realized what was going on. No, he put a great deal of thought and effort into his sin, and he went to greater trouble to cover it up. In fact, his life reads more like an Oliver Stone script than a Bible story. When the smoke finally cleared, two people were dead and two families destroyed. Most amazing, however, is the fact that this event didn't ruin the man. He recovered from his failure and got back on his feet. You probably already know that I'm talking about King David. He's the same one who as a teenager killed Goliath, and who later wrote the most recognizable passage in the Bible, *The Lord is my Shepherd I shall not want*.

Here's the story. One evening, King David couldn't sleep, so he took a walk on the balcony of his palace. In the distance he saw a beautiful woman named Bathsheba taking a bath. When he learned that her husband, Uriah, was a soldier at war, David sent for her and seduced her. Sometime later she told him she was pregnant. In an attempt to cover his tracks, David had Uriah come home from the battlefield for some "R&R".

When David urged Uriah to go spend time with his wife, Uriah politely refused—doing such a thing during a time of war would have been disloyal to his fellow soldiers. Since Uriah couldn't be persuaded to compromise, David sent him back to battle with a letter to deliver to the commanding officer. Uriah didn't know it, but he was delivering his own death warrant. The letter told the CO to put Uriah on the front lines and withdraw the other troops so Uriah would be sure to die.

This is exactly what happened. Uriah was killed in battle and David married Bathsheba. No one in Israel knew the story behind the story, but the bible says, *The Lord was very displeased with what David had done. (2 Samuel 11:27)*

It wasn't long before a prophet named Nathan confronted David with his sin. David knew he had done wrong, and I'm sure he knew he couldn't get away with it. To make matters worse, David and Bathsheba's newborn child was very sick, and Nathan said it was all David's fault. He said, "Because of what you have done, this baby will die." Imagine how David felt about that! He couldn't hide it any longer. He had blown it in a big way, and now it was time to face the music.

David did face the music. He made things right with God and got his life back on track. During this time of repentance and renewal, he wrote Psalm 51. David's story teaches how to make things right after you've made everything wrong. When you sin—even when you sin big—God forgives you and helps you get back on your feet. In order for this to happen, here's what you need to do. First of all, getting back on track requires a...

- **Change of heart**

In the first two verses of Psalm 51, David begs forgiveness, then says, *(v. 3-4) For I know my transgressions, and my sin is always before me. Against you, you only, have I sinned and done what is evil in your sight.* He was guilty and he knew it. He couldn't deny his wrongdoing any longer. He could only confess his sin and ask God for forgiveness.

Do you remember back when Dennis Rodman played basketball? Seems like he was always doing something outrageous on the court, like the time he made headlines for kicking a cameraman. He was suspended for 11 games and forced to pay $200,000 to the victim. Rodman took his punishment, but his attitude reflected anything but a change of heart. In fact, he insisted that what he had done wasn't all that bad. He said that he himself was the victim since he was being forced to pay money only because he's rich. After all, he said, he just gave the guy a little tap. He must have forgotten that everyone saw the footage (no pun intended) of the assault. The bottom line was, even after the payout and the suspension, Dennis Rodman didn't believe he had done anything wrong.

Too often, we're the same way about our sin. We justify it. We pretend it's not so bad. We explain why, in these special circumstances, it really isn't a sin. As long as we maintain this defiant attitude we can never be completely right with God. Getting right requires a change of heart.

When I was young and I would get into trouble, my mother would ask me if I was sorry. Of course, my answer was always yes. Then she would ask the tough question, "Are you sorry you did it, or are you just sorry you got caught?" A change of heart means that we're sorry we did it, regardless of who knows or doesn't know about our sin. Secondly, getting back on track requires a...

- **Change of mind**

Have you ever noticed how we gladly take credit for our accomplishments, but we often blame our failures on extenuating circumstances? How many times have you heard someone say something like, "I'm sorry I lost my temper. It's because I'm so tired...I'm under pressure...You were getting on my nerves."

Our tendency is to place blame elsewhere when we fail. When people say, "I'm not myself today" they usually mean they're at their worst, not their best. It's not easy to accept responsibility for failures, but it's necessary for anyone who wants to get back on track with God. You have to change your mind about who is in control of your life. You must stop blaming others and accept responsibility for your actions.

In 1980 New York City Mayor Ed Koch appeared on a local news program in the middle of the city's financial crisis. Koch had spent over a quarter of a million dollars to put up bike lanes in Manhattan, and they turned out to be a disaster. Cars were driving in the bike lanes, pedestrians were walking in the them, and bikers were getting crowded out. It was a mess and many New Yorkers were irate. Koch was coming up for re-election, so a handful of journalists cornered him on this show, planning to tear him to pieces for spending money foolishly when the city was nearly broke. One reporter said, "Mayor, in light of the financial difficulties New York City is facing, how could you possibly justify wasting $300,000 on bike lanes?" The stage was set for a half-hour confrontation.

Instead, Koch said, "It was a terrible idea. I thought it would work, but it didn't. It was one of the worst mistakes I ever made." Then he stopped. None of the other journalists knew what to say or do. They were expecting him to squirm and make excuses, but he didn't even try. The next journalist stammered and said, "But Mayor Koch, how could you do this?" Koch said, "I already told you. It was a stupid idea. It didn't work." Then he stopped.

There were still 26 minutes left to go on the news show, and the reporters had to find something else to talk about. The last thing they expected that day was for the mayor take responsibility for his actions. Ultimately, of course, Koch went on to receive both the Democratic and the Republican endorsements for re-election and repeated a term as mayor of New York City. (Taken from Roger Ailes's book, *You Are The Message* ©1996, Doubleday & Company)

You must change your mind about who's in control of your life. You can't blame your sin on anyone else. You are responsible for your actions. It does no good to say, "I am a victim of my environment, or a victim of my circumstances, or a victim of genealogy, or a victim of bad luck." We can't be like the character in West Side Story who said, "I'm depraved on account of I was deprived." David could have said, "It was Bathsheba's fault. Look what she was wearing." Or he could have blamed God. Or he could have blamed his other wives (yes, wives—he had hundreds of them) for not being sensitive to his needs. He could have placed blame in several different areas, but he realized that it was now time to take responsibility for his actions and take back control of his life.

That's why he said, (v. 4) *Against you, you only have I sinned...You are proved right when you speak and justified when you judge. I have been a sinner from birth.* He's saying, "I'm responsible for what I've done. I can't blame anyone but myself." Getting on track requires a change of heart, a change of mind, and a...

- **Change of direction**

David's life got off track because he started doing things his way and going his own direction. Suddenly, he recognized that his life had skidded out of control, and he needed to make it right. He also realized that he couldn't do it without God's help. Notice his words, *(v. 7-12) Cleanse me...wash me...blot out all my iniquity...create in me a clean heart...renew a steadfast spirit within me.* You can mess up your life without anyone's help, but it takes an act of God to get you back on track. You must depend on him to cleanse and forgive you.

Too often we try to clean ourselves up and make ourselves "good" in order to be acceptable to God—and that simply isn't acceptable to God! There is only one truly acceptable way to come to God—*Just As I Am*. When we come to him this way *he is faithful and just to forgive us and cleanse us from all unrighteousness.* (1 John 1:9)

Getting back on track requires a change of direction. You stop going your way and start going God's way. What does it mean to "go God's way"?

**a. Spend time alone with God on a consistent basis.** David said, *Do not cast me from your presence (v. 11)* because he recognized that spending time with God is what gives our lives direction.

**b. Be filled with the Holy Spirit.** David said, *Do not take your Holy Spirit from me (v. 11)* because he recognized that we need the Holy Spirit's power in our lives to overcome the power of sin.

**c. Ask God to give us a sense of joy.** David said, *Restore to me the joy of your salvation (v.12)* because he recognized that a relationship with God is supposed to make you happy, not miserable. We can't get back on track if we think that serving God is torture.

**d. Ask for the power to be consistent.** David said, *Grant me a willing spirit to sustain me (v.12)* because he recognized that we can't be changed if we're not willing to be changed on an ongoing basis.

**e. Look for the chance to help others.** David said, *Then I will teach transgressors your ways and sinners will turn back to you (v.13)* because he recognized the Good News is worth sharing with others.

## CONCLUSION
- A change of heart.
- A change of mind.
- A change of direction.

Do you know what all of this adds up to? Repentance.

When you blow it, you need to repent. Some people think that repentance is feeling guilty, but I've got "bad news" for those people: feeling guilty isn't enough. There's more to repentance than just feeling bad. Of course, when you sin you do feel guilty. That's natural. But if you feel guilty too long, you haven't really repented. Repentance removes guilt.

When David asked for God's forgiveness he also asked God to restore the joy of salvation. Repentance results in joy. If you've blown it, you need to get past feeling guilty and get back on track. Ask God to help you change your heart, and change your mind, and change your direction so that you can once again experience the joy of his presence.

# THE SIGNIFICANCE OF EASTER
MARK 16:1-8

The single most significant event in history took place on the Sunday after Passover around the year 30 A.D. It's the day we're celebrating today: Easter. Why is it important? Because the events of that day—the events we read about in Mark 16—confirm three very important things about life. Without Easter, the name of Jesus Christ would be about as recognizable as the name Theudas. Who, you may ask, is Theudas? That's my point. He lived in Israel several years before Christ. He was, in his time, a popular prophet and teacher. He attracted hundreds of followers, and when he offended the wrong people, he was put to death. Sound familiar? Then why haven't we ever heard of him? Because after his death his followers scattered and went on to other things, and the world soon forgot about Theudas.

When Jesus died, it appeared the same thing would happen—even before he died most of his followers deserted him. Do you remember the Apostle Peter? He was one of Jesus' key disciples. Jesus once said to him, "You are a rock, and on this rock I will build my church."*[Matthew 16:18]*But Peter the rock crumbled like sand when Jesus faced death. He deserted him, he denied having anything to do with him, and he disappeared. When Jesus died, it appeared that his "cause" would die with him, and that he would become as obscure as Theudas.

But it didn't happen that way. The followers of Jesus didn't fade into oblivion. In fact, they came back bolder and braver than ever before. What happened? What made the difference? Easter Sunday, that's what made the difference. When Jesus died he was placed in a tomb, and everyone assumed that was the end of it. Then, on the third day, he came back to life. He was dead and gone, and then he was alive and with them again. Seeing his resurrection firsthand changed his followers' perspective on life and death and everything in between.

Easter Sunday (and what it stands for—the resurrection of Jesus) confirms three important truths about life. Let's look at each one, and consider how they affect our lives today. First, because of the resurrection, we know...

- **Jesus is who He said He was.**

Jesus claimed to be God, and he proved it. He did what Theudas couldn't do: he beat death. You have probably heard people say something like, "Jesus was a great moral teacher, like Buddha, or Confucius, or Mohammed." You can't really say that, though. Here's why. Buddha and Confucius claimed only to be moral teachers, nothing more. Mohammed claimed to be a prophet of God, but never claimed to be more than just a man. On the other hand, Jesus made claims about himself that Buddha, Confucius, or Mohammed never made about themselves. Jesus claimed to be God. He claimed that he had always existed, that he would always exist, that all creation belonged to him, and that someday he would rule the world.

Now, if I made these claims—if I stood before you this morning and said, "Folks, I am God and someday I'll rule the world"—would you leave here today thinking, "What a good moral teacher our pastor is!"? Of course not. You would think, "He's lying, he's crazy, and he's dangerous." And, of course, if I made those claims, you would be correct. But when Jesus made these claims, he was telling the truth. Repeatedly Jesus claimed to be God, and it drove his enemies crazy. John 5:18 says, *For this reason the Jews tried all the harder to kill him; not only was he breaking the Sabbath, but he was even calling God his own Father, making himself equal with God. (John 5:18)*

When Jesus referred to God as his father, he didn't say it like we say it—"I have an earthly father and God is my heavenly father"—Jesus meant quite literally that "God is my Father and I have no earthly father." He claimed to be God, and he proved his claim by conquering death. This means that we have to take seriously everything he said. For example, he said, *"I am the way, and the truth, and the life. No one comes to the Father except through me." (John 14:6)* We must abandon the notion that "all religions lead to the same place" and "it doesn't matter what you believe as long as you're sincere." Jesus said specifically, *"I am the gate. Whoever enters through me will be saved." (John 10:9)*

Because of the resurrection, these words carry weight they never would have carried otherwise. If he had remained in the grave, the question of whether or not he is the only way to heaven would be a matter of debate. However, the resurrection answers the question and ends the argument once and for all. Is Jesus really the Son of God? Well, he has power over death, so I guess that means he is everything he claimed to be. Another important truth that Easter confirms is...

- **No situation is beyond God's power.**

On the surface, it appears that the death of Jesus initiated the death of his dream. It appears that God lost and the devil won. Jesus died the worst possible death a man can die. He was ridiculed, mocked, spat upon, beaten, stripped and hung on a cross—the ultimate humiliation for a Jew. [Galatians 3:13] The end of his life ran contrary to what everyone expected would happen when the Jewish Messiah appeared. They believed the Messiah would usher in a political kingdom. Instead, they watched him become the ultimate victim. For most people it was unthinkable that God would be behind the events of Jesus' death.

Yet, God had a plan. The death of Jesus would pay for the sins of the world. Through his death, all of creation would be reconciled to God. [Colossians 1:19-20] Through his death, the power of death would be defeated once and for all. And through his resurrection, he would be shown to be Lord of all. [1 Corinthians 15]

When you read about the death of Christ in the gospels, or when you see a movie like *The Passion of the Christ*, it's difficult not to be overcome with a sense of tragedy—a sense of loss—as Jesus is nailed to the cross. It appears, for a moment, that his enemies won the war. But God wasn't finished. Since we know how the story turns out, we can almost hear all heaven shout triumphantly as Jesus was laid in the tomb. You can almost hear the Father say, "Aha! I've got you right where I want you!" He knew on the third day the stone that closed his tomb would be rolled away. He knew that the blood in this lifeless corpse would flow again, his lungs would fill with air, strength would return to his body, and he would stand again.

Just as God brought his Son back from the dead, he can cause a resurrection in your life, as well. What has died? What dreams, what hopes, what relationship, what vision? What is happening in your world that appears to be beyond the hand of God?

Have you heard the sermon called "It's Friday...but Sunday's Coming!"? Oh, I wish I could preach it like the man who made it famous. His delivery, I'm afraid, is more dynamic than mine. But the idea of the message is: "It's Friday...Jesus has died...his followers are crying and the devil is laughing as Jesus lies cold in the grave...but Sunday is coming! It's Friday and it looks like the devil is winning...but Sunday is coming. It's Friday and it looks like the dream has ended...but Sunday is coming. It's Friday and the smell of death is in the air...but Sunday is coming. It's Friday and you may be tempted to give up and quit...but Sunday is coming."

Easter morning teaches that no matter what happens on Friday, Sunday is coming. Nothing is beyond God's power. The resurrection makes the word "hopeless" obsolete. It makes the word "impossible" meaningless. It makes the word "despair" powerless. That's why Paul said, *And if the Spirit of him who raised Christ from the dead is living in you, he ... will also give life to your mortal bodies through the Spirit. (Romans 8:11)* And it is why Paul said, *Now to him who is able to do immeasurably more than all we ask or imagine, according to his power that is at work within us, to him be the glory..."(Ephesians 3:20-21)* And it is why Paul said, *I can do all things through Christ who strengthens me. (Philippians 4:13)* No situation is beyond God's power to save; the resurrection proves it. Another important truth that Easter confirms is...

- **God's forgiveness is available to everyone.**

As the women stepped into the empty tomb that Sunday morning, they were met by an angel dressed in a white robe. He told them that Jesus had been risen from the dead. He said, *(v. 7)* "Go tell his disciples <u>and Peter</u>, 'He is going ahead of you into Galilee...'" Have you ever wondered why the angel mentioned Peter specifically? It was so there wouldn't be any doubt in anyone's mind that God intended to fully restore this fallen disciple. All of the disciples had deserted Jesus in his final hours, but Peter's failure was the most conspicuous. He denied Jesus. Three times. And remember, Jesus had once said, *"But whoever denies me before others, I will also deny before my Father in heaven." (Matthew 10:33 NRSV)*

I'm sure Peter believed that he was washed up as a follower of Christ. I'm sure most of Jesus' other disciples believed the same thing...about Peter. God wanted to make it clear to them, and he wants to make it clear to you now: His forgiveness is available to everyone—even you.

Here's the part about the death of Jesus that no one really understood at the time, but it became increasingly obvious over the years. When Jesus died on the cross, all the sins of the world were placed on his shoulders. Every sin ever committed—sins of the past, sins of the present, sins of the future—were placed upon Jesus. The Bible says, *God made him who had no sin to be sin for us, so that in him we might become the righteousness of God in Christ. (2 Corinthians 5:21)*

Jesus paid the price for your sin, and he paid it all. There's nothing left for you to pay. There's nothing left for you to do...except receive his forgiveness. During his earthly ministry Jesus went around forgiving sins. His promise of forgiveness would have been meaningless without the resurrection. The resurrection proves that he has the power to forgive your sins.

Pay close attention. If you struggle with sin and the guilt is eating you up, God will forgive you. Your spouse may never forgive you. Your co-workers may never forgive you. Your enemies may never forgive you. But listen! Forgiveness isn't theirs to give or withhold. The one who has power to forgive is the one who has power over death. He will forgive you, absolutely and completely, without fail, when you come to him in repentance. *If we confess our sins, he is faithful and just to forgive us our sins and cleanse us from all unrighteousness. (1 John 1:9)*

That's why the angel said, "Tell his disciples *and Peter.*"

## CONCLUSION

Easter Day is the most significant day in history. Were it not for Easter, our world would be unrecognizably different. Because of Easter, because of the resurrection, we know that Jesus is who he claimed to be. He is who the Bible says he is — God in the flesh. He has power over death and he has the power to change your life. He has the power — and the love — to wipe away your sins forever and welcome you back into his arms.

# IT DOESN'T MATTER WHO YOU USED TO BE
1 TIMOTHY 1:12-14

In the early months of 1998 many proponents of the death penalty stepped out of character momentarily to plead for mercy on behalf of Karla Faye Tucker, a murderer sentenced to be executed by the state of Texas. Karla had committed an unspeakably horrible crime. A drug addicted prostitute, she broke in to her ex-boyfriend's apartment armed with a pick axe and brutally murdered him and another woman. She was found guilty and sentenced to death.

Once in prison, Karla Faye met Christ. For the next 14 years she lived out her faith as a model inmate. As the day of her execution approached, the media picked up her story. She was featured on *Nightline*, *Larry King*, and *The 700 Club*. Viewers had a hard time imagining her as the cold-blooded murderer she once was. Her life had clearly changed, as those who knew her well would testify.

She petitioned the authorities for her sentence to be commuted from death to life-without-parole. Dozens stood up for her as character witnesses, including prison guards, former prosecutors, the detective who arrested her, and even the Pope. The petition wasn't granted; on February 3, 1998, Karla was executed by the state of Texas.

Karla isn't the first notorious killer to repent. Some people suspect the validity of these jailhouse conversions, but many times they're real — and the changes they produce are permanent.

Another high-profile criminal conversion in recent history is that of Charles Colson, former hatchet man for Richard Nixon. Though he was not guilty of murder, he committed crimes during the Watergate era that earned him a prison sentence. While serving time Colson met Christ. The change in his life was dramatic; it cannot be denied that the church (and society as a whole) has reaped the benefits of his conversion. After his parole,

Colson established Prison Fellowship, a jail ministry that spans the globe. He also became a leader and spokesman for the evangelical church. It's hard to imagine that a person can move in one direction for decades, and suddenly, miraculously, change course. But it happens. Some of you here today are living proof.

This phenomenon can be seen in scripture. There are many examples; the best known is Paul. For years he was an enemy of the church. He considered it his job to eliminate the threat of Christianity by killing Christians. Then on a trip to Damascus he had a face-to-face encounter with Christ that changed his life forever. Eventually Paul became the most significant man in the history of the church.

Let these examples remind you of a wonderful Biblical truth: *It doesn't matter who you used to be.* No matter how bad you've been, no matter how bad you think you are, God can and will forgive you. He can and will change your life. In today's text, Paul elaborates on this principle in three specific areas. Let's take a closer look. First of all...

- **God loves you in spite of your past.**

Paul acknowledges that he had a past to live down. He said, *(v. 12-13) I thank Christ Jesus our Lord, who has given me strength...even though I was once a blasphemer and a persecutor and a violent man...* In verse 15 he goes so far as to say that he was the worst of all sinners. Some of you may be thinking "He wouldn't say that if he knew me!" The fact is, God loves you in spite of the sins you have committed—no matter how bad they might be. There is nothing you can do to keep God from loving you. It doesn't matter who you used to be.

This is evident in the gospels. Jesus never judges a person based on his or her past. When people came to him who had committed sexual sin, or had dabbled in the occult, or had spent their lives cheating others in business, his message was the same: "I do not condemn you; go and sin no more." Jesus offered love and acceptance to everyone, even "sinners" — regardless of what their past had been.

Several years ago a woman told me that God could never love her because she had committed the worst possible sin. In a fit of rage, she said, because her baby wouldn't stop crying, she shook him so hard that his brain was permanently damaged. Every day she is reminded that her own child, now an adult, is forced to live with the consequences of her sin. She told me she had no right to be a mother, no right to be a Christian, and in fact, no right to live. "God couldn't possibly love me," she said. My response to her was exactly what I'm saying today: God loves you in spite of your past.

There is nothing you can do to change God's love for you. He loves you so much that he couldn't possibly love you more, and he will never love you less. I don't say this so you will have an excuse to sin; I say it so you will have a reason to hope. God doesn't see you as a second-class citizen. He doesn't consider you a has-been. His love for you is as great as it ever was. It doesn't matter who you used to be, God loves you in spite of your past. Secondly...

- **God will save you in spite of your past.**

Paul said, *(v. 14) The grace of our Lord was poured out on me abundantly, along with the faith and love that are in Christ Jesus.* He then reminds us of this Biblical truth: *(v. 15) Here is a trustworthy saying that deserves full acceptance: Christ Jesus came into the world to save sinners.*

When I say that God will save you, this is exactly what I mean. First, he will forgive you completely and wipe the slate clean. Second, he will change you into the type of person he wants you to be. When you accept Christ, you become a new creation [2 Corinthians 5:17].

This is only the beginning. Philippians 1:6 Paul says that God will finish the work he began in you. Romans 8:29 says that God will help you become conformed to the image of his son, Jesus Christ. It doesn't matter who you used to be, God will save you in spite of your past, and he will change you in spite of your past.

Too often we use the past as an excuse: "I've always been this way...I've always had a problem with my temper...Everyone in my family is overweight...I just don't have any self-control...I come from a long line of alcoholics..." and on and on. Many believe that "this is who I am and there's nothing I can do about it."

I'm telling you today: there is something you can do about it. Let God change you. He can part the Red Sea, he can make the earth stand still, he can hold back the rain for years at a time, he can heal the sick and he can raise the dead. And he can make you a better person. This is what Paul meant when he said, *He who raised Christ from the dead will also give life to your mortal bodies through his Spirit, who lives in you. (Romans 8:11)*

One day John Wesley (founder of the Methodist Church) was riding on horseback through the English countryside when he was stopped by a voice that said, "Your money or your life." As the man took Wesley's money, Wesley said, "Sir, you may someday regret this sort of life you are living. If you do, remember, the blood of Jesus cleanses you from all sin." Many years later, at the close of a Sunday evening service in which Wesley had just preached, a man requested the opportunity to speak to him. It was the same man who had robbed Wesley years before; he was now a successful businessman and a faithful Christian. The words Wesley had spoken to him had proven to be life-changing. He said to Wesley, "I owe it all to you." Wesley said, "No, not to me, but to the precious blood of Christ which cleanses us from all sin."

God can change you no matter what kind of past you've had. For some the change is immediate; for others it's a lengthy process. For everyone, it is a promise to cling to: It doesn't matter who you used to be, God will change you in spite of your past. Thirdly...

- **God can use you in spite of your past.**

*(v. 12, 16) [Christ] considered me faithful, appointing me to his service....I was shown mercy so that in me, the worst of sinners, Christ*

*Jesus might display his unlimited patience as an example for those who would believe in him and receive eternal life.* Look at some examples from scripture. Moses was a mighty man of God; God used him after he committed murder. David was Israel's greatest ruler; God used him after he committed murder and adultery. Peter and Paul were leaders in the early church; God used Paul after he committed murder, and he used Peter after he denied Christ. John-Mark was Paul's traveling companion; God used him even after he bailed out and quit the ministry. As long as you have breath, as long as you have a life to surrender to God, he can use you. It doesn't matter who you used to be.

## CONCLUSION

You can forget the past, because God has forgotten the past. He is concerned with who you're becoming, not who you've been. If you made mistakes years ago or months ago or even days ago, God is willing to put it behind you and give you a new start. You may have to live with the consequences of your mistakes, but you don't have to live with the guilt. It doesn't matter who you used to be. In spite of your past, God loves you, he'll change you, and he'll use you—if you open your heart to him.

SERIES: THE FAMILY CIRCLE
**HOW TO DEVELOP A TIGHT-KNIT FAMILY**
JOHN 10:22-30

It's obvious that in today's text Jesus is not talking specifically about the nuclear family. However, he is saying something here that all families need to learn. Our family relationships are to mirror the relationship that Jesus has with the father and that they have with us, the sheep. From this passage we can learn how to build a stronger family.

Let's think about what a family is. We know the traditional idea is a mom, dad, kids, and possibly a dog. The fact is, however, only one out of every six people in the United States live in the traditional setting of one mom being married to one dad one time with children from that marriage only. So, what about the remaining 84%? Is their family life doomed forever? Of course not. If your home has been broken by death or divorce, God hasn't turned his back on you. Whatever family situation you're in right now, he wants to help you be the strongest family you can possibly be.

The Census Bureau defines a family as people who live in the same house. Others would define a family as people who share the same last name. There's more to it than that. Today we'll look at six characteristics of a tight-knit family. First of all...

- **A tight-knit family listens to one another.**

(v. 27) *"My sheep [my family] listen to my voice."* The biggest obstacle in personal communication is not the inability to speak your mind, it's the inability to listen. Stephen Covey says, "Many people do not listen with intent to understand. They listen with intent to reply." This isn't really listening. The book of Proverbs says, *He who answers before listening — that is his folly and his shame. (Proverbs 18:13)* This describes how some parents listen to their children, and how some spouses listen to one another. This is why communication breaks down within families.

Chris Conway is a single parent, the father of two teenage sons. The boys had gotten involved with a youth group and were very enthusiastic about it. Mr. Conway asked them what they liked about the group, and the older son answered, "We can tell the leaders really care about us by the way they listen to us." This surprised Conway, and he said, "I listen to you." His son said, "I know that. But you are always doing something else. All you ever say is 'yes' 'no' or 'I'll think about it.'"

At that moment, Chris Conway decided that he was going to focus on listening to his sons. At dinner each night, whenever one of the boys would speak, he would stop eating, set down his fork, turn to his son and listen. This revolutionized his relationship with his sons. And since he spent so much time listening at the dinner table, he lost fifteen pounds during the first five weeks. Most importantly, the average length of their evening meal went from less than ten minutes to almost forty-five. Tight-knit families listen to one another. Secondly...

- **A tight-knit family gets to know one another.**

Once I led a family retreat. I spoke to the youth in the morning and the parents in the afternoon. During the morning session I asked the youth a series of questions such as "What is your favorite color? What is your favorite TV show? How do you spend your spare time? Who is your favorite recording artist?" They wrote down their answers, signed their name, and gave me their papers. That afternoon, when I met with the parents, I gave them a test. As I read the responses of the questionnaire, I asked the parents to identify which one belonged to their child. Of the more than two dozen parents there, only a couple got it right. Most were strangers to their own children.

One reason the TV show Frasier became so popular is that people could relate to it. The original premise of the show was that a father and son who know nothing about each other — and are as different as night and day — end up living together. The series is primarily about how these two grown men, father and son, finally get to know one another.

Jesus said about his sheep, *"I know them."* (v. 27) The great news of the gospel is that our relationship with God is personal...it is intimate...he wants to be close to us, and us to be close to him. He says, "I know you." The same bond we share with him he wants us to share with others.

My sister moved out of the house more than 30 years ago; we now live 300 miles apart. We don't get to see each other nearly enough, but we talk on the phone frequently. It's amazing how we never run out of things to talk about. If she suggests that I see a particular movie or TV show, I know I'm going to like it. Occasionally something funny will happen and I have to stop what I'm doing to call her, because only she will appreciate the humor in the situation. This is because we know each other. A family is more than just a group of people that live together, a family takes the time to get to know one another. Thirdly...

- **A tight-knit family is submitted to the Lordship of Christ.**

There's an important distinction in teaching children obedience. It's not a case of my children having to live by my rules, it's a case of our whole family being under the authority of Christ and living by his rules. Jesus said, *"[My sheep] follow me."* (v. 27) Children must understand that we have a path to follow; we're not making our own rules or calling our own shots. The parents, as well as the whole family, has a standard to live by — a standard that has been established by Jesus.

My kids hear me preach every Sunday. Hopefully they learn a little bit about Christianity in the process. Their greatest lessons, however, are not learned in the pew. They're learned at the little league field. I'm a coach, and each summer my kids get an up-close look at how serious I am about following Christ. They see how well I take losing, how well I take winning, how fair I am to the less gifted players, whether or not I show favoritism to my own kids, whether or not I coach with a "win at all costs" mentality, how I respond to criticism, and on and on. They've seen me get off track and get back on track. They have seen me make principled decisions that were based on priorities other than winning. Throughout the process they see first hand that I don't live according to my own idea of right and wrong. I am submitted to the Lordship of Christ; the rules that I challenge them to live by are the same rules that I strive to follow. Next...

- **A tight-knit family has spiritual values.**

(v. 28) *"I give them eternal life."* Jesus doesn't just want us to be happy, he wants us to be holy. He teaches that there is more to life than meets the eye. We are to live with an eternal perspective. It's not enough for your children to get into the right school and make good grades and get a good job and earn lots of money. If your children don't learn spiritual values at home — if they don't learn to live with an eternal perspective — they will not be prepared to face the world as an adult.

Whether you're a football fan or not, you probably know the reputation the Oklahoma Sooner football program had in the 1980's. To be blunt, it was a program out of control. Recruiting rules were disregarded. Players were, at the same time, pampered and exploited. A significant percentage never made it to graduation. More than a few found themselves in serious legal trouble, facing charges of rape, robbery, drug possession, drug dealing, assault with a deadly weapon and on and on. In fact, Jay Leno once commented that University officials should work out an arrangement with prison officials so players could wear the same number in prison that they wore on the field. Barry Switzer had not exactly built a program known for academic excellence; he was no Joe Paterno. (Barry joked that the reason OU had a recruiting advantage over state rival OSU was because the name of his school was easier to spell.)

Into this program came J.C. Watts. He played quarterback for the Sooners, leading them to two consecutive Orange Bowl victories. Watts was exposed to the same life-style that ambushed so many others, but it didn't phase him. He earned a degree in journalism, had a career in the Canadian Football League., and eventually returned to Oklahoma to serve four terms in Congress. He's now in business for himself. Clearly, his life has taken a different path than that of many of his teammates. What made the difference? According to J.C. Watts, it was his family. His father was a pastor, and the Watts' home life was more than just religious, it was spiritual. He grew up knowing that he had a calling to serve God. When you hear him today, you discover that his life is more about ministry than career. This is because he grew up in a family committed to spiritual values that taught him to live life with an eternal perspective. Next...

- **A tight-knit family offers one another security.**

Jesus has a long term commitment to his sheep. Your relationship with him is permanent. He said, *(v. 27) "No one can snatch them out of my hand."* God's love for you is not based upon your goodness. Paul said, *God demonstrates his love toward us in that while we were yet sinners Christ died for us. (Romans 5:8)*

A high school student once said to me, "I've been saved nine times." Imagine that! He was 16 years old, and in his opinion he had fallen in and out of grace nine times! He believed he was part of God's family only as long as he was perfect. Every time he failed, he was sure that God had disowned him. This is not how God treats his children. There is security in our relationship to him. *"No one can snatch them out of my hand."* In the same way, there should be security in our family relationships. Children need to hear the message: "There is nothing you could do that could make me stop loving you...You are, and will always be, an important part of this family."

A friend told me that whenever he would get into trouble as a child his mother would say, "I ought to leave and never come back." Imagine how that made him feel. This is the exact opposite of the message we get from Christ. He offers us the security of his never-ending love and his never-failing protection. Families need to offer one another this same sense of security: "You belong to us...forever."

- **A tight-knit family has the bond of unity.**

*(v. 30) "I and the father are one"*. In saying this he asserted his divinity. He was saying, "I am God in the flesh." He was also

saying, "I and the father are of one mind and purpose." There is a unity of purpose between the father and the son, and being in God's family means that we share that purpose. God's purpose is that all the world should come to know Christ, and as members of God's family, this is our purpose as well.

You've heard the old saying "A family that plays together stays together" It's true. A family that pursues common interests together is a strong family. I once heard a man give a speech called *Multi-Level Marketing Saved My Marriage..* He was serious. He had lost his job and he was under tremendous financial pressure. As a result, his marriage was rocky and he was losing his grip on his home life. Then he signed up in a multi-level business. He convinced his wife that this was the answer to their money problems. They recruited their children to help them run the business. They sectioned off part of the house as a work area and spent hours together filling orders. As their business grew, and their financial problems began to disappear, they found that they had gained something more valuable than money: family unity. His story is about much more than "how to get rich in multilevel marketing." It is a lesson about the power of family unity. This is a good example to follow. Do things together that everyone in the family will enjoy. Go places together where everyone will have a good time. Get involved in a project that everyone believes in. This strengthens the bond of family unity.

## CONCLUSION

The relationship between Jesus and his father, and their relationship to us, teach us about family life. Families need to listen to one another, know one another, obey Christ together, grow spiritually together, accept one another unconditionally, and share a common purpose.

A family is more than just a group of individuals with the same last name or the same address. A family is a team, a circle of people committed to one another. The gospel message is that God is committed to us; the hope of the family is that together we remain committed to him and committed to one another.

SERIES: THE FAMILY CIRCLE
**HOW TO REAR EXCRUCIATINGLY PERFECT CHILDREN**
JOHN 14:23-24

Several years ago a couple named John and Luanne "Doe" wanted to have a baby, but were unable to conceive. They found a solution at a fertility clinic: anonymous male and female reproductive donors whose conceived "test-tube" baby would be implanted into a surrogate mother. Everything went as planned; the surrogate mother (who was paid $10,000) gave birth to a little girl named Jaycee.

Unfortunately, the Doe's marriage had been troubled for quite some time. Before Jaycee was born, John filed for divorce. He decided that since he is not the child's biological father, he shouldn't have to pay child support. A California judge ruled in his favor. In fact, the judge said that since Luanne is not the biological mother, she has no right to custody. The little girl (two years old at the time of the trial) was ruled to have no parents at all—not even the surrogate mother who gave birth to her, since they were not genetically related. As for the male and female donors, no one who knows who they are and they do not themselves know they have a child. Luanne retained custody, but did not pursue adoption. An appeals court later overturned the lower court's decision, ruling that John and Luanne are the legal parents, and therefore John was forced to pay support.

Some will hear this story and conclude, "Technology will be the ruin of the human race." I beg to differ. Technology is not the villain in this story; that role is being played by the parents and their co-conspirators. One would think that people who go to such lengths to have a child would take their parental responsibilities more seriously. There is a crucial element of family life that is conspicuously absent in this entire drama: Love. You can't help but wonder where the love is in this family.

Instead of casting judgment upon this couple and the California court system, we should each take a look at our own family situation. The very same element that is desperately needed in the "Doe" household is desperately needed in your household as well. The key to a great family is love. Today we'll look at words of Jesus that weren't spoken specifically and exclusively for the family, but can certainly be applied to any family situation. He said... *(v. 23-24)* *"If anyone loves me, he will obey my teaching...He who does not love me will not obey my teaching."* This principle can be applied to every area of life — your family life, your spiritual life, your marriage, your job, your church, and on and on. The principle: *Love Comes First.*

In my early twenties I had a job I didn't really enjoy. It was not a "career" job; I just needed the money. When I showed up late for the third time in a week, my boss called me into his office and said, "Steve, it's obvious you don't care anything about me, my business, or your job." I said, "That's not true. I love this job." (My fingers were crossed.) My boss replied, "Clearly you don't. If you loved this job you would show up on time."

I didn't realize at the time just how wise my boss was. Most employers would have attacked my "lack of character" and would have told me I was lazy and undisciplined. Not this guy. He just said, "Anything you love you will give yourself to 100%." We talked about the job awhile and I began to realize some things I hadn't considered before. It really was a good job. I was earning good money (for a college student), I enjoyed the people I worked with, and I really did like my boss.

In fact, suddenly I realized that this was a great job, and I was lucky to have it. Just as quickly as my attitude changed, my work habits changed. I began showing up on time, and I began approaching my work more enthusiastically. In the process, I learned that *Love Comes First.* The key to growing in obedience is growing in love.

All parents want their children to be well-behaved. Some, however, are more successful than others in getting this result. Different parents use different strategies, and you can witness their efforts at any family restaurant. Or just listen to the way they get the kids to do their chores. Have you noticed how they do it?

• Some parents beg: "Please, will eat your food? Please, will you clean up your room? Please, will do your homework? Please, will you do it for mommy?"

• Some parents approach it like Frank Burns would. Their attitude is "We're going to get some discipline in this camp!" and all conversations are reduced to orders, ultimatums and threats: "Eat your food, or there will be no dessert!...Clean up your room or you will be grounded!...Do your homework, and I mean right this minute!" Kids obey these orders, but only because you're bigger than they are. (A word of warning: be careful how you phrase your orders, because they might do exactly what you say. One mother told her son, "Eat every carrot and pea on your plate" — and he did!)

• Other parents use guilt to get their children to mind: "I can't believe that after I work my fingers to the bone and bring you to this nice restaurant you repay me by playing in your salad. I don't know why I do for you the things that I do. I spent $500 buying you school clothes and you can't even bring yourself to carry the laundry up the stairs." Implied, but not said, is, "You're a bad person and a major disappointment to me."

• Others try the art of persuasion. They're not going to come right out and make their kids do anything, they just try to talk them into it: "Don't you want to eat your corn? It's so good for you. It'll make you strong. You'll feel so much better when your room is clean. Don't you think cleaning your room is the right thing to do?"

• Other parents use role models: "I'll bet LeBron James eats all of his oatmeal." Of course, the totally ineffective derivative of this strategy is to use a sibling as the shining example. "Your brother Johnny gets good grades. Your sister keeps her room clean. Don't you want to be like her?"

• There's also the pragmatic approach. It's the old standby — bribery: "Here, kid. Here's $10 bucks. Finish your mashed potatoes and go clean your room...And if you make all A's on your report card there's another $20 in it for you."

Parents try different methods to get their children to behave, with varying degrees of success. In contrast, Jesus tells us exactly what it takes to be obedient. His words apply to our relationship to him the same as our relationship to our children. In your spiritual life, if you've got an obedience problem—if you're not following Jesus the way you know that you should—the problem resides in your heart. How much do you love him? The more you love him, the more you'll obey him.

When children don't obey their parents, the solution is not—and I'm speaking very carefully here because I'm afraid I'm about to sound like a Democrat—the solution is not that they need more rules and a stricter form of punishment. The solution is that they need to grow in love, and learn to act in a loving way. The more children learn to love, the more they will obey.

Do children need to live in a disciplined environment? Of course. Do they need rules? Absolutely. There must be clear lines drawn by the parents so that children know the difference between right and wrong. They need to know what's expected of them. And they need to know that they obey these rules, not out of guilt or fear or intimidation, but out of love.

I've always told my children, "You don't treat people you love disrespectfully. You don't speak hatefully to someone you love. If you love your brother (or sister) then treat him (or her) in a loving way." Now, they're typical kids, and they have the occasional squabble. We are not the "Ozzie and Harriet Show." But neither are we the Osbornes. The primary rule in our family is that we act in a loving way toward one another. The best way to teach children obedience is to teach them that the way you act stems from the way you love.

Remember, of course, that kids are kids, and they're going to make mistakes. When they do, don't accuse them of not loving you, or you'll catch yourself saying things like, "You don't love me or you wouldn't put your socks in the t-shirt drawer." Instead, when they make a mistake, show them how to act in a loving way. This makes the parents' job much more difficult; you have to pay attention to how you treat your spouse and children. You have to watch every word that comes out of your mouth. Quite frankly, it's easier to just bark out orders. However, it's more effective to lead your children in the way of love.

St. Augustine summed up the life of obedience in this way: "Love God, and do whatever you want." He meant that if you love God, your behavior will take care of itself. If you love God you won't want to sin against him. If you love God, you will obey him. Jesus said the same thing: *"If you love me, you will obey me."* It works at home, too. If you teach your children how to love their parents and love one another, you won't have major disciplinary problems. Yes, you'll have to correct them from time to time, and you'll have to restore order on occasion, but you won't be living in constant turmoil. You'll find that when love comes first, it makes a difference in the way the members of your family treat one another.

Here are three suggestions for how you can help your family grow in love and help your children to be more obedient.

- **Do things together.** This involves more than just being in the same room with them. *Do something*. Play a game. Play catch. Clean the garage. Go to the park. When you participate together in activities that you both enjoy, it reminds you both, "This is a person I love and I really like to spend time with."

- **Move to the middle.** Whatever parental tendency you have (as described above), move in the other direction. If you're a drill-sergeant, lighten up a little bit. Give them some breathing room. If you have a tendency to be too lenient, then don't be afraid to lay down the law. In our Home Bible Study one person said to the group: "My parents were so strict that as soon as I got out of the house I went wild." Another person then said, "My parents gave me no boundaries at all, and when I moved out of the house I didn't know how to make good choices, so I went wild."

The parents of both of these individuals needed to temper their parenting style with love. When you do that, you'll find yourself moving to the middle. When you move to the middle, the children find it easier to do what is right.

• **Give them a chance to practice.** Dads can say to the kids, "You know how much we love Mom; let's cook dinner for her." Or you can say to your son, "Let's go to the mall...and buy something for your sister." Let them find opportunities to act in a loving way toward other members of the family.

## CONCLUSION

Jesus taught an important principle to live by: *Love Comes First*. You want your children to be obedient? Love comes first. You want your marriage to be stronger? Love comes first. You want to be a better Christian? Love comes first. You want this church to grow and reach people? Love comes first. The way you act stems from the way you love. If you're struggling with obedience in any area of life, learn to love more. Grow in love, and you'll grow in obedience.

SERIES: THE FAMILY CIRCLE
**HOW TO INFLUENCE YOUR FAMILY**
ACTS 16:16-34

Imagine for a minute that a man is hired to manage a professional baseball team—the Yankees, let's say. But he doesn't go to all the games. He only shows up about half the time. When he's at the ball park, he offers no direction to his players. For example, it's the bottom of the ninth, the Yankees are a run behind, there are runners on first and third. The team needs to know what to do. Pinch-hit? Bunt to advance the runners? Attempt a sacrifice fly? The players look to him for leadership, but he sits in the dugout, watching TV.

"Do whatever you think is best," he tells his players. "My job is to see that you have plenty of bats and baseballs; I make sure that the field looks good, the team bus is running, and you have brand new uniforms to wear. I've done my part, now go out there and win." Needless to say, his team doesn't stand a chance. Can you imagine the manager of a major league team doing his job this way?

The sad truth is, this is the way many men in America manage their team—their family. By and large, men have not lived up to their responsibility to their families. As a result, families are falling apart. The Bible makes it clear that the man is to be the spiritual leader of his family. The *Spiritual Leader*. That doesn't mean he's a bully, a dictator, or a despot. He's to be spiritual, and he's to be a leader.

Now men, I'm not trying to make you feel guilty. The fact is, nothing in society prepares us for this role, and it is an enormously difficult role to fill. But it can be done, even when you start from scratch. Today we'll see how one man became the spiritual leader in his household. I'll tell you right now how he did it: *he led by example.* As a result, his family life was revolutionized.

Here's the story. Paul and Silas were preaching in the town of Philippi. They raised a bit of a ruckus and wound up in trouble with the city officials. They were stripped, beaten, and thrown in jail. The officials told the jailer to guard Paul and Silas carefully, so he put them in a dungeon and placed them in stocks. Late into the night, Paul and Silas were praying and singing hymns loud enough for all to hear.

Suddenly, there was a mighty earthquake, shaking the foundations of the jail. The doors flew open and everyone's chains came loose. The jailer (who probably lived next door to the jail) panicked. It was his job to guard Paul and Silas, and it appeared they had escaped. He knew his punishment would certainly be a slow and painful death, so he took out his sword and prepared to take his own life. At this point Paul called out, "Don't harm yourself! We're all here!"

This was more than the jailer could take. He had been intrigued, I'm sure, when he heard Paul and Silas singing hymns after being beaten and bound. Now they had a chance to escape and they didn't! The jailer realized that these prisoners had something in their lives that was sadly lacking in his own. He asked them, "What must I do to be saved?" Paul said, *"Believe in the Lord Jesus and you will be saved—you and your whole household."*

Before the night was through, the jailer and his family had all committed their lives to Christ and had been baptized in his name. The story of the jailer ends here, but in these few verses we see four examples he set that established him as the spiritual leader of his home. If you want to give your family the leadership they need—if you want to coach a winning team—they need to see these four examples in you. First...

- **Take a spiritual inventory.**

Every man must ask himself, "Where do I stand spiritually? What is my relationship with God?" During my ministry more than one man has told me that his wife handles the religion in the family. Many parents send their children to church because they think that the kids will learn good moral lessons there—and of course they will—but the lessons lose their impact if your kids don't see evidence of your own spirituality. The salvation of the jailer's household began with his own realization that he was spiritually empty and needed something more in his life. So he asked Paul, *"What must I do to be saved?"*

A few years ago at the National Prayer Breakfast in Washington, Senator Connie Mack spoke to the group. He admitted that he had always found it difficult to ask his wife to pray with him. He said, "There was a void in my life—a part of me that I was not dealing with." In search of something more, he began attending the weekly Senate prayer breakfast. Then, on October 26, 1995, he moved his chair to the center of the room where his colleagues surrounded him, laid their hands on his shoulders, and prayed for him. He said, "On that day I began the process—*began the process*—of turning my life over to God."

Spiritual leadership begins with taking a personal spiritual inventory; this begins the process of letting God have control. A second way to lead by example is...

- **Treat others with dignity.**

When Paul and Silas first arrived at the jail, the jailer did the very least he had to do in order to take care of them. They had been stripped, severely beaten and sent to jail. The jailer's response was to toss them in the dungeon and shackle them. He wasn't concerned that they were bruised and bloody; he was more concerned with his own well-being. Then, during the night, he had a spiritual awakening. What did he do next? *(v. 33) At that hour of the night the jailer took them and washed their wounds.* Paul and Silas were still his prisoners; he couldn't set them free. But he did treat them with dignity and compassion: he washed their wounds. He could have done that when they were first thrown into his jail, but he was a different man then. A spiritual man treats others with dignity.

In his autobiography, Norman Vincent Peale tells a story about his father that taught him a great lesson in the dignity of others. They were walking down the street in Cincinnati on

Christmas Eve. A dirty, ragged man approached Norman, asking for a handout. Norman shook the man off and kept going. His father said, "Never treat a man like that, Norman." Then he reached into his wallet and said, "Go after that man and say to him, 'Sir I give you this Christmas gift in the name of our blessed Lord Jesus Christ.'" Norman said, "Oh Dad I don't want to do that." His father was firm, "Go on and do as I tell you."

Norman ran up the block, stopped the beggar and said, "Sir, I give you this Christmas gift in the name of our blessed Lord Jesus Christ." The man looked surprised, and with a bow said, "Young man, I accept your gift in the name of our Lord Jesus Christ." As he said these words, Norman said, a wonderful smile illuminated his face and dignity seemed to possess him. Later, his dad asked him what he learned from the experience. Norman said, "I saw the man he really is." His father replied, "Always remember, and never forget: Jesus Christ can make men and women what they can be." (*The True Joy of Positive Living*, Norman Vincent Peale, ©1998)

A man once told me "My father views everyone as an opponent, and all social interaction as competition. He is always afraid someone is going to get the best of him." Can you see how this attitude prevents the father from having a spiritual influence on his children?

- **Model generosity.**

*(v. 34) The jailer brought them into his house and set a meal before them.* The jailer went above and beyond the call of duty by feeding prisoners in his home. In doing this, he made a point for his family to see: "My new religion makes a difference in the way we share with others." A non-Christian woman once made a revealing comment to me about her ex-husband. She said that for years he had been a "deadbeat" dad, always behind on child-support and never available for his daughters. She said, "But he's religious now and pays on time." In fact, she complained that now her daughters want to be with him every weekend so they can go to church with him—a great imposition on her schedule.

There is a connection between your attitude toward money and your ability to influence your family. A woman at church said, "My husband spanks the children for leaving the lights on." He probably thinks he's running a tight ship. In reality he is sowing seeds that will destroy his credibility with his children. When they are old enough to reason things out for themselves they will resent his miserliness and cruelty.

If your family consistently gets the message that your money is more important to you than anything else, you will have a hard time providing leadership for them in other areas of life. A fourth way you can lead your family by example...

- **Practice obedience.**

*(v. 33) Immediately he and all his family were baptized.* The first step in following Christ is identifying with him in baptism. Baptism symbolizes dying to an old way of life, and rising to walk with Christ in a new way of life. The jailer showed his family that when it came to obeying Christ, he would lead by example. It stands to reason that if he was willing to be baptized in the middle of the night, he was willing to be obedient in other areas, too. If you want to lead your family by the example of your obedience, here are some areas where you can start.

- **Attend church.** Today, you get an "A" on this one.
- **Pray with them.** This may seem difficult to do at first, since prayer is such a personal thing and we men are terminally macho. Begin, at least, to say prayers at meal time.
- **Have a family devotion.** This causes many fathers to panic. (And many children to be overcome with a sense of dread.) It doesn't have to be that way. You're not creating a church service. Don't be rigid about it; let them offer input. Tell them, "We're definitely doing this together. What are your suggestions for how we do it?"
- **Serve with them.** Give your family the opportunity to see you serve others—in a church ministry, a homeless shelter, a short-term missions trip, or some such thing. Let your family hear you say: "I do this because it is what God wants me to do."

## CONCLUSION

Every father wants to manage a winning team. Every father wants to have a positive influence on his family. Understand: you cannot be a positive influence without being a spiritual leader. And there is only one way to accomplish this—you lead by example.

You are called to be the spiritual leader of your family. That means you have to be *spiritual*. For some of you that means, like Senator Connie Mack, you need bow your head in prayer and begin the process of turning your life over to God. For some of you that means that you need to begin to show your family an example of obedience. For some of you that means you need to make some changes in the way you treat others, and in your attitude toward money. For all of us today it means that we must answer the challenge to lead our families by our example. You've been given a team to manage. You can have a winning team, if you'll be the example they need you to be.

SERIES: THE FAMILY CIRCLE
**TREAT YOUR MATE TO A BETTER MARRIAGE**
GENESIS 2:18-24

The outspoken feminist activist and publisher Gloria Steinem once said, "A woman needs a man like a fish needs a bicycle." She also often referred to marriage as "legalized oppression." Her attitude throughout her career has been, basically, "men—who needs them?" Well, apparently Ms. Steinem decided that men aren't so bad after all. In fact, she found one she plans to keep for awhile. In September 2000 the founder of Ms. Magazine officially became a Mrs. — Gloria Steinem got married.

It makes you wonder: What is the appeal of marriage, that someone who has blasted the institution for almost 40 years would suddenly decide that she wants it for herself? Don't get me wrong; I'm not criticizing her. I wish her and her husband all the happiness in the world. But, isn't it interesting that after saying for so many years that she doesn't want or need a man in her life, she later decided that she does? Interesting, but not surprising, because the Bible teaches that we are created to desire this kind of companionship. In fact, after God had created the first man, he said, *(v. 18)* " *It is not good for the man to be alone.* " We were made to be together, to have someone to share our lives with, to love, to grow old with. For most people, that's God's plan—not to spend your life alone, but with a mate.

Notice I said "for most people." If you're single, let me quickly interject a couple of things. First, being single doesn't mean you're missing out on God's will. Chances are you'll eventually meet someone you want to share the rest of your life with. If it doesn't happen, it's because God has something better planned for you, not something less.

Also, if you're single, I encourage you not to be in a rush to get married. You're exactly where God wants you to be right now. And, frankly, you're right where a lot of married people wish they could be. Marriage counselors hear it again and again: "If only we had waited a little while longer...if only we hadn't been in such a rush to get married." If you're single, take your time. Today's message will help you prepare for the day when you take that step. If you're already married, today's message will help you relate to your spouse in such a way that it strengthens your marriage.

It takes two people to make a great marriage. Some of you are in a situation in which the person you've married isn't interested in improving the partnership. Frankly, there's nothing you can do about that. You can't change your spouse. (It's been said that a woman marries a man hoping he'll change, a man marries a woman hoping she won't, and they're both wrong.) You can't change your spouse, but you can change the way you treat your spouse. Even though it takes two to make a great marriage, it only takes one to make a marriage better. And if you make some changes in the way you relate to your spouse, chances are he or she will take notice and become more cooperative.

Today we'll look at three ways you can treat your mate to a better marriage. They're found in the second chapter of Genesis. You're probably familiar with the story. There's an old joke about how it took place. God created man, took a long look at him and said, "I think I can do better" and then created woman. That's not exactly how it happened. The way it *did* happen teaches us the first principle in how we should treat our spouse. First of all...

- **Treat your spouse as your soul mate.**

In creating Eve, God staged a rather elaborate production for Adam. First he said, *(v. 18) "It is not good for the man to be alone. I will make a helper suitable for him."* Then he created all the beasts of the field and the birds of the air, and Adam named each one. The strongest evidence we have that the woman wasn't around for this ceremony is in the names the man came up with. I mean, would a woman have come up with the name "hippopotamus"?

I don't think so. She would have named him something like "Bubbles". Regardless, Adam went through this procedure, and when it was done, the Bible says, *(v. 20) But for Adam no suitable helper was found.*

Then God caused Adam to fall asleep. From Adam's own body God took a rib and created the woman. Why is the story told this way in the Bible? It's because God wanted to underline the fact that men and women are created equal. Yes, we're different from each other—physiologically and psychologically—but we are, according to scripture, equal. Some societies and cultures throughout history have oppressed women and forced them into a lesser role, but this was not God's plan. He created us to be partners.

When Adam was awakened from his sleep, he saw Eve and said, *"This is now bone of my bones and flesh of my flesh"(v. 23)* Do you know what Adam was saying? "I found my soul mate. This is the partner God created for me."

This is how you need to see the person you've married—as your soul mate, as the partner God created for you. Some may object, "Impossible! This person isn't my soul mate. He's a Neanderthal. He burps at the table. He uses his sleeve as a napkin. When you ask him a question he answers in monosyllabic grunts. He has the depth of a mud puddle, and the personality of one, too. I don't know what I was thinking when I married him. How can I treat him as a soul mate?"

Well, I didn't say it would be easy. But it's possible. How do you treat your spouse as your soul mate, as "flesh of your flesh and bone of your bones"? It begins by blurring the line between your needs and your mate's needs.

Many people enter the marriage relationship asking, "What about me? What about my needs?" This kind of self-focused living is death to a relationship. The solution, however, is not found in the extreme opposite, in which our sole focus is, "What about you? What about your needs?" This leads to martyrdom. The key to treating your spouse as a soul mate is asking the question, "What about us? What about our needs?" Before the marriage you lived separate lives; now you have become one. That's what the Bible says. *(v. 24)...they will become one flesh.* In the old Calvin Klein "Obsession" commercial the woman says, "I don't know where you begin and I end." Now, typically I don't recommend using advertising slogans as the basis of your relationships — especially Calvin Klein — but this one has the right idea.

Treating your spouse as your soul mate begins with the attitude: "You are an indelible part of me. It's no longer a question of you or me, it's a question of 'us' because we're in this together." That's why there are times in every marriage that decisions must be made based not on what is best for the husband or the wife, but what is best for the marriage. Your spouse is a gift from God. When the two of you came together you became, in God's eyes, one flesh. You became soul mates. You stopped being "me and you" and became "us." Treat your spouse that way. Secondly...

- **Treat your spouse as your top priority.**

*(v. 24) For this reason a man will leave his father and mother and be united to his wife...* This was written at a time when it was assumed children had a lifelong obligation to their parents. Today, in our culture, it tends to be the other way around. The point this verse makes is that even though you have other obligations in life, your top priority is your spouse. The King James Version translates this verse, *(v. 24) Therefore a man shall leave his father and mother, and shall cleave unto his wife...*

The word that is translated *"cleave"* in the King James, and *"be united"* in the NIV, is, in the Hebrew, based on the root of the word "glue." Do you realize what the Bible is saying? You're stuck with each other! Actually, there's a better way to say it. The two of you are to stick together. Your spouse is to be the most important person in your life...your top priority.

In the early stages of a relationship, this usually happens without much effort. It's how you got that person to marry you in the first place. But as time goes on, it's easy to let your spouse slide into a secondary role. After a while it seems like the children, the job, the lawn, the garden, the golf course, or even church becomes more important than the person you married. This doesn't happen overnight; it takes years to become noticeable. But it can cause a marriage to fall apart. Maybe you've heard about the *Seven Stages of A Married Cold*.

Year One: (the husband says) "Sugar, I'm really worried about my girl. You've got a bad sniffle. So, I'm putting you in the hospital this afternoon for a few days' rest. And since I know you don't like hospital food, I've arranged to have your meals delivered by Rozzini's."

Year Two: "Listen, darling, I don't like the sound of that cough. I've called Dr. Schwartz to rush over here. Now, go to bed and get some rest."

Year Three: "Maybe you better lie down, honey. There's nothing like a little rest when you feel lousy. I'll bring you something. Have we got any canned soup?"

Year Four: "Now look, dear. Be sensible. After you feed the kids and wash the dishes and sweep the floor, you should lie down."

Year Five: "You look awful. Why don't you take some aspirin?"

Year Six: "Look, I wish you'd gargle or something, instead of sitting around barking like a seal all evening."

Year Seven: "For crying out loud, stop sneezing! Are you trying to give me pneumonia?"

This is an example of the erosion of priorities in marriage. Can you relate to it? If you want to strengthen your marriage, start treating your spouse as your top priority. With your words and with your actions make an effort to let your mate know: You are the most important person in my life.

The pastor of one of the largest churches in America went through a divorce a few years ago. There was no adulterous scandal involved. The couple just decided they couldn't stay together. In a statement to the press, his wife said, (paraphrasing) "Years ago my husband chose his priorities in life, and they didn't include me." He became a success in the ministry, but not in marriage. And though the minister spent almost a decade attempting to reconcile with his wife, it was too late. Now, there are two sides to every story, and I won't speculate on who was right and who was wrong. But I'll say this: If your marriage is important to you, treat your spouse like your top priority. Thirdly...

- **Treat your spouse with unconditional acceptance.**

*(v. 25) The man and his wife were both naked, and they felt no shame.* This verse symbolizes the need for transparency between married people. Spouses need to know that they are accepted unconditionally...that you love them as they are, and even if they never change, you would still want to be married to them.

A man said to me once, "My wife wouldn't divorce me in a million years, but she told me if she had it to do all over again, she wouldn't have married me in the first place. I've been nothing but a disappointment to her." I don't know everything this guy did wrong, but I do know that lack of unconditional acceptance is choking the life out of his marriage.

Your spouse doesn't need you to pretend that he or she is perfect. Do you know what your spouse needs? He or she needs to you say, "So, you're not perfect. So what? I love you anyway. And I wouldn't trade you for anyone else in the world." In fact, I'll take it a step further. It would be good for your spouse to hear, "I love you so much, that most of the time I'm not even aware of your faults."

When a friend of mine was dating the woman who later became his wife, he said to her, "Why would you choose me? You could have any handsome, successful man you wanted." She said, "I don't want a handsome, successful man. I want you." Believe it or not, he found a certain security in that statement. It's good to know that someone loves you exactly as you are and accepts you so that you don't feel shame for your inadequacies.

Some friends were going through a divorce last year. Like all breakups, it was complicated and painful. He had been going through some pretty serious financial problems which undoubtedly contributed to the breakup. She told me once that he wasn't willing to be open with her and talk about what's going on his life. I repeated this to him and asked, "Have you considered opening up and sharing your heart with your wife?"

He looked at me and said, "You go share your heart with her and see what happens." I said, "What do you mean?" He said, "To begin with, she's the answer queen. When I try to talk to her about something that's bothering me at work, she interrupts and give me the answer." (By the way, most marriage counselors say men are guilty of this more often than women.)

My friend went on to say, "When I try to talk to her about something that's wrong between us, she cuts me off mid-sentence and explains how it's all my fault. She never does anything wrong. And if she does, it's because I did ten things wrong first." He then said, "Do you know what was the final straw? Because of my financial problems we're losing our house. She told me that she would rather move to another city than go through the humiliation of moving to a smaller home."

Sounds like it was all her fault, doesn't it? Well, more than likely it wasn't. I only heard his side of the story in detail. But I know this: What he needed at that time more than anything was unconditional acceptance. Sure, they had a lot of problems, but if he had heard, "Honey, I don't care if we live in a box as long as I can be with you", he might have been willing to try again.

Your spouse needs unconditional acceptance. Just as God accepts you unconditionally, you need to accept your spouse. Just as God forgives you completely, you need to forgive your spouse. Give your spouse the freedom to be transparent with you, without risk of shame. Do this and—believe me—it will not be long before they're bending over backwards to become the kind of person you deserve to have.

## CONCLUSION

Preaching on marriage is a difficult task, because the state of the marriages in any congregation cover a wide range. Some of you live in a state of perpetual honeymoon; some of you live in a state of impending doom. Obviously, marriages with serious problems can't be fixed in twenty five minutes, but I hope today's message will inspire you to take the next step in salvaging your marriage by pursuing counseling. Most of us, however, live somewhere in the middle of doom and the honeymoon. As Rodney Crowell sang...

*Sometimes it's diamonds, sometimes it's dirt*
*Sometimes it's magic, sometimes it's work.*

Your marriage may not be in danger of falling apart, but it may be in danger of becoming bland. Treat your mate to a better marriage. That person you met at the altar is your soul mate; that person to whom you said "I Do" is your top priority, and that person deserves — and desperately needs — your unconditional acceptance.

SERIES: THE FAMILY CIRCLE
**A MOTHER'S FAITH**
JOHN 2:1-11

It's a tradition to honor Mothers on this day, and we want to extend special honor to you today—though I hope we don't make the same mistakes that have been made in the past. For example, one year I ordered roses for all the moms at church. Shirley, the church secretary, picked them up on Friday. Apparently Shirley's husband had never sent her flowers because she didn't know to put the roses in the refrigerator. She left them on her kitchen counter over the weekend. Sunday morning she placed them on the altar, limp and lifeless. As we went through the ritual of handing them out, I worried about the symbolism behind giving someone a dead flower on her special day, and I prayed no one would be offended.

A pastor I know followed the tradition of giving flowers to Moms of Special Distinction—the mother with the most children, the mother with the oldest child, the mother who had traveled the farthest to come to church, and on and on. To spice things up, he added a new category: a special flower for the mom who had gained the most weight during her pregnancy. For some reason, no one claimed it.

And then there's the story of the young associate pastor who was called upon to read the scripture on Mother's Day. He was to read from 2 Timothy 1, the passage which says, *I have been reminded of your sincere faith which first lived in your grandmother Lois, and in your mother Eunice, and, I am now persuaded, lives in you also.* It's a lovely homage to Christian motherhood; quite appropriate for Mothers' Day. But the young associate was nervous; when he stepped into the pulpit, instead of reading from Second Timothy, he read from First Timothy. To make matters worse, he began by saying, "I would like to dedicate today's reading to the wonderful women in our congregation."

And then he began: *"Some of you have wandered from the faith and have turned to meaningless talk. You want to be teachers of the law, but you do not know what you're talking about...The law is not made for the righteous, but for lawbreakers and rebels, the ungodly and sinful, for those who kill their fathers and mothers..."* Not surprisingly, shortly thereafter, the young associate pastor felt a call to another avenue of ministry.

So....today, when we honor all the mothers in our congregation, we hope to do it right! There's an old saying that "God couldn't be everywhere at once, so he made mothers." This statement may not be theologically accurate, but it does convey the right attitude toward motherhood—moms fill a place in our lives that no one else can fill. I remember seeing a cartoon once in which a little boy was talking on the phone, saying something to the effect of, "That's right, Grandma. Mom's out of town, so me and Dad and Tommy and Sarah and Fido are here all alone." I don't know how it is at your house, but at our house, that's the way it feels when Mom is away.

I don't think we do it on purpose...but we tend to place different expectations on moms than we do on dads...especially at meal time. For example, maybe this has happened in your house: The husband says, "What's for dinner?" The wife says, "I'll need to run to the store first...we don't have any food in the house." The husband says, "Can't you just 'whip something up'?"

Sound familiar? Why is it that we think our wives can go in the kitchen and create a meal out of nothing? (I'll tell you why...because they can!) This scene plays out differently if mom isn't around. The kids come in and say, "What's for dinner?" Dad looks in the freezer, and if there's nothing microwavable, he says, "Who wants Domino's?" No one ever says to Dad, "Can't you just go in the kitchen and whip something up?"

Now, I'm not trying to perpetuate stereotypes, and I'm certainly not implying that a woman's place is in the kitchen. I *am* saying that in our society women are bombarded with many dual roles and mixed messages. It is typically expected of them to contribute to family finances through outside employment, to consistently "whip something up" on a limited budget, to get the kids off to school with matching socks and shoes on the correct feet, to maintain the family's social calendar, and on and on. It's not an easy job, which is why we say today, "Thank you!"

Every mom here is aware that her job involves much more than cooking and cleaning and carpooling. It involves nurture, guidance, and building character. And, as I have learned with my own mom, the job doesn't end when a child moves out of the house. Today, we'll look at a story that shows it was the same way with Jesus and Mary. In the gospel of John we see that Mary played a vital role in the life of Jesus throughout his ministry...she remained with him till the very end. [John 19:25 ff] She was also there at the beginning of his ministry, playing a role in his first miracle.

You've heard the story. Jesus and his disciples attended a wedding in Cana of Galilee. Mary was there, too. The Bible doesn't say whose wedding it was. Other (non-Biblical) sources speculate that it was the John the Disciple's wedding, and that his mother was Mary's sister. Maybe, maybe not. It's just a guess. It's not in the Bible. However, Mary's involvement in the wedding was such that she felt obligated to do something when the bridegroom ran out of wine. (Joseph isn't mentioned in this story—or in any story about Jesus' life as an adult. It's assumed that he had passed away by this time.)

Weddings in Palestine were a cause for great celebration. They were feasts that lasted several days. A crucial part of the celebration was an abundance of wine. This wasn't because everyone attending the wedding got drunk. In fact, drunkenness was considered a social disgrace. But their social custom required that there be plenty of wine for everyone. Hospitality was sacred in their culture; running out of wine would have been humiliating for the wedding host. So, when the wine ran out, Mary came to Jesus and said, "They have run out of wine." Jesus' answer may seem almost rude if we don't read it in context. He said, *(v. 4) "Dear Woman, why do you involve me? My time has not yet come."* The King James Version sounds even more harsh than that. It says, *(v. 4) "Woman, what have I to do with thee? Mine hour has not yet come."*

If you were to address your mother as "Woman" it would be disrespectful, but Jesus didn't speak to his mother in English, he spoke to her in Aramaic. He used a term of honor that can be translated, *"Dear Woman"* or *"Gracious Lady"*. The phrase *"What have I to do with thee"* is a Hebrew idiom that doesn't mean (as it may sound to us) "Mind your own business." Rather, it means, "Leave things to me, and I will settle them my way." Mary said to the servants, *(v. 6) "Do whatever he tells you."*

There were a half a dozen 20-30 gallon stone water jars nearby that were used for ceremonial washing. Jesus told them to fill the jars with water. They did, and then he told them to draw some out and take it to the master of the banquet. The master of the banquet was not the bridegroom, he was more like a head-waiter. His job was to make sure the feast ran smoothly. The servants drew water from the stone jars and took some to the banquet master, who said, *(v. 10) "Everyone brings out the choice wine first and then the cheaper wine after the guests have had too much to drink; but you have saved the best till now."*

As we look at the relationship between Jesus and Mary, there are three lessons that both mothers and children can learn from this story, three lessons that teach us something about how a mother's faith can impact the life of her child. Moms, you can learn something about the positive role you can continue to play in your children's lives; the rest of us can learn something about how we should listen to our moms, even as adults. The first lesson we can learn is...

- **Be involved in your child's life.**

It's no coincidence that Jesus and Mary attended the wedding together. He stayed involved in her life and she stayed involved in his. They continued to spend time together. Parents often joke about getting the kids out of the house and out of their hair forever, and kids often joke about getting out from under their parents control. George Burns said, "Happiness is having a large, loving, caring, close knit family...in another city!" The fact is, however, the closer we remain to our parents or our children, even in adult years, the better off we are. Keep the lines of communication open, continue to do things together, and enjoy one another's company.

Moms, this is your responsibility. Make sure your children enjoy being with you. Just as you tried to brighten their day when they were young, just as you nurtured and comforted and encouraged them back then, continue doing it today. I say this because you have the power to do it. More than anyone else, you can brighten your children's day just by being pleasantly present.

A man called his mother to ask how she's doing. "Not good," she says. "I'm weak." He asks, "Why are you weak?" She says, "I haven't eaten in 32 days." He asks her, "Why in the world haven't you eaten in 32 days?" She says, "Because I didn't want my mouth to be full of food in case you should call." Moms, as tempting as it may be, this is not the message to communicate to your children. They don't need more guilt (though they sometimes might deserve it). Strive to be a source of joy, so that being with you is always an uplifting time of fellowship.

Children (of all ages), follow the example of Jesus in this story. Speak to your mom using words of honor: *Dear Woman...Gracious Lady.* A second lesson in this story is...

- **Be aware of your child's potential.**

A few years ago I had a business meeting on the east coast involving some serious negotiations, so I asked my friend Don to attend the meeting with me. His mother asked, "Why did you want Don to go with you? What does he know about your business?" Don has an MBA; I was thrilled that he agreed to help out. But I felt bad for his mom because she didn't recognize her own son's talent and knowledge.

Fortunately, moms like Don's are in the minority. Most mothers swing to the opposite extreme—and that's great! Most moms are more like Jerry Seinfeld's mom. When crazy Joey Davola wanted to beat Jerry up, his mom (on the show) kept saying, "You're such a nice boy. How could anyone not like you?!" That's the way moms should see their children.

When the wine ran out, Mary immediately approached Jesus because she knew he could do something about it. In this story you get the impression that if she hadn't mentioned it to Jesus, the water wouldn't have been changed to wine, because no one else there recognized his potential. No one else there knew he had the capacity to perform a miracle. Not even his disciples were fully convinced until after this miracle occurred. The Bible says, *(v. 11) This, the first of his miraculous signs, Jesus performed at Cana in Galilee. He thus revealed his glory, and his disciples put their faith in him.* Mary was the one who recognized his potential.

Wendell Burton is an actor and musician. In the early 70's he was in *The Sterile Cuckoo.* Sometime later he became a Christian and began recording Christian music. Wendell's mother is a Christian, too. She attended a home Bible study in Los Angeles that Bob Dylan also attended. One day she said to him, "Oh, Mr. Dylan, you should meet my son. He's a songwriter. I'll bring you one of his records." When he heard this, Wendell was embarrassed. He said, "Mom, please don't bother Bob Dylan. He's not interested in my music." She said, "Sure he is! [How could anyone not like your music?]" She gave Bob one of Wendell's records. A few weeks later, Wendell got a call...from Bob Dylan. He said, "I like your music. I'm working on a song that could use your input. Can you stop by my house when you get a chance?" Wendell said, "Only a mother would assume that Bob Dylan and I are on the same level as song-writers."

That's the kind of mother every son and daughter needs—one that recognizes his or her potential—even before anyone else has a chance to. Moms, look for your children's strengths. Remind them of the good they can do. To children of all ages I say: Your mom may see things in you that others don't see. She may see potential that you don't know exists. Listen to her. The third lesson in this story is...

- **Be willing to let your child do things themselves.**

Mary told Jesus about the wine, she told the servants to do whatever he said, and she stepped out of the picture. Then Jesus solved the problem his way, using his method.

In reading this story, we have an advantage Mary didn't have. We know what ultimately happened. Jesus performed this miracle and many, many more. He taught thousands how to live God's way. Then he died on the cross for our sins, rising again on the third day. We know this now, but Mary didn't know any of it then. She didn't know any details of the upcoming events of Jesus' life. But she knew that he was no ordinary son. She knew that she had to let him to do his work his way. So she said to the servants, *(v. 5) "Do whatever he tells you."*

Mary didn't try to tell Jesus how to perform miracles or how to be the Messiah. She let him make those decisions on his own. Every parent must learn when to step back and allow their child to make his or her own decisions. Sometimes they'll make decisions you don't agree with—decisions that you don't understand—but you have to be willing to let them to do it for themselves.

A friend of mine—a grown man in his twenties, married, with children—said to me, "If I grew my hair long my parents would never let me hear the end of it." Can you imagine that? Moms, remember: While it is important to stay involved in your child's life, it's also important to step back and let them make their own their decisions. This is difficult because parents (moms especially) will always see their children as children. My daughter is now a young woman, but to me she's still the little girl I held in my arms.

It's the same with my mom. A while back she said she showed her boss my picture. I asked, "Which picture?" She said, "The family reunion picture taken at your Uncle Ernie's farm." I said, "Mom! That was 20 years ago. I don't look anything like that now." She said, "Well, you still look the same to me." That child will always be your child, but you have to step back and let him make his own decisions. You have to be willing to let him do things his way. It doesn't mean that you're not involved. It doesn't mean that you don't care. It doesn't even mean that you trust their judgment. It means that you recognize their responsibility to make their own decisions.

## CONCLUSION

We see from this story that a mother never stops being a mother. I also want you to realize that a son or daughter never stops needing a mother. As Mordkhe Gebertig said, "A child who has all his teeth still needs his mother to sing him to sleep."

When your child was little, you were the only one who could offer the kind of love, nurture, encouragement, and support that he or she needed. Now that your child is fully grown, you're still the only one who can do it. He or she may no longer live at your house, but you're still needed. Your children need you to be involved without being intrusive. They need you to recognize potential that they may not be able to see in themselves. And they need you to stand by them as they make their own way in life.

A mother's role in the life of her child is so important...this is why we take this special day to honor you. Dear Woman, Gracious Lady...thank you.

SERIES: THE FAMILY CIRCLE
**A FATHER'S LOVE**
LUKE 15:11-24

Bud Welch was, indirectly, one of the victims of the bomb that destroyed the Alfred P. Murrah building in Oklahoma City in April, 1995. His 23 year old daughter died in the explosion. Bud struggled for years to overcome his grief, first through rage, then through an addiction to alcohol, and, finally, through forgiveness. He recalls an incident that took place shortly after the bombing—one that he suppressed for many years. He saw Bill McVeigh, father of convicted bomber Timothy McVeigh on TV. Bud says:

"...when he [looked at the camera] I could see a deep pain in his eye...I recognized his pain immediately, because I was living with that same pain." [Newsweek, June 18, 2001, page 30]

As a father, Bud understood what Bill McVeigh was experiencing. Fortunately, very few fathers will ever experience the kind of hurt—the kind of shame—that Tim McVeigh's father lives with every day. Even though he didn't detonate the bomb, he must feel in some way responsible. He's probably heard the verse in the Bible that says... *Train a child in the way he should go, and when he is old he will not turn from it. (Proverbs 22:6)*

Maybe he asks himself: Where did I go wrong? Where did I fail? Whether they believe the Bible or not, most people understand Solomon's teaching that parents are mostly responsible for the way their children turn out. If their children succeed, they're proud. If their children fail, they blame themselves.

In the movie *Gladiator* Caesar Aurelius is the father of Commodus. (If you've seen it, then you know he lives up to his name.) Early in the story, Aurelius tells his son that he will not be pass the title of emperor to him. Commodus gives a long speech, saying that he realizes he could never live up to his father's expectations. He says, "All I ever wanted was to live up to you." Aurelius says, "Commodus, your faults as a son are my failures as a father." There's truth in that. We're responsible for shaping our children's character, helping them develop traits that will empower them as they go through life. In many ways, the faults of our children reflect our failures as parents.

However, even the best parents aren't exempt from having children that rebel. Jesus told a story of a father who had a rebellious son. He was a good father, yet his son made some awful mistakes. Actually, the father in this story is an example of our heavenly father. He is a perfect father, and sometimes we, his children, disobey him. But this story in the gospel of Luke shows us how our heavenly father responds to us when we sin, and it shows fathers how to respond to a child's rebellious attitudes and actions.

Most parents never have to deal with a child as blatantly rebellious as the Prodigal Son. Your child's disobedience will probably be more subtle, but there's a pretty good chance, at some point in your child's life, that you'll have to deal with rebellion in some form or another. At the first sign of a defiant attitude, you might be tempted to crack the whip a little louder and bear down a little harder. It rarely works. The best way to handle disobedience is to deal with your children the way your Heavenly Father deals with you.

Today, we'll talk about how to do that—how to treat your children like your Heavenly Father treats you. If you follow this example, you may not ever have to deal with serious rebellion in your family. But even if you do, following these principles will help your children find their way back home, just as the prodigal son did. There are three things a father must strive to do. The first is...

- **Build a foundation for your children.**

My favorite verse in this story is verse 17 of the 15th chapter of Luke. *When he came to his senses...* Fathers, it's your job to make sure your children have 'senses' to come back to. It's your job to give them a foundation for good living. The primary characteristic of dysfunctional families is that the children have to guess at what 'normal' is. When home life is erratic and unpredictable, they assume it's that way for everyone. They assume all parents scream at each other 24 hours a day, that all family conversations end with a slam of the door, that all fathers work 80 hours a week, and so on. They lack a solid foundation. They have to guess at what normal is because they've never seen normal. As they get older, they're more likely to drift.

Fathers, here is where you make a significant contribution. You can build for your children a foundation upon which they can build the rest of their lives. You can make sure they have 'senses' to come back to. Ideally, this happens in the traditional environment of a father and mother living together and raising their children together in harmony. That's the ideal, but in real life it doesn't always happen that way. Maybe you've already been through a divorce, maybe your spouse is neglecting his or her parenting responsibilities, and you're having to play the role of both mother and father to your children. Your situation may not be ideal, but that doesn't get you off the hook. You need to do all you can to give your children a solid foundation in life. What kind of foundation do children need?

**They need to know that they are loved.** You need to show them and you need to tell them. Some men have trouble saying, "I love you." Dennis Byrd was a defensive back for the New York Jets. When I read his autobiography, *Rise and Walk*, I was surprised that he and his football buddies ended conversations with "I love you." It's this simple: if professional football players can say it to each other, you can say it to your kids.

**They need to know that they are not alone.** When they have a problem at school, or at Little League, or on their part-time job, they need to know they're not facing it alone. It's not about solving all their problems for them, it's about letting them know you're with them.

**They need to know right from wrong.** J. Edgar Hoover once told the nation, "Send your children to Sunday School so they don't end up in reform school." That's certainly a start, but they also need to see those "Sunday School" values lived out at home.

When I was in grade school, a friend of mine's bicycle was stolen from my front yard while he was visiting me. He got a new bike for free, though, because his father told the insurance company the bike was stolen from their garage. My friend's family was much more "religious" than mine. His dad went to church more times in a week than my dad went in a year. But I remember thinking, "There's no way my dad would ever lie to the insurance company just to get my bike back." He would have told me to start saving for a new bike. (And, fondly remembering my father, I'm sure the word "knucklehead" would have worked its way into the conversation.)

Children need a foundation upon which they can build their lives. It's what the Prodigal Son had, and it helped him find his way out of the mess he created for himself. He was able to "come to his senses" because he had grown up in an environment that taught him some sense in the first place. He knew what normal was, and he knew that there was a better way of living than the way he was living on his own.

At some point your children may insist on going their own way. In the process, they may make a number of foolish mistakes. I hope it never happens, but if it does, keep this in mind: The foundation you built for them will help them eventually to come to their senses.

Fathers, you need to deal with your children the way your heavenly father deals with you. He has given you a foundation for living: he revealed his love to you through his son Jesus Christ, he promised that he would never leave you or forsake you, and he has given you his Word to teach you right from wrong. It's the same foundation your children need.

- **Give them an example of fairness.**

After the Prodigal Son came to his senses, he said, *(v. 17-19) How many of my father's hired men have food to spare, and here I am starving to death! I will set out and go back to my father and say to him: Father I have sinned against heaven and against you. I am no longer worthy to be called your son; make me like one of your hired men.* The Prodigal Son realized that his father was a fair man, and that he was much better off being his father's hired hand than his rebellious son. He made his decision to go home based on what he knew about his father: that he was a man of honor, a man of character. He knew his father would treat him at least as fairly as he treated his hired hands.

What if the son didn't have that example of fairness to fall back on? Imagine if he had said, "I'd like to go home, but what if my dad treats me like he treated the insurance company? What if my dad humiliates me the way he humiliates his employees? What if my dad turns his back on me the way I've seen him turn his back on others who have disappointed him? I don't dare go home, because Dad might treat me the way he treats everyone else." Your kids notice how you treat others. If you're fair, they see it. If you're unfair, they see it. And it affects the way they relate to you.

Also realize that the Prodigal Son knew his dad wasn't a pushover. It didn't cross his mind to say, "Maybe I can go back home and talk Dad out of some more of his money." He knew he couldn't manipulate his dad, and he didn't try. But he knew he would be treated fairly, because his dad was a man of honor. I once had a job in which I was in a supervisory position. One of the workers I supervised was my bosses' son. If he wanted to take the day off, he wouldn't call me, because he knew I would say "No." He would call his dad, because he knew his dad could not say "No" to him. His dad was a soft touch, and he could easily manipulate him.

Dads, being a pushover is as bad as being a bully. A parent who allows themselves to be cajoled and persuaded by their children is doing great damage to the emotional well being of the child. If every time you go to the store your child scans the shelf until he or she finds a toy for you to buy, and then begs and pleads and whines until you finally give in and buy it—you're teaching your child some lessons that will haunt both of you for many years to come. You're teaching that "No" doesn't really mean "No". And you're teaching that he or she is stronger than you are. The child may be temporarily happy to get the toy, but long-term effect is that he or she will feel a little less secure. And he or she will be more likely to try to manipulate their way out of situations, instead of coming clean and doing the right thing.

The father in this story gave his son an example of fairness. It was an example that the son could cling to, even in his darkest moments. If you want to be an effective father, you need to deal with your children the same way your heavenly father deals with you. He exemplifies fairness. He's not a bully, and he's also not a pushover. He's fair. That's the example your children need to see. Thirdly...

- **Be quick to show forgiveness.**

When the Prodigal Son came to his senses and decided to return home, his father saw him approaching from a distance. The father then did something that was, at that time, culturally unexpected. Normally, a father would wait to be addressed in a respectful manner by the son before responding. This father didn't wait. The Bible says, *(v. 20)...he ran to his son, threw his arms around him and kissed him.*

The son then began the speech that he had, no doubt, practiced all the way home: *(v. 21) "Father, I have sinned against heaven and against you. I am no longer worthy to be called your son."* But the Father didn't wait to hear the rest. He said to his servants, *(v. 22-24) "Quick! Bring the best robe and put it on him. Put a ring on his finger and sandals on his feet. Bring the fattened calf and kill it. Let's have a feast and celebrate. For this son of mine was dead and is alive again; he was lost and is found."*

What do you do when your children repent? Do you fold your arms and say, "Prove you mean business first!"? Do you remind them repeatedly of the mistakes they've made? Or do you allow them to bury the past? There's a rule at my house: we don't bring up one another's faults and mistakes. We leave the past in the past. It's a good rule; I recommend it for everyone. We need to deal with our children in the same manner that our heavenly father deals with us. According to the Bible, when he forgives, he forgets.

The Bible says, *In your love you kept me from the pit of destruction; you have put all my sins behind your back (Isaiah 38 v17)* The Bible also says, *Once again you will have compassion on us. You will trample our sins under feet and throw them into the depths of the ocean! (Micah 7:19)*

I sat in horror in the living room of a friend's house one evening as he told me in detail about the sins of his teenage son—as his son sat humiliated in the room with us. First, it was none of my business. Second, he didn't tell me the story to express joy over his son's repentance, but to express shame over his son's behavior. Third, his son already felt guilty enough without getting me in on it. If Biblical forgiveness was ever to be made available to his son, I could tell it wouldn't be for quite some time.

Your children will make mistakes throughout their lives. If you have given them a solid foundation, they'll eventually come to their senses. When they do, forgive them, celebrate with them, and bury their sins in the past—*and then throw away the shovel.* Don't make your children wait for your forgiveness. Deal with them the way your heavenly father deals with you: forgive them immediately and totally.

It's a fact that cannot be denied: your child will sin. Maybe in little ways, maybe in big ways, but he or she will do things that are wrong. When they come to their senses, you must be quick to forgive—like the Prodigal Son's father...like our heavenly father.

## CONCLUSION

Do you know what this story illustrates? A father's love for his son. To be an effective father, you have to spell out your love for your children. Of course, you say it with your words, but you say it much louder with your actions.

Build a foundation for them, a foundation of love, security, and morality...a foundation upon which they can build their lives. A foundation they can come back to if they ever wander away. Give your children an example of fairness. You have to be a person of character so that you can pass it on to them. Be quick to forgive your children when they fail, because they will certainly fail. When they do, they need to know forgiveness is available.

This is how a father expresses love to his children. You can't do it in a day; it takes a lifetime. It takes a commitment to treat your children the same way your heavenly father treats you. That's a father's love.

*SPECIAL MESSAGE: GRADUATION SERMON*
**WHAT DOES GOD WANT ME TO DO?**
2 THESSALONIANS 1:11-12

Good evening, Students. I'm not sure what thoughts are foremost in your mind right now, but knowing how hectic the month of May is for graduating seniors, you're probably grateful for the chance to sit down for a few minutes—for the chance to listen to someone talk without having to take notes and without having to worry what parts you'll need to know for the exam.

Well, here's the bad news. There will be a test on tonight's message...in about sixty years. This sermon is that important. In the next few minutes I'll tell you about something that has the potential to change the direction of your life forever.

If you've ever been to a youth group meeting, you've probably sat through a lesson on how to know God's will for your life. I would venture to say that every person on the planet asks this question at some point: *What does God want me to do?* Some of you already wrestle with this question, and the rest of you eventually will—it's that important.

When you begin to think about doing God's will, you first have to overcome a few mental obstacles. What if God's will is too hard? What if it's something I'm afraid to do? Or something that I don't want to do? What then? We've all heard the horror stories from the missionaries. They say things like, "I told God that I would do anything but be a missionary in the jungle, and sure enough, he called me to be a missionary in the jungle." Is that how it works? Does God look for the thing you least want to do when he chooses his plan for your life? I tried to fool God into thinking that what I least wanted was a lot of money and a house by the beach, but it didn't work.

I once heard a preacher say, "Every morning I ask God what he clothes he wants me to wear. One day God said, 'Wear the blue tie with yellow dots on it.' Later that morning a man commented on my tie and I took the opportunity to witness to him." I remember thinking, "How in the world am I supposed to hear God's voice on which tie to wear when I can't even decide what career path he wants me to follow or which city he wants me to live in?"

The idea of seeking God's will is intimidating for many. They're not sure what to expect. They're usually full of questions. Does surrendering to God's will make you a robot? Is God's will so detailed that every morning you pray about which shirt or pair of white socks to put on? Will God's will conflict with what you most want to do in life? And if you really want to do something, does that automatically mean that it is God's will, or does it mean that it isn't God's will? And most of all, how do I go about finding God's will, and how will I know it when I do?

God's will isn't all that mysterious. Neither is it complicated. Simply put—and I want you to get this, because it'll be on the exam—God wants what's best for you. His will is nothing to be afraid of because he cares for you more than you care for yourself. He wants what's best for you. What's more, he's willing to help you get it. Not everything you want, but what's best. There's a difference—the difference between a life of happiness and a life of misery; it's the difference between a life of failure and a life of success.

In order to follow God's will, you need to prepare yourself. Tonight we'll look at two Bible verses that help you do that. This is 2 Thessalonians 1:11-12 [NLT]. *(v. 11-12) And so we keep praying for you, that our God will make you worthy of the life to which he called you. And we pray that God, by his power, will fulfill all your good intentions and faithful deeds. Then everyone will give honor to the name of our Lord Jesus because of you, and you will be honored along with him.* As you consider the question *What Does God Want Me To Do?* there are three things to consider. Here they are. First...

- **Be ready to stretch.**

God has a plan for your life. Though I don't know all the details about his particular plan for you, I'm sure of this: God's plan is bigger than you are. It will require some stretching on your part. You can't coast through life and do God's will at the same time. You're not yet what you need to be...you're not yet completely worthy of his calling—but he'll make you worthy. Paul says, *(v. 11) We keep praying for you, that our God will make your worthy of the life to which he has called you...* He's saying that God will make us worthy of his calling. He wants what's best for us, and he helps by making us worthy to do his will.

You've probably heard this before. It's as true today as it ever was: God doesn't give you challenges to match your strength; he gives you strength to meet your challenges. This can be applied to God's will—he gives you the strength to do his will.

A good example is the disciple named Peter. God called him to be the leader of the early church even though he did not seem to be a good candidate for the job. He was obstinate, impulsive, argumentative, sometimes violent, selfishly ambitious, undependable, likely to give in to peer pressure, and he had a bad habit of saying the wrong thing at the wrong time. God's call on Peter was a tremendous stretch for this unpredictable disciple; Peter had to stretch way beyond his own skills in order for God to make him the man he needed to be. What eventually happened?

Peter became a man of such power that when he preached, thousands committed their lives to Christ. When he prayed, people received miracles. In fact, Peter became such a powerful man that crowds used to bring the lame and sick to the streets where he walked so that at least his shadow might fall on them. [Acts 5:15]

An example we've seen in our own lifetime is the lead singer of U2, Bono. A couple of things that some people don't know about him. First, the driving force of his life is to do what Jesus wants him to do. Second, when the band first started, people used to say to the other members, "Your band is OK, but you've got to get rid of that singer—he sounds terrible!" Bono stretched himself to become a good singer, and the band eventually became one of the biggest rock bands in history. But even after he became rich and famous, he continued to stretch himself to fulfill God's will in his life. He's not perfect; he's made some mistakes along the way. But he's also made a tremendous contribution to improving the lives of millions, especially those in poverty-stricken nations of Africa. This is quite an accomplishment for a rock singer—especially one who was told that he can't sing.

People ask, "What exactly is God's will for my life?" I can answer only part of that question, because there are two aspects of God's will. First, there is...

*a. God's General Will.* This is the same for everyone. He wants us all to be like Jesus. He wants everyone to pray, read the Bible, go to church, worship, and live by the ten commandments. God's general will is that we should work for peace and justice, treat one another with dignity, make disciples, build up one another, strive to be good, help the poor, and live a simple, quiet life. God's General Will consists of principles that can applied to our lives in a variety of ways, but the principles are the same for everyone. Next, there is...

*b. God's Specific Will.* This is the part that I can't tell you about, because it is for you and you alone. God has a plan that he wants you to accomplish with your life. You discover this plan through prayer and self-examination. God's Specific Will involves your career, certainly, but much more than that. His will encompasses all that defines you, every aspect of your existence—who you marry, where you live, how you invest your time, and on and on.

Deciding to do God's will isn't just a one-time experience. It lasts your whole life. When I finished high school my primary concern was knowing and doing God's will. Today, almost 30 years later, it's still my primary concern. Of course, most of the major pieces of the puzzle are in place, but I'm still learning new aspects of his will.

God has a plan that is much bigger than you are, and you'll have to stretch to do it—but he'll give you the strength you need. That's because God wants what's best for you, and he'll help you get it. Be ready to *stretch*. Secondly, to do God's will, you must...

- **Be ready to dream.**

God's revealed will isn't a blueprint. It's more like a sketch. We fill in many of the details for ourselves. In Hollywood there are producers who put deals together with nothing more than a 30 second pitch. They don't have a director, they don't they don't have actors, they don't even have a script — they just have an idea for a movie. They pitch this idea to various studios — and often they're able to sign multi-million dollar contracts on the strength of this "rough sketch".

One producer had an idea for a film about a mad dog terrorizing a town. He described it to the studio executive in four words: "It's Jaws on Paws!" The executive offered the producer a contract on the spot. (The movie was *"Man's Best Friend"* — maybe you've seen it on cable.) Now obviously, on a deal like this, there are a lot of specifics to be determined by the writers, directors and producers, but the general direction of the film is established by the studio who bought the pitch.

Similarly, God doesn't reveals His will with a complete manuscript. He gives you an outline. You participate in the process of fulfilling God's will for your life by adding some of the details. Paul indicates this when he says, *(v. 11)...God, by his power, will fulfill all your good intentions and faithful deeds.*

Paul says it works like this: Your good intentions and God's power come together to make it happen. It's your idea, your dream, your vision, your goal — you supply the intentions, God supplies the strength to make it happen. God wants what's best for your life; if you're willing to reach for your dreams, he's willing to help you achieve them. The only restriction is that your dream must be compatible with God's call on your life. Maybe God has called you into business. It's up to you to dream about how you can use your business to fulfill God's will. Maybe he's called you into the arts. It is up to you to dream about what you accomplish through your artistic talents.

Have you heard of Ricky Freeman? Probably not. He spent ten years playing minor league baseball in places like Tennessee, Canada, North Dakota, and many towns in between. He never made it to the big leagues, but he accomplished some big things in his life. First, he got to play baseball for a living—which isn't bad, since most people only get to play it for free. Second, he used his position as a platform to tell others about Jesus. This enabled him to touch thousands of lives. Ricky Freeman probably had a dream of playing in the pros. He didn't make it, but he was still able to accomplish great things. It happened only because he dared to reach for his dream.

Do you have a dream? Every person who aspires to do the will of God must cultivate the art of dreaming. This isn't daydreaming about what will never happen—it's stretching the limits of your faith and the limits of your imagination to consider the great things you can do for God. God will give you the power to make your dreams come true. That's because he wants what's best for you and he's willing to help you get it. If you want to do God's will, be ready to dream. Finally...

- **Be ready to bend.**

God promises to help you stretch so that you're worthy to do his will. He promises to help you dream so that you're able to do his will. But he never guarantees any particular result. Sometimes the results will be, in your eyes, spectacular. Sometimes they'll be miserable. You have to be ready to react to both. You have to roll with the punches. You have to be ready to bend in each and every situation.

Two tests await everyone who wants to do God's will. First is success. Second is failure. Some can live with one but not the other. As you strive to do God's will, you'll experience both. The way you react makes a big difference in who you are. Everyone has seen examples of success changing a seemingly nice guy into a spoiled brat. Everyone's seen failure change a good sport into a cry baby. You have to be ready because you will experience both.

You remember Deion Sanders. He seemed to have it all. He was one of a handful of athletes who played both professional baseball and professional football. In football he was one of the few athletes who played both offense and defense. He was one of the best—rich, powerful, and successful. And, as it turns out, he was completely miserable. He wrote a book about his life called *Money, Sex, and Power: How Success Almost Ruined My Life*. Fame and fortune was more than he could handle. It almost destroyed him. Eventually Deion Sanders discovered that the only way he could handle the pressures of life is through a personal relationship with Jesus Christ.

Some people can't handle success, others can't handle failure. Have you ever known someone who didn't get they wanted, so they just gave up? You have to be ready to pass both tests. You will have some success along the way, and you will face some failure. Be ready to bend no matter what comes your way. In success and failure, there's only one proper way to react. The Bible says, *(v. 12) Then everyone will give honor to the name of our Lord Jesus because of you...*

Doing God's will isn't about success or failure...it's about glorifying Christ in your life. As long as this is your attitude, nothing can defeat you. While everyone else faces the futility of winning the world's way, those committed to doing God's experience lasting fulfillment. This fulfillment isn't based on money, promotions, relationships, or possessions—it's based on God's presence. Notice again how the Bible says it. *(v. 12) Then everyone will give honor to the name of our Lord Jesus because of you, and you will be honored along with him.*

God says that when you glorify Christ, he'll honor you. This means, first, that when you do God's will, you'll eventually receive the recognition you deserve. It may not happen immediately...it may not happen in your lifetime...it may not happen until you're in heaven, but the truth remains: If you honor God, he'll honor you.

Secondly—and more importantly—this means that those who do God's will can experience fulfillment right now. When Christ is honored in you and you are honored in him, you can be sure that insignificant matters such as money and prestige won't make a difference. It's much more fulfilling to know that what you're doing is in the center of God's plan.

To do God's will, you need to be ready to bend. You react to failure by not letting it get you down. You react to success by not letting it go to your head. God gives you the ability to do this, because he wants what's best for you, and he's willing to help you get it.

## CONCLUSION

In *The Lion, The Witch, and the Wardrobe*, little Lucy is about to meet Aslan, the Lion who rules Narnia. She nervously asks, "Is he—safe?" Mr. Beaver answers by saying, "Of course he isn't safe. But he's good. He's the king."

God's will isn't always safe. Sometimes you'll have to stretch beyond your capabilities. He may give you a dream that makes it necessary to reach beyond your comfort zone. You may find yourself having to bend to challenging situations day in and day out as you experience different levels of success and failure. God's will isn't always safe, but it is always *good*. He wants what's best for you, and he'll help you get it.

SERIES: SOUL SURVIVOR
**JESUS LOVES ME THIS I KNOW**
1 JOHN 5:9-13

Today we're beginning a new series called *Soul Survivor*. It's about getting through life with your faith intact. We will examine four key elements necessary for a dynamic spiritual life. In week two we'll talk about the importance of being filled with the Spirit; in week three we'll examine living a life of worship; week four will address dealing with the storms of life. Today we're talking about one of the foundational benefits of a relationship with God — assurance.

Assurance. Certainty in the midst of uncertainty. We can have it. It's about knowing that God loves us, knowing that our sins are forgiven, knowing that we have eternal life in him. This world is full of uncertainties. We have no idea what the future holds for us — in fact, we've learned how our entire world can change in an instant. In the midst of all the uncertainty of life, there is one thing we can be sure of: we are eternally secure in the hands of God. And what's more, God has promised that we can approach this uncertain future with a sense of certainty, a sense of assurance in him.

I've worked in several different types of churches throughout my ministry — from the casual, laid-back atmosphere of a California beach community to a fast-paced metropolitan congregation to the relaxed, easygoing atmosphere of rural West Tennessee. One thing I have noticed in each setting — no matter where people are geographically, no matter where they are on the socio-economic scale, they tend to ask the same question: "How can I know where I stand with God? How can I know if I am on the right track? How can I be sure?"

Today's message is about how you can know that you know that you know that you know that you are right with God and you are secure in your relationship with him. Let's look at a passage from 1 John. 1 John was written by the Apostle John—the same John who wrote the gospel—and this passage contains a key verse that I want to zero in on. *(v. 13) I write these things to you who believe in the name of the Son of God so that you may know that you have eternal life.*

So that you may know, he says. Some of you may say, "I've done a lot of things wrong in my life, and sometimes I just don't feel forgiven...I would like to know for sure where I stand with God." Some of you may say, "Hey, I've been in church all of my life, and I've never been sure...I want to get this nailed down." This passage of scripture can help you find that kind of assurance. Today we'll look at three things you need to do that will help you know that you know that you know that you are right with God. First of all, you need to...

- **Identify the source of your uncertainty.**

We've all heard that God loves us. We've all heard that our sins are forgiven through the blood of Jesus Christ. The majority of people here today have already made the decision to follow him...so why do we feel uncertain about where we stand spiritually? We feel uncertain because we tend to place our faith and hope in the wrong things. Listen to what John wrote...*(v. 9) We accept man's testimony, but God's testimony is greater because it is the testimony of God, which he has given about his son.*

John is saying, in effect, "If we're willing to believe what man says, how much more should we believe what God says, since God is so much more reliable than man." The problem is that when we're faced with a choice, many of us choose to believe the words of men rather than the Word of God. We choose to believe the world's wisdom rather than God's wisdom—especially in matters of religion.

I've heard people say "It's not fair that Christianity should claim to be the one true religion and claim that all other religions are wrong. What about all the people who live in Muslim countries, or communist countries, or in the remote regions of Africa or Asia? These people may never hear about Jesus; will he condemn them to hell simply because they didn't have a chance to hear? Certainly God must judge us on our character—whether or not we are faithful to our own personal value system."

The problem with this philosophy is that it places the burden of salvation on us—we have to be good enough to earn God's acceptance. I have yet to meet anyone who can meet this standard. When we put our faith and our hope in ourselves, on good days we'll feel optimistic about our chances and on bad days we'll feel pessimistic about our chances—but we're never sure. The reason some of you struggle with uncertainty is because your hope is built on you—and you're never able to measure up. You think, "One of these days I'll be good enough, and then I'll know that God loves me." It will never happen. As long as we place our hope in ourselves and not in God, we will always lack assurance.

Another mistake is that we put our faith in the church instead of in God. This doesn't work. The church is made up of imperfect people who will inevitably disappoint you. I've known too many people who spend their spiritual lives bouncing from church to church looking for the perfect one, and they leave each one a little more discouraged than before. If you're looking for a church to believe in—a perfect church where everyone loves one another all the time, where there is never any conflict, any disagreements, where the leaders don't make mistakes, and where things are done exactly the way you think they should be done—you'll never find it. This is a great church, but it's not perfect. I could name a dozen areas in this church that need improvement. If you put your faith and your hope in this church, you'll be disappointed.

If you're uncertain about where you stand with God, you need to identify the source of your uncertainty. You need to ask yourself, "Where am I placing my faith and my hope?" Is it in yourself? Is it in your own goodness? No wonder you feel uncertain. You'll never be good enough to earn God's love. Is it in the church? Are you expecting other people to be perfect for you? You'll never find the perfect church.

If you're uncertain about where you stand with God, it's because you're putting your faith and your hope in the wrong place. So what do you do? Here's the second thing I want you to notice. To establish (or re-establish) assurance in your relationship with God, you need to...

- **Go back to square one.**

Square One is found in verse one of this passage of scripture. *(v. 1) Everyone who believes that Jesus is the Christ is born of God...* That's where the Christian life begins. This is the foundation of our relationship with God, and it never changes. John goes on to say in verse 10...*(v. 10) Anyone who believes in the Son of God has this testimony in his heart. Anyone who does not believe God has made him out to be a liar, because he has not believed the testimony God has given about his Son. And this is the testimony: God has given us eternal life, and this life is in his Son.*

That's square one. That's the essence of Christianity. We have life in Jesus. He is our source. If you want assurance — if you want to know that you are right with God — look no further than Jesus. Going back to square one requires two things. First of all, it requires repentance. John said... *(v. 10) Anyone who does not believe God has made him out to be a liar.*

We need to come to God in repentance, saying, "God, I haven't trusted in you as I should. I have put my faith in myself and in my own goodness, not in your mercy. Forgive me for trying to earn what cannot be earned; forgive me for trying earn what you have given freely in your Son." The word repentance means to change your mind — to stop thinking one thing and start thinking another. If you want to experience assurance, then stop thinking about your own worthiness and start thinking about God's mercy.

Going back to square one also involves determination. We must remember that faith is a choice. It is not a feeling. You can't always choose which direction your feelings go, but you can choose which direction your faith goes. To experience assurance we must make the determined choice that we will believe God, not our feelings, not what the world says, or anything else. There's an old hymn that goes...

> *My hope is built on nothing less*
> *Than Jesus' blood and righteousness.*
> *I dare not trust the sweetest frame*
> *But wholly lean on Jesus name.*
> *On Christ the solid rock I stand*
> *All other ground is sinking sand,*
> *All other ground is sinking sand.*

There's a ton of truth in that old hymn. Jesus is our foundation. He is our hope. We have assurance because of who he is, not because of who we are. As the old saying goes, we have assurance not because of who we are, but because of whose we are. To experience assurance, then go back to square one. Put your faith in Jesus, and in Jesus alone. Trust him to forgive you. Trust him to save you from your sins. Trust him to give you new life. He is your only hope. If you want to get grounded in the assurance of your salvation, there's a third thing you need to do.

- **Send in the re-enforcements.**

What re-enforcements am I referring to? Listen John's words... *(v. 13) I write these things to you who believe in the name of the Son of God so that you may know that you have eternal life.* John's purpose in writing this letter was to re-enforce the assurance of his readers. His letter is all about the certainties of the Christian life in the midst of this uncertain world. The word "know" is a key word throughout this book.

*2:3 We know that we have come to know him...*
*2:5 We know that we are in him...*
*3:2 We know that when he appears, we shall be like him...*
*3:14 We know that we have passed from death to life...*
*3:19 We know that we belong to the truth....*
*3:24 We know that God lives in us...*
*4:13 We know that we live in him and he in us...*
*5:15 We know that God hears us...*
*5:19 We know that we are children of God...*

John wrote this letter to re-enforce our assurance in God. In fact, all of scripture serves this purpose. If you want to experience assurance in this life, spend time in the Word. When someone begins to study the Bible, he or she usually makes two quick discoveries. Discovery number one is, "I didn't realize how much God loves me." Discovery number two is, "I didn't realize how far I am from being truly holy."

When we read the Word we become convinced of God's love for us, and we also become convicted of sin. The Word challenges us to become holy. It demands that we become holy. And it also constantly reminds us that our good works can never save us. The Word helps us to remember that salvation is a free gift of God. Salvation is not the result of our obedience, obedience is the result of our experiencing salvation.

In order to experience the assurance of God's salvation, you need to re-enforce it: spend time in the Word, spend time with the Lord. Spend time in his presence. The most valuable lesson I learned as a new follower of Christ was to spend time alone with God on a daily basis. I was taught to spend time each day reading a passage of scripture, asking God to speak to me through his Word. I was taught to spend time each day in prayer—praising him, confessing my sins, bringing my requests to him. These "quiet times" are what have kept me going throughout the course of my Christian life. They have re-enforced me in my journey.

I went to Disney World a few years ago. I was driving to the park, following directions as best as I could, but every now and then I would begin to wonder: "Am I still on the right track? Did I make a wrong turn somewhere?" Sure enough, about the time I would begin have these doubts, I would see a road sign or a billboard reminding me: Disney World is straight ahead. I was so grateful for those bits of assurance along the way. God has given us the same kind of reminder for our journey. His Word re-enforces us along the way. Therefore, we need to spend time in his Word.

## CONCLUSION

I could spend all day talking about the things in this life that you'll never be sure of: your health, your finances, your career, your relationships—these can all change in an instant. There's one thing that will never change—one thing you can be absolutely sure of no matter what happens. You can be sure of your relationship with God. You can be sure of where you stand with him. You can know that you have eternal life. You can know that you are saved. You can know that you are forgiven. And you can be sure that he wants you to be sure.

How can you have this assurance? Go back to square one. Stop trusting in yourself and start trusting in him. Stop trusting in your righteousness and start trusting in his righteousness. Put all of your hope in his mercy. Re-enforce your hope by spending time in his Word. And you will know that you know that you know that you are right with God—for now, and for all eternity.

SERIES: SOUL SURVIVOR
**COME HOLY SPIRIT**
EZEKIEL 37:1-14

How many of you have heard the song *Dem Bones*? Did you sing it when you were a kid? The only part I remember is...
*The toe bone's connected to the foot bone*
*The foot bone's connected to the ankle bone*
*The ankle bone's connected to the shin bone...*
And on and on it goes through the remainder of the human anatomy. We sang it when we were kids, but I didn't realize until many years later that it was connected to a passage of scripture — the text we read earlier in Ezekiel 37.

Today is *Pentecost Sunday*. Churches throughout the world are celebrating the presence and ministry of the Holy Spirit which began on the day of Pentecost approximately 2000 years ago. You may be familiar with the story. Jesus told his disciples to wait in Jerusalem until they were filled with power from on high. On the day of Pentecost — which was a festival day for Jewish people — the disciples were gathered together praying in an upper room, and the Holy Spirit came upon them in a powerful way. A mighty wind blew through the place, tongues of fire fell on each of them, and they began speaking in other languages. Later that day Peter preached a sermon and 3000 people were saved.

It is the work of the Holy Spirit that has made the difference in the life of the church. It is he who empowers us; it is he who convicts us and strengthens us. Bill Bright, founder of Campus Crusade for Christ, said that if there was one message he could preach to the church, it would be a message about how to be filled with the Holy Spirit. That's how much of a difference the filling of the Holy Spirit can make in a person's life.

I've known many people who have given up trying to live the Christian life — it's too hard. The fact is, it's not just hard, it's impossible. It's impossible to live the Christian life without the Holy Spirit's power. The Holy Spirit is the oil that makes the machinery of your life run smoothly. Have you ever driven a car without oil? You know what happens, don't you? The engine locks up and breaks down. It's the same way for a Christian who lives without the oil of the Holy Spirit in his or her life.

Some of you have been walking in the Spirit for many years; for others the idea of being filled with the Holy Spirit is a new concept. But the fact is that all of us—from the greatest to the least of us—need the power of the Holy Spirit in our lives. Today we'll look at a passage of scripture that teaches in plain detail what the Holy Spirit can do for you, how you can be filled with the Holy Spirit, and how you can live a Spirit-filled life. The passage we'll look at is in Ezekiel 37, the story of the Valley of the Dry Bones. First, please notice…

• **What the Holy Spirit can do for you**

When you're filled with the Holy Spirit, it will benefit you in three ways. First of all…

**a. He revitalizes your life.**

*(v. 5) This is what the Sovereign Lord says to these bones: I will make breath enter you, and you will come to life. I will attach tendons to you and make flesh come upon you and cover you with skin; I will put breath in you and you will come to life. (v. 14) I will put my Spirit in you, and you will live.*

That's what the Holy Spirit does for you. He revitalizes you. He takes you from the point of merely surviving to the point of truly living. He changes your life from black and white to the wonderful world of living color. He changes your life from mono to stereo, from VHS to DVD, from DOS to Windows XP, from a moped to a Mercedes. He revitalizes your life. He infuses you with freshness, and with newness.

**b. He renews your hope.**

*(v. 11-12) Then he said to me, "Son of man, these bones are the whole house of Israel. They say, 'Our bones are dried up and our hope is*

*gone; we are cut off.' Therefore prophesy and say to them: 'This is what the Sovereign Lord says: O My people I am going to open your graves and bring you up from them; I will bring you back to the land of Israel. Then you, my people, will know that I am the Lord."*

What's he doing? He's renewing their hope. Have there been times when you felt like the people of Israel did? Have there been times when you have said, "My bones are dried up and my hope is gone"? I think we all have. The presence of the Holy Spirit changes your perspective on life. One of the best benefits of the Spirit-filled life is the absence of despair. He renews your hope.

In Ephesians 1 Paul says that the Holy Spirit is given to us as...*a deposit guaranteeing our inheritance until the redemption of those who are God's possession...(Ephesians 1:14)*

He's saying that the presence of the Holy Spirit guarantees that you will get through this life—no matter how dark it may seem, no matter dry you may feel, no matter how desperate things might be—the Holy Spirit will keep your hope alive. A wonderful benefit of the Spirit-filled life is the absence of despair.

**c. He restores your dreams.**

*(v. 14) I will put my Spirit in you and you will live, and I will settle you in your own land.* The people of Israel had a dream of living in their own land. When these words were spoken to Ezekiel they had been living for years in exile. God was saying to them, "Do you remember that dream I gave you—the one about living in your own land? Don't give up on it. I'll restore your dreams." He'll do the same for you.

Too many of us go through life like we're living in exile. We live like we've been banished from our homeland, banished from the benefits and promises that all children of God can claim. If you're not walking in victory, you're living in exile. If you're not experiencing power over sin, you're living in exile. If you're not filled with joy, and peace, and hope, and love—you're living in exile. God didn't create us to live in exile. He created us to experience the benefits of our heavenly citizenship here on earth.

It is through the fullness of the Holy Spirit that we experience the fullness of life. In him we experience life as it should be lived.

That's what the Holy Spirit can do for you. He'll revitalize you, he'll renew your hope, he'll restore your dreams. He'll give you life as it should be lived. Now, some of you are saying, "I want that. I want to go from the Valley of Dry Bones to the Valley of Life. How do I get there? How do I experience this difference in my life?" Let's take a look at that right now—how to be filled with the Holy Spirit. I want to warn you up front, though, it is very easy.

- **How to be filled with the Holy Spirit**

Let's pause for a moment to split a theological hair. Sometimes we use the term "receiving the Holy Spirit" in a way that is synonymous with being filled with the Spirit. Technically, you received the Holy Spirit when you were saved—the Holy Spirit came into your life and gave life to your spirit. You received all of the Holy Spirit then...so being filled with the Holy Spirit is not about you receiving more of him, it's about him receiving more of you. So, how do you experience the fullness of the Spirit? First of all...

**a. Ask for it.**

In fact, "asking" may not be a strong enough term. A better term might be "speak it" or "claim it." Take a look at verse 4.

*(v. 4) "Prophesy to these bones and say to them, 'Dry bones, hear the word of the lord! This is what the Sovereign Lord says to these bones: I will make breath enter you, and you will come to life...'"*

The fullness of the Spirit is God's promise to all believers. It's a promise that we can all claim; it's a promise that God will certainly deliver. But if we don't claim it, if we don't speak it, if we don't ask for it—we'll never experience it.

There are times when I have to speak to myself the same way that Ezekiel spoke to the bones in the valley. I have to say, "Self, hear the word of the Lord. The Spirit of God is going to breathe life into you. Receive it! Stop feeling sorry for yourself. Stop doubting him. Stop courting despair. Let God do his work."

In the book of Ephesians Paul commands us, *Be filled with the Holy Spirit. (Ephesians 5:18)* The fact that he expresses it this way, as an imperative command, tells us that being filled with the Holy Spirit is an act of obedience on our part. It's something we do; it's something we initiate by asking for it...by claiming it as God's promise. If you want to be filled with the Holy Spirit, ask for it. Step One is that simple. Step Two is also simple. After you've asked to be filled with the Holy Spirit, you need to...

**b. Accept It.**

Another way to say it is "Receive it." That's what Jesus said to his disciples, *And with that he breathed on them and said, "Receive the Holy Spirit." (John 20:22)*

Even though we initiate the work of the Spirit in our lives by asking for it, being filled with the Spirit is not something we can do for ourselves. It's something God must do for us; it's something we must receive. We receive the Holy Spirit by yielding to him...by allowing him to have his way in our lives. Being filled with the Holy Spirit is that simple. You ask for it. You accept it. And you...

**c. Act on it.**

Imagine if your banker called and said, "Someone just deposited $1 million into your bank account. It's there...and it's all yours." What would you do? You could do one of two things. You could say, "But I don't feel like a millionaire. I don't look like a millionaire. I don't deserve to be a millionaire. And I don't see any money...where is it?" Or, you could go write checks, pay bills, make investments, give gifts, and so on. Even though you haven't actually seen a stack of money, you can begin living like a millionaire if you're willing to act on the word of your banker.

Likewise, God has made a deposit into your spiritual account—he's given you the Holy Spirit. In your account there is joy, peace, love, patience, kindness, goodness, faithfulness, gentleness, self-control. They're yours, but to receive you have to act. You have to start writing checks, so to speak. Don't wait till you feel it—just do it.

I have prayed before: "Lord, I need strength, but I don't have any...Can I take some from my account? Lord, I need to love this person, but I don't have any love to give...Can I take some from my account? Lord, I need power over temptation and I'm completely powerless today...Can I withdraw some power from my account?" Now, this may sound silly, but it reminds me that I live according to God's resources, not my own—and everything I need in order to do his will is available when I need it.

Being filled with the Holy Spirit is not an elusive experience. It is the promise of God, and it is available to all believers. If your heart is right with God, you can be filled with the Holy Spirit right now. Ask for it. Accept it. Act on it. It's that simple. Next...

- **How to walk in the Spirit**

Bill Bright taught this principle called S*piritual Breathing:* Day by day, throughout the day, as you become aware of impurities, you "exhale" them by confessing them to God. And then you "inhale" his presence by surrendering to his control.

When you realize you've just had an impure thought, don't wait until later to repent, don't wait until later to confess it—take care of it immediately. Ask God's forgiveness and surrender to his control. Do this all day long, every day. Whenever you think something or say something or do something that breaks the flow of the Spirit, confess it immediately and surrender control to him. You exhale what is impure, you inhale his presence. The idea is that you recognize and acknowledge the presence of the Holy Spirit throughout the day. You walk with him all day long. This is how Paul said it: *Since we live by the Spirit, let us keep in step with the Spirit. (Galatians 5:25)*

I like that phrase—*"let us keep in step with the Spirit."* This is how this verse is translated in the NLT... *If we are living now by the Holy Spirit, let us follow the Holy Spirit's leading in every part of our lives. (Galatians 5:25 NLT)*

Walking in the Spirit is an all-day, every-day experience. It's the key to a dynamic relationship with Jesus. And it's the key to victory.

## CONCLUSION

God's promise in Ezekiel is, *(v. 14) I will put my Spirit in you and you will live.* Anything less is just existing. Anything less is black and white TV. God wants to fill your life with living color. He wants to revitalize you. He wants to renew your hope. He wants to restore your dreams. He wants to fill you with the Holy Spirit so that you can live in his power.

Is this what you want? Then ask for it. Accept it. Act on it. He will do it: he will fill you with his Spirit. And then, beginning this very moment, practice spiritual breathing. Keep in step with the Holy Spirit throughout the day, every day. I can promise this: his presence means that you will never be the same.

SERIES: SOUL SURVIVOR
**THE HEART OF WORSHIP**
ISAIAH 6:1-8

When we talk about worship, many think it refers exclusively to the meeting that takes place between 11:00 and 12:00 on Sunday morning. That's true to a certain extent; the Sunday morning service should be a worshipful experience. But that's not all there is to worship, because that's not all there is to life. We need to realize that worship (like walking in the Spirit) is a lifestyle; it's a 24 hour a day, seven day a week experience.

Because we have so many great churches in this country—and so many great churches in this community—we can develop a bad habit if we're not careful: the habit of "critiquing" the worship service instead of fully participating. Sometimes we find ourselves evaluating the band, evaluating the song list, evaluating the drama, evaluating the message—not on how well these things impacted us spiritually, but on how well they were performed. And if they don't measure up to our standards, we'll say something like, "I don't know...I just couldn't get into worship this morning....there was too much treble in the guitar, the keyboard was too loud, the guy in the drama missed his cue. There were too many mistakes...I couldn't get into the worship."

On a side note, I want to say quickly that as worship leaders we strive to make every aspect of the service excellent. We want the music to cook, we want the drama to be powerful; we want the message to be uplifting and life-changing. We do that because we should do everything in life with a spirit of excellence. But the simple truth is that we don't hit a home-run in every area every week—and if the only way you can get into worship is for us to be brilliant, you're missing out on the heart of worship.

Mike Pilavachi is the pastor of a contemporary church in England that has been home to some incredible worship leaders (i.e. musicians) in the past several years. A couple that come to mind are Matt Redman and Tim Hughes. Matt wrote a number of songs you've heard: *Better Is One Day, Blessed Be Your Name, Let My Words Be Few*, among others. Tim wrote *Here I Am To Worship, Consuming Fire, May the Words of My Mouth*, among others.

Mike noticed that a tendency had developed among his congregation to focus too much on the performance aspect of the worship. He noticed that the focus of the services had become about the music, not about Jesus. He decided the church needed to be brought back to the place where each one is bringing their own contribution to the worship, not just watching the band and grading their performance. So he made a drastic move. He "banned the band" and said, "We're not doing any music for a while—we're going to take some time to get re-focused on who it is we're here to worship." They had several meetings with no performed music; this became a time of renewal in their fellowship. Eventually they began doing music again with a band leading the worship songs—but it was with a new focus.

Out of this experience, Matt Redman wrote one his best known songs. It goes...

> *When the music fades, and all is stripped away*
> *And I simply come,*
> *Longing just to bring something that's of worth*
> *That will bless your heart*
> *I'll give you more than a song*
> *For a song in itself*
> *Is not what you have required*
> *You search much deeper within*
> *Through the way things appear*
> *You're looking into my heart*
> *I'm coming back to heart of worship*
> *And it's all about you, All about you Jesus.*
> *I'm sorry Lord for the thing I made it*
> *When it's all about you, it's all about you, Jesus.*
> *(The Heart of Worship © Kingsway 1999 Thank You Music)*

That's the heart of worship. It's all about him. It's all about Jesus. It's not a matter of how well everyone performs on this side of the stage; it's a matter of where your heart is. I've been in all kinds of churches throughout my life. I've been in services where the guitar was hopelessly out of tune, the organist played like she was wearing mittens, the sermon was long and dull—and I have connected with God in a very real, very personal, very intimate way. I have also been in services where the music was awesome, the drama was thought-provoking, the sermon was dynamic—and I have left some of those services just as self-willed and hard-hearted as when I walked in the door. It's not about the production quality of the service, it's about the state of your heart. So, today we're going to look at getting back to the heart of worship.

This is a crucial lesson to learn if you want to get through life with your faith intact. Being a soul survivor means that you will be involved with a church, but you can't focus your eyes on the church. It means that you will participate in the songs we sing, but you won't focus your eyes on the worship leaders. It means that you will learn from the messages and Bible studies, but you won't focus your eyes on the pastor.

Today we'll look at a story in Isaiah 6 that teaches three things you can do to get back to the heart of worship. First of all, this passage teaches us to...

- **Get focused on God.**

A common obstacle to worship is resentment toward leaders in the church. Let's not kid ourselves. We're all human and sometimes there's friction in our relationships. If your eyes are on a person rather than God, it will hinder you. A woman said to me recently, "I went to church today, but my heart wasn't into it. Knowing what I know about the pastor, I just couldn't worship." Now, her pastor is not involved in anything illicit, he's just a little hard-headed. He and she don't see eye-to-eye on a couple of administrative issues. She got ticked when he was abrupt with her husband in a board meeting, and now she can't get into worship. Interestingly, her husband shrugged the whole thing off. He just said, "I don't go to church to worship the preacher. I go to worship Jesus." That's the right attitude.

We see this in Isaiah 1. Listen... *(v. 1) In the year King Uzziah died, I saw the Lord seated on a throne, high and exalted, and the train of his robe filled the temple.* Isaiah mentioned King Uzziah. In some ways he had been a good king, but he was just a man and he made many mistakes. His reign was a time of prosperity for Judah, but the book of 2 Chronicles says... *But after King Uzziah became so powerful, his pride led to his downfall. (2 Chronicles 16:16)*

Basically, King Uzziah decided to rewrite the rules of Judaism, and he was eventually struck with leprosy. Isaiah begins this chapter by saying, "Regardless of what happened with King Uzziah, I saw the Lord. My eyes weren't on the king; my eyes were on God." If you want to get through life with your faith intact, you need to do the same thing: get your eyes off people and get focused on God.

Instead of looking at people, focus on **God's majesty**. Notice what Isaiah said... *(v. 1) ... I saw the Lord seated on a throne, high and exalted, and the train of his robe filled the temple.* Instead of looking at people, focus on **God's holiness**. *(v. 3) And they [the angels] were calling to one another: Holy, holy, holy is the Lord Almighty...* Instead of looking at people, focus on **God's glory**. Isaiah said...*(v. 3) ...the whole earth is full of his glory.* When you come to church, don't look at people. Look at God. Look at his majesty. Look at his holiness. Look at his glory.

This doesn't just apply to Sunday morning. It applies to every day of the week. If we're not careful, we can let the imperfections of others prevent us from focusing on God. Maybe your spouse isn't a model Christian. Don't let his or her imperfections prevent you from seeking God every day. Or maybe your boss claims to be a Christian but you don't like the way he or she does business. Don't let your boss's imperfections prevent you from seeking God's presence. If you want to get back to the heart of worship—if you want to develop a worship lifestyle—get your eyes off people and get focused on God.

If we, as a congregation, will do this, the same thing will happen here that happened in Isaiah. Listen to what Isaiah wrote...*(v. 4) The glorious singing shook the temple to its foundations.* Let's get focused on God. The second thing we need to do to get back to the heart of worship is that we need to...

- **Get cleansed by grace.**

There is something about seeing God for who he is that causes us to see ourselves for who we are. Isaiah eye-witnessed the glory of God, and then he said...*(v. 5) "My destruction is sealed, for I am a sinful man and a member of a sinful race."*

There's a story in Luke where Jesus told Simon to put his net into the deep water. Simon answered by saying that they had worked all night and had caught nothing, and continued by saying, *"Yet if you say so, I will let down the nets."* Simon didn't exactly sound enthusiastic about it. You know what happened next: *they caught so many fish that their nets were beginning to break. (Luke 5:6)* In fact, when they began to load the fish into the boat, there were so many that the boat began to sink. Peter realized that he was in the presence of more than a man—he realized he was in the presence of the living Christ. His response was that... *he fell down at Jesus' knees, saying, "Go away from me, Lord, for I am a sinful man." (Luke 5:8)*

This happens in the presence of God. Pride suddenly melts away and you become aware of your own sinfulness, your own inadequacy. You can't help but respond the way Isaiah did. I like the way this verse is written in the King James Version...*(v.5) Then said I, Woe is me! for I am undone; because I am a man of unclean lips, and I dwell in the midst of a people of unclean lips.*

It's not that God wants us to acknowledge our sinfulness merely for the sake of talking about how wretched we are. We acknowledge our sinfulness to experience the transformational power of his grace. Listen to what happened next to Isaiah...

*(v. 6-7) Then one of the seraphim flew over to the altar, and he picked up a burning coal with a pair of tongs. He touched my lips with it and said, "See, this coal has touched your lips. Now your guilt is*

*removed, and your sins are forgiven."* That's the purpose of being in the presence of God. We acknowledge our sin so that we can experience his forgiveness. Getting back to the heart of worship means that we recognize this crucial truth: we aren't able to approach God on the basis of our own worthiness. We approach God only because he made us worthy through the blood of Jesus. Because Jesus died on the cross for our sins, we can be in the presence of our holy God. The book of Hebrews says...*We have been made holy through the sacrifice of the body of Jesus Christ once for all. (Hebrews 10:10)*

The act of worship involves recognizing our total dependence upon God's mercy in our lives. We don't approach him proudly. We don't approach him on the strength of our good deeds. We approach him with humility, with a sense of gratitude for his forgiveness. When you have this attitude, it's impossible to get distracted by the bass player hitting a bad note. It's impossible to get distracted by any superficial thing, because your heart is directed toward God.

What this means in our day-to-day life is that we don't need a concert atmosphere to enter into worship. We don't need a band, a song-leader, or anything else. You can worship him alone, in the privacy of your room, just you and him. Now obviously it is important that we come together as a body and worship together each week—but this isn't the only time worship takes place. It's a seven day a week experience. Getting back to the heart of worship requires that we get focused on God, get cleansed by grace, and thirdly...

- **Get ready to go.**

*(v. 8) Then I heard the Lord asking, "Whom should I send as a messenger to my people? Who will go for us?" And I said, "Lord, I'll go! Send me."* Worshipping God and working for God go hand-in-hand. Our best response to worship is to say, as Isaiah said... *(v. 8) "Lord, I'll go! Send me."* Here are a few things I've learned about worship. First, right worship leads to right living. Our struggle with sin is not so much a matter of badness; it is a matter

of "awayness." The "awayness" leads to the badness. When you have a one-on-one encounter in the presence of God, it affects the way you spend the rest of your day. It affects what you say. It affects how you treat people. Do you want to become a better person? Do you want to be holy? Spend time in the presence of our holy God each day. Right worship leads to right living.

Also, right worship leads to acts of compassion. It is impossible to be unmerciful to others when you have just been drenched in the mercy of God. It's impossible to be unforgiving toward others when you have just basked in God's forgiveness. And it is impossible to turn away from the needs of others when you have had a personal encounter with God's goodness.

I mentioned Mike Pilavachi earlier. I once heard him say something I will never forget. He said: "You can't worship God and ignore the poor." We tend to think of social justice as an addendum to the gospel. The fact is, though, that there are 500 verses in the New Testament on social justice and caring for the poor. How we treat others matters to God. The only way to get to where we need to be is to become worshipping people. We cannot be satisfied with just a weekly nod-to-God. Worship must become an everyday priority.

## CONCLUSION

As a church and as individuals, we need to stick to the heart of worship: we need to get focused on God, get cleansed by his grace, and get ready to go into the world and do his work. That's the lifestyle of worship. Now, in the event that someone says: "How? How do I worship God when I'm alone?" Here's what to do, and it's very simple. Get alone with God. Sing some songs to him. Spend some time in prayer. Open your Bible and let him speak to you through his Word. If you don't do this every day, I challenge you to start. Make it a habit. It will change the way you treat your wife and children, it will change the way you do your job, it will change your perspective on what happens here on Sunday morning...most of all, it will change you, through and through, into the likeness of Jesus.

SERIES: SOUL SURVIVOR
**WHEN THE STORMS OF LIFE ARE RAGING**
PSALM 107:23-32

Recently I had a chance to play catch-up with a friend I was in ministry with about 20 years ago. We talked about scheduling a family reunion of sorts to get back together with some of the others we worked with back then, and I noticed something rather alarming: many of them are no longer in the ministry and some are no longer walking with the Lord. I wondered: How can the fire that once burned so bright have been snuffed out in so many of us?

It happens for a number of different reasons. Often it's because life just became too difficult. Some gave up because they were discouraged with the church. Some gave up because someone close to them died. Some gave because their marriage crumbled. The underlying misconception is that life is supposed to be easy—or, at the very least, it's not supposed to be this hard. But there is nothing in the Bible to support this idea. In fact the Bible teaches the opposite.

Today we're in part four of a four part series called *Soul Survivor: Getting Through Life With Your Faith Intact.* In the last three weeks we've talked about three things that will help you keep your faith alive.

Number one is nailing down the assurance of your salvation, putting your hope in Jesus alone. Number two is living the Spirit-filled life, learning to walk day-by-day in the power of the Holy Spirit. Number three is to cultivate the art of worship, not only in church on Sunday morning but in your day-to-day life, spending time with God on a daily basis. Number four is learning how to handle the storms of life. In the first section of this message we'll look at what you need to *know* about the storms of life, in the second section we'll look at what you need to *do* about the storms of life. First you need to know that...

- **Storms happen to everyone.**

On an intellectual level we all know this is true, and yet, when we're hit by a storm our first reaction is often, "This shouldn't be happening to me...I don't deserve this." Whether we deserve it or not, we all have to endure the occasional storm. None of us are strangers to the rain. Jesus said... *He [God] causes his sun to rise on the evil and the good, and sends rain on the righteous and the unrighteous. (Matthew 5:45)*

For years I tried to defy this principle. I thought if I organized my life a certain way—if I could just get my income to a certain level, if I could just get a handle on my relationships, if I could just get my schedule under control—there would be no more storms. That's not how it works; the rain falls on everyone.

Some storms are the result of our sinfulness and our own bad decisions. But many are not. Someone in my family has been struggling with vision problems for several years, and it has created hardship for her in a number of areas. When she was first diagnosed, she asked her doctor, "What did I do to cause this? What could I have done to prevent it?" His answer was, "This one you'll have to blame on your ancestors. It's not your fault." And yet she has to endure the storm.

The first thing to remember is that storms happen to everyone. If your storms are the result of your bad behavior, clearly you need to change what you do. But if it's not your fault, you need to accept the fact that storms happen to everyone—the rain falls on the righteous and the unrighteous—and nothing will change that. Secondly...

- **The pain doesn't last forever.**

If you're going through the storm of divorce right now, you need to remind yourself that it won't hurt this much forever. If you've lost someone you love, you need to remind yourself that the emptiness you feel won't last forever. There may be damage to deal with, you may have to pick up the pieces and move on, you may have to rebuild your life—but the pain caused by the suddenness of the storm will not last forever. Thirdly...

- **Sometimes, in the midst of the storm, God seems to be silent.**

In Mark 4 Jesus and his disciples were in a boat crossing the Sea of Galilee, and suddenly a huge storm arose—the Bible calls it "a furious squall" — and began to rock the boat. The waves were crashing against the vessel to the point that it almost capsized, and the disciples were convinced that they were about to die. The wind was ferocious, and the disciples all panicked. Where was Jesus in the midst of this? Mark tells us...*Jesus was in the stern, sleeping on a cushion. (Mark 4:38)*

I love the little detail that Mark adds. While the disciples were staring death in the face, he was sleeping comfortably—on a cushion! Of course, we know how the story ends. Jesus calmed the storm and they made it safely to the other side of the sea. But that doesn't change the fact that in the midst of the storm, he seemed to be unaware of the crisis. Cold hard fact: there will be times when it seems like God isn't paying attention. There will be times when he is frustratingly silent. During these times, all you can cling to is your faith.

When we read how the disciples panicked in the midst of the storm, we tend to think, "How foolish of them. Why would they be afraid? Jesus was right there with them, didn't they know he would take care of them?" The same can be said about us: How foolish we are to be afraid during the storm. Jesus is right here with us. Don't we know that he will take care of us? After all, he said...*Never will I leave you; never will I forsake you. (Hebrews 13:5)*

It may seem that God is unaware of the crisis in our lives, but we have his promise that he knows every detail, and he is with us every step of the way.

Now let's talk about what you need to do about the storm. Being in a storm forces you to walk your talk. It forces you to put your faith in action. How do you do that? How do you walk your talk in the midst of the storm? Let's take a look at Psalm 107...there are three simple things to do when the storms of life are raging. First of all...

- **Cry out to God.**

In this Psalm David describes merchants experiencing the same kind of storm at sea that the disciples experienced. He says...(v. 26-27) ...*in their peril their courage melted away. They reeled and staggered like drunken men; they were at their wits' end.*

Have you ever been there—at your wits' end? When the storm is so overwhelmingly destructive that you have run out of ideas? Maybe you're there right now. Maybe you've done everything you know to do and your marriage is still crumbling. Maybe you've done everything you know to do and your children continue to rebel. Maybe you've done everything you know to do and your health is deteriorating. Maybe you've done everything you know to do and your business is failing anyway.

If you are at your wits end in the midst of the storm, you have two options. You can give up—you can decide that "Christianity doesn't work after all, my life is falling apart and God seems to be asleep, so let's forget the whole thing." That's one option. Or you can do what the disciples did in Mark 4. They went to where Jesus was and woke him up, crying..."*Teacher, don't you care if we drown?*" (Mark 4:38)

It's not the most eloquent prayer in scripture, but it was certainly effective. In the midst of your storm, you need to do the same thing: Cry out to God, and keep crying out to him until the storm has passed. Listen to what David wrote...(v. 28-29) *Then they cried out to the Lord in their trouble, and he brought them out of their distress. He stilled the storm to a whisper; the waves of the sea were hushed.*

I hear people say, "I tried that. It didn't work. I cried out to God for help, and nothing happened." My question is always, "How long? How long did you cry out? For an hour? For a day? For a week?" It could possibly take longer. The idea is to pray as it long as it takes to get an answer. Sometimes I think that we're not crying out to God in holy submission to him, we're snapping our fingers and demanding that he do our bidding. There's a big difference. We need to cry out to him in surrender to his Lordship...in a such a way that we explicitly put our faith in him:

"Lord, you're in control of the storm, you're in control of my life, and I trust you for the results." The results may not always be what we think we want, but we can be the sure that the results will always work out for our good. *And we know that in all things God works for the good of those who love him, who have been called according to his purpose. (Romans 8:28)*

In the midst of the storm, cry out to God, and keep crying out to him for as long as you have breath. He will hear you and he will bring you out of your distress.

- **Let God guide you.**

There is an amazing principle in the Christian life that I have seen many people forget—including pastors, preachers, teachers, theologians, leaders, and people who have been believers for decades. I've forgotten it, too, at times. The principle is this: *If you ask for God's guidance, he will give it to you.*

You can say, "God, I have completely messed things up. What can I do to get back on track?" He will guide you. You can say, "God, I have run my business into the ground. What can I do to rebuild it?" He will guide you. You can say, "God, my husband has abandoned me and I'm all alone. How can I make it on my own?" He will guide you. When we seek his guidance, he guides us. When we seek his direction, he gives us direction. When we place our future in his hands, he takes care of our future. Listen to what David wrote...(v. 30) *They were glad when it grew calm, and he guided them to their desired haven.*

To their desired haven. There's a place where you want to be. A place of peace. A place of security. A place of hope, comfort, and rest. A place of joy, love, and fulfillment. He can get you there, if you let him guide you. You have to let him map out the course. The journey may take you on a route you wouldn't have chosen for yourself. It may include some high winds and hard rain, but if you follow his leadership, he will get you to your desired haven. Let God guide you.

Some of you may say, "Good advice...but how? How do I 'let God guide' me?" Learning to follow the leadership of God is a life-long process, but I'm convinced that about 80% is a matter of the heart. If we want to make the right decision, he will reveal the right decision to us.

I thought of this several years ago when we were having a big family-wide Easter Egg hunt. We had hidden eggs all over the back yard, and the older kids were having no trouble finding them. We kept giving hints to the younger kids: "Maybe there are some eggs behind the tree...maybe there are some eggs under those flowers..." and so on. So everyone was finding roughly the same number of eggs. Everyone except my youngest son, who was about two at the time. He couldn't have been less interested in the whole Easter Egg hunt idea. Maybe he had ideological objections to the secular commercialization of a religious holiday—who knows? But he didn't care about the eggs—he would rather pull flowers, throw rocks and chase the cat. The other kids, however, truly appreciated the hints we gave them along the way. This illustrates how God gives us guidance. If we're looking for the eggs, he gives us hints—obvious hints, sometimes—to make sure we find them. If we're not looking for the eggs, though, no amount of hinting will help.

Having God guide you to your desired haven begins with turning your heart toward him. Open your eyes, look for his guidance. Open your ears, listen for his leading. He will guide you. The third thing you need to do about the storm...

- **Remember to remember God's faithfulness.**

I began by saying that I have known some people over the years who have stopped walking with the Lord. Some were in ministry and had experienced his powerful work in their lives. Yet, for whatever reason, they chose to forget about God's prior faithfulness. When the storms of life came, they didn't remember God's provision in the past, and therefore they didn't see any hope for the future. So they gave up in the present.

Here's my challenge to you. When you're going through the storm, make an effort to remember all that God has done for you in the past.

David wrote Psalm 77 while he was going through a time of trial. Listen to his words...*Has his [God's] unfailing love vanished forever? Has his promise failed for all time? Has God forgotten to be merciful? Has he in anger withheld his compassion? Then I thought, "To this I will appeal: the years of the right hand of the Most High." I will remember the deeds of the Lord; yes, I will meditate on all your works and consider all your mighty deeds. (Psalm 77:8-12)*

He says something similar in Psalm 107: 31: *Let them give thanks to the Lord for his unfailing love and his wonderful deeds for men. Let them exalt him in the assembly of the people and praise him in the council of the elders.*

He's saying, "Once you're through the storm, talk about it. Sing praise to God, tell everyone how good God has been to you." God will get you through this storm like he has done in the past. When it happens, remember to remember to thank him.

A while back a friend of mine made this comment: "If I never experience another miracle or receive another blessing, it's OK. I have already been given more than enough to last a lifetime." In truth, the blessings and miracles never end, but my friend has the right idea. An attitude of gratitude gets you through the crisis. When the storms of life are raging, our attitude must be, "God, you've already given me so much more than I deserve; I trust you to get me through this storm, too."

**CONCLUSION**

Even though storms happen to everyone, they have a way of making you feel like you're the only one this has ever happened to. They make it seem that God has forgotten you—while you're overcome with a crisis, he has fallen asleep. Regardless of how you feel, this isn't the case. He is with you. He will get you through it. *Now is the time to cry out to him.* Keep crying as long you have breath. *Now is the time let him guide you.* Turn your heart to him and anticipate his leadership. *And now is the time to remember his faithfulness.* Thank him for all he has done for you in the past, and prepare even now to thank him for seeing you through this storm...and (while you're at it) the next one, too.

## A LESSON IN FORGIVENESS
LUKE 7:36-50

In New Testament times, the Pharisees were a strict group of fundamentalists who believed in keeping the letter of the law in minute detail. Generally speaking, you could say they were religious, but not spiritual. The Pharisees were also the most outspoken enemies of Jesus. They played a major role in bringing him to death. This is not to say that all Pharisees were enemies of Christ, or were all bad, or that their theology was all wrong. In fact, Jesus never challenged their theology. He challenged their legalistic way of applying it. Some Pharisees were followers of Christ; most viewed him with suspicion or hostility.

One evening a Pharisee named Simon invited Jesus to dinner. In those days, affluent people often had a large dining area in the courtyard of their home. On special occasions, such as when a visiting rabbi or a distinguished guest was invited for a meal, people in the community would come to the courtyard area and listen. They weren't invited to eat and they weren't included in the conversation; they were allowed only to listen and observe.

The Bible says that Jesus was reclining at the table. This is how they ate their meals. They didn't sit on chairs with their feet under the table. The dinner table was low to the ground and the guests would lay on mats, with their head near the table and their feet away from the table. They would prop themselves up with their left elbow, and eat with their right hand. Kind of like your kids do when they eat in front of the TV. (Next time you tell them to quit eating on the floor, they'll say "I'm just trying to preserve a Biblical tradition.) This is how all meals were eaten.

While Jesus was lying at the table, eating and talking with the other guests, a woman from the crowd of onlookers approached him. The Bible describes her as a "sinful" woman. In that patriarchal society, there was only one way a woman could get a reputation for being sinful. If you said a man was a "sinful man" that might mean he was a liar, or a cheat, or violent, or cruel, or unfair, or immoral—it could mean any number of things. But when a woman was called a sinful woman, it meant one thing: she had lived a promiscuous life.

This woman was so drawn to Jesus that she broke social custom and approached him. As she listened to him speak she began to cry, and her tears spilled onto Jesus' feet. She washed his feet with her tears. This was an important symbol in Jewish culture. Since people wore sandals and since the streets were dusty, people's feet were always dirty. Some had slaves whose job it was to wash their feet. Those who didn't have slaves would offer guests a bowl of water and a towel when they entered their home so they could wash their own feet.

A similar custom today is that we offer to take a guest's coat when he enters our home. Simon didn't offer water Jesus' feet, so this woman washed his feet with her tears, then dried his feet with hair. Jewish women did not appear in public with their hair unbound, so this woman broke another custom by doing this. In fact, her overall behavior was, according to the standards of the day, rather scandalous.

While she was washing his feet with her own tears, she also kissed his feet repeatedly. Today, in the Western world, we interpret a kiss a gesture of romance. In the days of Jesus, in the Eastern world, the kiss was also a gesture of friendship and devotion. When a guest entered a house, the host placed his hand on the guest's shoulder and gave him the kiss of peace. This was a mark of respect that Jewish custom allowed never to be omitted in the case of a distinguished rabbi. However, when Jesus entered Simon's house, no kiss was offered.

After the woman washed and dried Jesus feet, she opened an expensive alabaster vial—it was common for women to carry such a vial around their neck—and she began to anoint Jesus' feet with the costly perfume. This, too, was a sign of devotion. Whenever a special guest entered the home, the host would show his welcome by burning special incense upon their arrival, or by anointing the forehead with a small amount of rose oil. Simon didn't do this when Jesus entered his home, but the woman anointed Jesus' feet with oil.

As all this happened, Simon watched with a critical, judgmental eye. He thought to himself, "If this man were really a prophet, he would know what kind of woman is touching him—that she is a sinner." He thought this, but rather than discuss the matter with Jesus—who always welcomed sincere inquiry—Simon kept his thoughts to himself. Now, I'm straying from the passage just a little bit here when I say that it wouldn't surprise me at all if Simon was the type who, on the following day, would take great delight in telling all of his Pharisee friends, "I had him over for dinner and you wouldn't believe who he let wash his feet. And this man claims to be a prophet!" Whether or not that is the case, it is obvious that Simon didn't view Jesus with the respect that he deserved.

Simon was like the worst kind of church member. He went through the motions of doing what he was supposed to do—he invited Jesus into his home—but he didn't treat Jesus with respect, he didn't treat him as a spiritual leader, he didn't even treat him as an equal. He just observed Jesus with a critical eye. He was not openly hostile, but neither was he openly devoted. He was, in the words of the book of Revelation, lukewarm.

He didn't recognize his own spiritual bankruptcy; he was too sidetracked by what was taking place in his dining room. A sinful woman was washing and kissing and anointing with oil the feet of a man who was supposed to be a prophet. In Simon's opinion, this just wasn't proper. Jesus read Simon's thoughts, and I don't think he had to rely on his supernatural power to do it. People like Simon are pretty easy to read. In response to what Simon was thinking, Jesus said to him...

Two men owed money to a certain moneylender. One owed him [the equivalent of] $5,000, and the other $50,000. Neither of them had the money to pay him back, so he canceled the debts of both. Now which of them will love him more?" Simon replied, "I suppose the one who had the bigger debt canceled."

Jesus said, "You have judged correctly." Then Jesus said to his host, "When I came into your house you did not give me water for my feet, but she wet my feet with her tears and wiped them with her hair. You did not give me a kiss, but this woman, from the time I entered, has not stopped kissing my feet. You did not put oil on my head, but she has poured perfume on my feet."

Jesus finished by saying…*"Therefore, I tell you, her many sins have been forgiven – for she loved much. But he who has been forgiven little loves little." (Luke 7:41-47)*

The Bible doesn't say how Simon responded to Jesus' words. It only says that the other guests were surprised that he claimed to forgive her sins. Pharisees believed that since only God could forgive sins, no one – not even a Rabbi – had the authority to say "you are forgiven." Jesus said this on more than one occasion, and every time it led to trouble. He said it again here…*(v. 48) "Your faith has saved you. Go in peace."*

I don't know if Simon learned the lesson that Jesus was teaching that evening; we never hear from him again. But this is a lesson that Jesus continues to teach us today – one of the most important aspects of a relationship with God: The more you understand forgiveness, the more you are able to love. There are three aspects of forgiveness that are seen in this story; let's take a brief look at them. First…

- **We all have much to be forgiven.**

*(v. 47) "Therefore I tell you her many sins have been forgiven – for she loved much."* Jesus isn't suggesting that we commit many sins so we can love God more. He's giving Simon a hint about his need for forgiveness, but Simon didn't get it. Instead, he made a tragic mistake: he graded himself on the curve. He compared himself to others, and came to the conclusion that the woman at the feet of Jesus was a sinner, but he wasn't.

If Simon had been truly perceptive, instead of judging Jesus and condemning this woman, he would have asked himself, "Why is this prophet in my home? I am not worthy of his presence." This was Peter's attitude when he realized that Jesus was the Messiah. He said, *"Depart from me, Lord, for I am a sinful man."* [Luke 5:8] God doesn't grade on the curve. You don't score points by being better than the worst people. You need his forgiveness as much as anyone. The biggest mistake you can make is to think that you need his grace less than any other sinner. Like this sinful woman, Simon had much to be forgiven — but he was too smug to acknowledge it.

Do you remember Jim Henson, the creator of the Muppets? He died unexpectedly in 1990. He was sick, but he didn't know it. He thought he had a cold. He thought it was a touch of the flu. He thought he would soon be better, so he did nothing about it. He had no idea that it was life-threatening. He could have saved his own life with a trip to the doctor, but he didn't know how sick he was.

In the very same way, there are millions of people on this planet who think that because, in their own opinion, they are basically good — that "basically good" is good enough. They will never be able to receive God's forgiveness because they will never bring themselves to acknowledge their own sinfulness.

"After all," they will say, "I've never killed anybody. I do my job, pay my bills, try to help my fellow man, and I'm a productive member of society. At least I'm not a drug addict or prostitute." They say this, but they don't see how their lives are filled with bitterness, or envy, or gossip, or resentment, or self-righteousness, or pride, or hate, or jealousy — they don't see how sin has corrupted them and driven a wedge between themselves and a holy God. As a result they go through life thinking "I'm not that bad; in fact, I'm better than most."

When Jesus preached the Sermon on the Mount he began by saying, *Blessed are the poor in spirit, for theirs in the kingdom of heaven. (Matthew 5:3)*

It is only when we recognize our own spiritual poverty that we can experience the riches of God's forgiveness. Simon didn't get it. The sinful woman did — and she experienced the forgiveness of God. We all have much to be forgiven, and...

- **If you want to be forgiven, you can be.**

God's forgiveness is not based on how much we deserve forgiveness. It's based on how much we want forgiveness. Do you want to be forgiven? Do you want to be forgiven enough to ask for forgiveness? If you go to God, in sincerity, asking to be forgiven of your sins, he will forgive you—every time, without fail. *He who conceals his sin does not prosper. He who confesses them and renounces them finds mercy. (Proverbs 28:13)*

There is a sin that you probably struggle with from time to time. Maybe it's "big," maybe it isn't—but you've given in to it in the past, and maybe you'll do it again in the future. It could be gossip, or anger, or lust, or pride, or any number of things—but you have a problem with it. For the sake of this example, let's say you have a problem with speaking hatefully to people. And one day, you fly off the handle as you have so many times before, and let someone have it, up one side and down the other. When that happens you can have one of two attitudes. You can take the attitude that says, "Well, he had it coming. I sure set him straight." If that's your attitude, there's not much God can do for you. That's concealing your sin. If you don't think you did anything wrong, how can he forgive you?

On the other hand, if your attitude is "Lord, I am sorry that I said what I said. It is wrong and I don't want that kind of talk to be part of my life ever again. Please forgive me." Guess what happens. God forgives you. If you want to be forgiven—if you ask him for forgiveness—he forgives you. But then, what if you do it again the next day? What then?

Well, God forgives you again. And what if the next day, it happens again, and you ask forgiveness again? God forgives you again. Now, how many times do you think this can happen before you reach the saturation point and he no longer forgives you? 10 times? 20 times? 100 times? The truth is, the Bible teaches that God will forgive you as many times as it takes until you get victory. That's what Jesus told Peter about forgiveness...*If your brother sins against you seven times in a day and seven times comes back to you and says, "I repent," forgive him. (Luke 17:4)*

God expects you to forgive others without limit, because he forgives you without limit. Now, that's not a license to sin. People who think that way are simply missing the point. Sin causes pain. It breaks the heart of God. It wrecks lives. Part of wanting to be forgiven is wanting to be free from sin forever—even though you lose the battle from time to time. If you want to be forgiven and if you want to be free from sin, you will be forgiven immediately and you will be set from sin's power ultimately.

Some say, "If you're sincere when you repent, you won't do it again." These people rarely, however, apply the same standard to themselves. You can ask them: Have you ever had a hateful thought? Did you repent? Were you sincere? They will answer "yes" to each question, but the question they can't answer "yes" to is: Are you saying that will never again have a hateful thought? Never, ever, ever?" If the answer is "no" then, by their standard, they weren't really sincere when they repented the first time. The truth is, we struggle with sin even after we repent—and sometimes we have to keep coming back again and again for forgiveness. You know if you're sincere, and God knows if you're sincere. Don't let others judge your heart.

God's forgiveness is not based on how much you deserve it, because you don't deserve it all. Why should he forgive you for gossip, or lying, or lust, or anger, when you're going to do it again? It's not a question of whether you deserve God's forgiveness, it's a question of whether you want God's forgiveness. If you want to be forgiven, you can be. The third lesson this story teaches is...

- **Accepting forgiveness is an act of faith.**

*(v. 34) Jesus said to the woman, "Go in peace. Your faith has saved you."* An Aramaic translation of this verse reads, *"Your trust has made you alive."*

Receiving forgiveness is an act of faith. You don't wait for a feeling to confirm it; you ask for it and by faith you accept it. Trust God to keep his promise. You might feel a weight being lifted from your shoulders—or you might not. How you feel doesn't change the fact that God has promised to forgive you, and he will.

The sinful woman was saved because she put her faith in Jesus, not in her own goodness. Simon missed out because he trusted in himself. If you will put your faith in Jesus, your faith will make you alive. It will, literally, save your life.

## CONCLUSION

The more you understand about forgiveness, the more you are able to love. That's what this passage teaches us. If Simon had only known. If he had only recognized that he, too, had much to be forgiven. If he had only been willing to ask for God's forgiveness, the pain of his past could be wiped away forever. If he had understood this, then he, like the sinful woman, would have been on his knees before Jesus, washing his feet with his own tears.

This is what God wants. The more you understand forgiveness the more you are able to love. And that is the response God is looking for. He wants your love. The more you understand forgiveness, the more you are able to love.

## DEALING WITH DIFFICULT PEOPLE
LUKE 12:57-59

When people get together, some level of conflict inevitably develops. It can't be avoided. The sign of a spiritually mature church, or family, or marriage, or friendship, is the willingness to resolve disagreements. When you examine the life of Jesus, the lives of his disciples, and the example of the early church, you won't discover an absence of conflict. You will discover, however, a commitment to work through conflict to achieve unity. The only church I have ever worked for that was free from conflict was a dead church. No one disagreed with anything because no one cared. On the other hand, when a church—or any organization—commits to moving forward, at some point, they must learn to resolve conflict.

I don't have to convince you that conflict is an enormous waste of time. A church can't do what God called it to do if the people are mired in petty bickering. The same goes for your business and your family. The insane thing about conflict is that it often starts with something insignificant.

One of the most famous conflicts is the feud between the Hatfields and McCoys. In 12 years it claimed the lives of 12 people—3 Hatfields, 7 McCoys, and 2 outsiders. The feud began over a dispute about the ownership of a hog. Though both sides despised the other, and both believed their view was absolutely right, I'm sure neither Mr. Hatfield or Mr. McCoy believed a hog was more valuable than the lives of his children.

Conflict has a way of mushrooming in churches, too. I heard a preacher tell a story about a church that had grown to the point of needing a new building. After the building was completed, a disagreement arose among the members as to which side of the auditorium to put the piano. Words were exchanged, tempers flared, and the church ultimately split. The side that "won" kept the building, but they no longer needed the extra seating space, and couldn't afford the mortgage payment. This is how futile our conflicts become. These seem like extreme examples, but are they? Have you and your spouse ever fought—and later couldn't remember what started it? Maybe you went days or weeks without speaking—and now you can't remember what you were fighting about. (Some would say, "Not in my house. The person I married never forgets a thing!")

In today's message we will examine what Jesus taught about resolving conflict; he offers some rather straight-forward advice. He said...*(v. 58-59) As you are going with your adversary to the magistrate, try hard to be reconciled to him on the way, or he may drag you off to the judge, and the judge turn you over to the officer, and the officer throw you into prison. I tell you, you will not get out until you have paid the last penny.* There are three ways to deal with difficult people. First of all...

- **Recognize that you might be wrong.**

Jesus said, in effect, "On the way to court try to patch things up with your adversary, because when you stand before an impartial judge, he may decide that you are the one who is wrong." Whenever you disagree with someone, of course you believe you're right. It only makes sense. No one would hang on to an opinion that they believed was wrong. As a safety measure, however, no matter how right you think you are, remind yourself there is a possibility that you could be wrong.

H.L. Mencken was a well-known publisher in the early part of the twentieth century. He used to write scathing criticisms of American politics and culture. In return he received thousands of angry letters expressing outrage and indignation. Mencken responded to every critical letter the same way. He would write the person back and simply say, "You may be right." Resolving conflict begins with recognizing that you may be wrong. Think about this: if you're right only 55% of the time you can make a million dollars a day on Wall Street. Yet, who among us is doing it? When dealing with other people, admit to yourself, and admit to them, that you don't think you're always right.

That doesn't mean you have to go the other extreme. You don't have to become spineless. I am not saying you should compromise what you know to be the truth. I am saying choose your battles carefully. The question is: How important is it to be right in this situation? Mr. Hatfield and Mr. McCoy were each sure he was right. Was a hog really that important? The smart thing would have been to say, "You know, I may be wrong. What difference does a hog make anyway?" One small concession would have saved the lives of 12 people. When you're in conflict with another person, recognize that it could be you who is wrong. Secondly...

- **Make the offer of reconciliation.**

*(v. 58) Jesus said, "Try hard to be reconciled with him on the way..."* The old song *Tie a Yellow Ribbon Round the Old Oak Tree* is about a man just been released from prison and is on his way home. He doesn't know if his wife has forgiven him, so he asks her to Tie a Yellow Ribbon Round the Old Oak Tree as a signal that he is welcome there. If he doesn't see the ribbon he "will stay on the bus, forget about us, and put the blame on me..." You remember how the story ends. The bus approached his hometown and in the distance he could see "a hundred yellow ribbons round the old oak tree."

Most of the people you have conflict with are willing to resolve it and put it in the past—regardless of who's at fault. When you take a step toward reconciliation, most often the other person will take a step, too.

Barry McGuire was a protest singer in the sixties (his big hit was *Eve of Destruction*.) In the seventies he became a Christian. Years later, he found himself struggling in an unhappy marriage. Though he was committed to Christ, he and his wife lived in constant turmoil. They had lost their ability to communicate, and couldn't even carry on a conversation without conflict. One day after a major disagreement, when it appeared all hope of reconciliation was gone, he entered the room and sat down beside her. At this point, he was ready to give up. But he made one final effort. He turned to her and said, "Can I get you some tea?" A little surprised at the kindness of the offer, she said, "That would be nice." He got up and poured her a cup of tea, handed it to her, and sat down again. They began to talk, and a miracle of reconciliation took place. He had taken a step in her direction, and she took a step toward him.

Unfortunately, reconciliation is usually more complicated than offering someone a cup of tea. The fact is, some people are not at all interested in the prospect of reconciliation. They prefer to let the barriers remain. You can't control their reaction, you can only make the offer of reconciliation and leave it at that.

In a passage similar to the one in Luke, Jesus said...*If you are offering your gift at the altar and there remember that your brother has something against you, leave your gift there in front of the altar. First go and be reconciled to your brother; then come and offer your gift. (Matthew 5:23-24)*

The principle that Jesus is teaching is the one echoed by Paul...*If it is possible, as far as it depends on you, live at peace with everyone. (Romans 12:18)* Once you have tried to bridge the gap between you and someone else—either by admitting that you were at fault and asking forgiveness, or by expressing a desire to restore broken communication—you've done almost as much as you can do. There is one more thing...

- **Decide that you won't make matters any worse.**

Another famous conflict existed between Winston Churchill and Lady Astor. Their mutual contempt is legendary. I don't know who was at fault, but there are numerous stories about how Mr. Churchill kept the battle going with his one-liners. When Lady Astor said to Churchill, "If I were your wife I would fill your cocktail glass with poison." Churchill replied, "Lady Astor, if you were my wife, I would drink it." When Lady Astor made the public accusation: "Mr. Churchill, you are disgracefully drunk!" Churchill said, "Yes I am. And you, dear lady, are disgracefully ugly. What's more, tomorrow morning I will be sober." Maybe Mr. Churchill couldn't do anything to change

Lady Astor's animosity, but he could have, with a little effort, kept the relationship from deteriorating further simply by keeping his comments to himself.

For many of us, this is an impossible task. We think we have to have the last word. We think we have to return insult for insult. The result is that we keep things stirred up much longer than necessary. Paul said..."*Do not repay anyone evil for evil.*" *(Romans 12:17)* This means you approach conflict with the attitude: "I may not be able to make this situation better, but I don't have to make it worse. I will bite my tongue and keep my comments to myself."

## CONCLUSION

These attitudes—recognizing that you might be wrong; taking steps toward reconciliation; deciding that you won't make the conflict worse than it is—will go a long way in helping you resolve conflict.

When Norman Vincent Peale wrote *The Power of Positive Thinking*, many people decided they didn't like him. Some liberals didn't like him because he was too fundamental—he emphasized prayer, Bible study, and salvation through faith in Christ. Some conservatives didn't like him because they didn't think he talked enough about sin and hell. He was blasted in pulpits throughout the country and criticized in journals left and right. In all of his writings and public speaking, he never made a counter-attack. When Peale was in his nineties, someone made the comment that he outlived his enemies. A friend of his, who knew him well, said, "No. Norman has out loved his enemies."

Jesus had enemies, too. Though he never compromised the truth, he never stopped loving them. You will have conflicts with others from time to time, and you will not have the power to single-handedly fix the problem. However, you do have the power to love that person, to shower that person with grace, and to keep the door of reconciliation open at all times.

## HOW TO TREAT A MISTREATER
GENESIS 45:1-15

The tagline to A & E's *Biography* once was "You're either biography or you're not." Today we'll look at the story of a man who is definitely Biography material. In fact, his life story has been made into a movie and was the subject of a successful Broadway show. The show was *Joseph and the Amazing Technicolor Dreamcoat*. His story, told in the book of Genesis, is fascinating, to say the least.

Joseph's story begins with the story of his parents, Jacob and Rachel. Jacob loved Rachel with all his heart. He wanted to marry her, but Rachel had an older sister named Leah who, according to custom, should be married first. Their father tricked Jacob into marrying Leah instead, but told him that he could marry Rachel too (such things were allowed in those days) if Jacob worked for him for seven years. Jacob agreed, and eventually he and Rachel were wed.

Unfortunately, this isn't the happy ending; Rachel was unable to have children. Jacob fathered 10 sons with his other wives, but Rachel was unable to conceive. Finally, after years of waiting, Rachel gave birth to a son, Joseph. A few years later, while giving birth to another son, Benjamin, Rachel died. In the meantime, God had changed Jacob's name to Israel, which means *struggles with God*.

Jacob/Israel had a special affection for his son Joseph. The Bible says...*Israel loved Joseph more than any of his other sons, because he had been born to him in his old age; and he made a richly ornamented robe for him. When his brothers saw that their father loved him more than any of them, they hated him and could not speak a kind word to him. (Genesis 37:3-4)*

To make matters worse, Joseph kept having these strange dreams that infuriated his brothers—dreams that indicated he would one day rule over his brothers. They finally decided they had just had enough. One day they saw Joseph coming towards them as they were tending their flocks, and they devised a plot to kill him. After some debate and discussion, the decided rather than killing him outright, they would toss him into a deep well and let him starve to death.

Then they saw in the distance a traveling band of Arabs ("Ishmaelites") approaching, and their plan crystallized. They would sell Joseph as a slave and tell their father that he had been devoured by a ferocious animal. After collecting 20 shekels from the merchants, they splattered some blood on the fancy coat and went home to tell Israel that his favorite son was dead. Heartbroken, Israel (Jacob) mourned the death of his son. Meanwhile, Joseph was taken to Egypt and purchased as slave to Potiphar, a high-ranking official in Pharaoh's government. The Bible says...*The Lord was with Joseph and he prospered, and he lived in the house of his Egyptian master. When his master saw that the Lord was with him and that the Lord gave him success in everything he did, Joseph found favor in his eyes and became his attendant. Potiphar put him in charge of his household, and he entrusted to his care everything he owned...the Lord blessed the household of the Egyptian because of Joseph. (Genesis 39:2-5)*

Sounds like Joseph landed on his feet, doesn't it? Unfortunately, things soon took a turn for the worse. The Bible says...*Now Joseph was well-built and handsome, and after a while his master's wife took notice of Joseph and said, "Come to bed with me!" But he refused. (Genesis 39:7-8)*

Joseph held his ground in spite of this woman's repeated efforts to get him to sleep with her. He was determined to do the right thing. But his rejection offended her, so she framed him. She accused him of making untoward advances and Potiphar became furious and threw him in jail. Then the Bible says...*But while Joseph was there in the prison, the Lord was with him; he showed him kindness and granted him favor in the eyes of the prison warden. (Genesis 20-21)*

It wasn't long before Joseph was running the prison for the warden. A little while later, Pharaoh became angry with a couple of his officials and threw them in jail, too. While in prison, these men began to have strange dreams. Joseph was able to explain their meaning, telling one official that he would soon be set free, and the other official that he would soon be executed. To the one being set free, Joseph said, "Remember me on the outside; help me get out of jail, too." Sure enough, the dreams came true. One man was freed, the other executed. The one set free was Pharaoh's cupbearer, and after his release the Bible says...*The chief cupbearer, however, did not remember Joseph; he forgot him. (Genesis 40:23)*

That's gratitude for you, isn't it? It seems like Joseph couldn't get a break. Sold as a slave, he made the best of his situation and ended up in prison. As a prisoner, he made the best of his situation, and ended up forgotten by the one who could have helped him gain his freedom. Two full years passed. Pharaoh began having strange dreams, and when he asked Egypt's greatest magicians and wisest men to explain, they had nothing to offer. The cupbearer suddenly remembered Joseph and told Pharaoh about the prisoner who could interpret dreams. The Bible says...*So Pharaoh sent for Joseph, and he was quickly brought from the dungeon. When he had shaved and changed his clothes he came before Pharaoh. (Genesis 41:14)*

Joseph listened to Pharaoh's dreams, and with God's help, was able to give him this interpretation: "Seven years of abundance are coming to Egypt, followed by seven years of famine. Find a wise man to put in charge of the land, collect food during the good years and store it away so that Egypt won't be ruined by the famine." Pharaoh took a look at Joseph and said, "You're the man. You're my second in command. Since God has made this known to you, I put you in charge of my palace and the whole land of Egypt. Only with respect to my throne will I be greater than you."

So, at the age of 30, Joseph—the former slave, the former prisoner—was now the second most powerful man in the most powerful nation of the world. For the next seven years he did his job well, storing enough food to help the entire nation prepare for the years of famine. And sure enough, after seven years, famine struck. Now, back to Canaan land. The famine affected their country, too. Jacob heard that there was plenty of food in Egypt, so he sent his sons on a journey to buy grain. The ten older brothers made the journey — these were Joseph's half-brothers. His full-brother, Benjamin, stayed home.

*Now, Joseph was the governor of the land, the one who sold grain to all its people. So when Joseph's brothers arrived, they bowed down to him with their faces to the ground. As soon as Joseph saw his brothers, he recognized them...(Genesis 42:6-7)*

Joseph recognized his brothers, but they didn't recognize him. In the next series of events of this story, Joseph's motives are sometimes difficult to discern. Maybe he was still working out a strategy for dealing with them, maybe he was testing them to determine whether or not they were being honest with him, but clearly his long-range plan was to re-unite with all of his brothers and his father.

Joseph accused them of being spies, and said, "One of you must stay here as a hostage, while the rest of you go home and bring back your youngest brother." They reluctantly agreed, took the grain they purchased and left. When the brothers got back to Canaan and told their father (Jacob/Israel) what had happened, and that they must return with Benjamin, Jacob said, "Forget it! You're not taking Benjamin away from me!" But eventually the grain they had purchased in Egypt was all used up, and to prevent his family from starving to death, Jacob was forced to agree to allow Benjamin to make the next journey to Egypt.

When Joseph learned that his brothers had returned, he invited them to have lunch with him in the palace. He asked about his father—if he was still alive. And when he saw Benjamin, his younger brother, he was overcome with emotion and left the room to cry. When he regained his composure, he came back and said, "Let's eat." Joseph had made seating arrangements for them; the brothers were shocked to discover they had been seated in order of their ages. When the food was served, Benjamin was given more food than everyone else.

Later, after the brothers purchased the grain they needed, Joseph told his steward to put the money they had paid for the grain back in their sacks, and to plant his silver cup in Benjamin's sack. The men received their grain and began the journey home. Before they had gotten far from the city, Joseph sent his soldiers after them. Their bags were inspected, Joseph's silver cup was discovered, and the brothers were all arrested. They pleaded their innocence before Joseph, but he said, "Only the one who had the cup in his possession must remain here as my slave. The rest of you may go home."

Of course, Joseph knew that it was Benjamin, his younger brother, who had the cup. I'm not sure what his reason was for staging this event — maybe it was an elaborate scheme to rescue Benjamin from his older brothers before they did to him what they had done to Joseph. But I don't think he was prepared for what happened next. His older brother, Judah—the one whose idea it was to sell him as a slave, broke down before him and said, "Please don't take my youngest brother. Take me instead."

This brings us to today's text.

*(v. 1-2) Then Joseph could no longer control himself before all his attendants, and he cried out, "Have everyone leave my presence!" So there was no one with Joseph when he made himself known to his brothers. And he wept so loudly that the Egyptians heard him, and Pharaoh's household heard about it.*

*(v. 3) Joseph said to his brothers, "I am Joseph! Is my father still living?" But his brothers were not able to answer him, because they were terrified at his presence.*

*(v. 4-7) Then Joseph said to his brothers, "Come close to me." When they had done so, he said, "I am your brother Joseph, the one you sold into Egypt! And now, do not be distressed and do not be angry with yourselves for selling me here, because it was to save lives that God sent me ahead of you. For two years now there has been famine in the land, and for the next five years there will be plowing and reaping. But God sent me ahead of you to preserve for you a remnant on Earth to save your lives by a great deliverance.*

*(v. 8-11) So then, it was not you who sent me here, but God. He made me father to Pharaoh, lord of his entire household and ruler of all Egypt. Now hurry back to my father and say to him, 'This is what your son Joseph says: God has made me lord of all Egypt. Come down to me; don't delay. You shall live in the region of Goshen and be near me — you, your children and grandchildren, your flocks and herds, and all you have. I will provide for you there, because five years of famine are still to come. Otherwise you and your household and all who belong to you will become destitute.'*

*(v. 12-13) You can see for yourselves, and so can my brother Benjamin, that it is really I who am speaking to you. Tell my father about all the honor accorded me in Egypt and about everything you have seen. And bring my father down here quickly."*

*(v. 14-15) Then he threw his arms around his brother Benjamin and wept, and Benjamin embraced him, weeping. And he kissed all his brothers and wept over them. Afterwards his brothers talked with him.*

Incredible, isn't it? Who ever came up with the idea that this book is boring? Not only is this a great story, but today, thousands of years later, there are lessons that we can learn from these events.

At a young and tender age, Joseph was on the receiving end of some rather cruel treatment, but he never gave in to despair, and he never gave in to bitterness. He made the most of every situation, even when he was treated unfairly. And when the opportunity came to reconcile with his brothers, he received them with open arms.

Though our individual stories may not be as extravagant as Joseph's, we share this in common with him: we are all, at one time or another, treated unfairly. We all know what it's like to be given worse than we deserve. We've all been mistreated by someone at sometime in our lives — maybe it was a parent, or a sibling, or an employer, or a coach, or spouse, or a child, or a friend — regardless of who it was, we learn from Joseph's story how to treat a mistreater. We've spent most of our time this morning learning about the events of Joseph's life; this was necessary to understand the significance of his reconciliation with his brothers. In these last few minutes I want us to look at four things we can do in response to mistreatment. First of all, if you've been mistreated...

- **Recognize how God has adapted the situation for good.**

Notice what Joseph said to his brothers...*(v. 5) "...it was to save lives that God sent me ahead of you."* Even though the events of his life had been challenging, to say the least, Joseph recognized God's hand in the details. Listen to this...*(v. 8) "So then, it was not you who sent me here, but God."*

I don't know where you are in your story—sold into slavery, falsely accused, wrongly imprisoned, all but forgotten—regardless of where you are, God has not abandoned you. Do you remember how the Bible said that the Lord was with Joseph when he was a slave, and the Lord was with Joseph when he was in prison, and the Lord was with Joseph when he served before the Pharaoh — in the very same way, the Lord is with you...in your slavery, in your prison, in your pain. Maybe today you can see how God has worked out negative events for good, or maybe that hasn't yet been made clear to you, but either way, God is at work, as the book of Romans says...*causing all things to work together for good. (Romans 8:28)*

Obviously, Joseph's brothers didn't have his best interests in mind when they sold him into slavery. It wasn't done with the idea of helping him establish a political career in Egypt. They intended to hurt him, but their intentions backfired—because God was with Joseph all the way. Guess what. He's also with you. Remember this verse...*Our God, however, turned the curse into a blessing. (Nehemiah 13:2)* For you, God can and will turn your curse into a blessing. Recognize his work in your life. Secondly...

- **Release the offender.**

Joseph reveals his spiritual depth in the words he speaks to his brothers...*(v. 5) "And now, do not be distressed, and do not be angry with yourselves for selling me here..."* Joseph could have given his brothers a long speech about the terrible things they had done. He could have said, "Now it's your turn; you will suffer as

I have suffered." But Joseph wasn't interested in revenge. He just wanted to let the offense go. Joseph understood this: When you release the offender, you release yourself. As long as you hang on to your bitterness and resentment, you will never be free, no matter how much success you achieve. God is willing to turn the curse into a blessing—don't waste it by clinging to the past. Let it go. Release the offender.

Augustine said, "If you are suffering from a bad man's injustice, forgive him, lest there be two bad men." Archibald Hart said, "Forgiveness is relinquishing my rights to hurt back." Don't hang on to the hurt. Don't cling to the past. Forgive whoever you need to forgive. Release the offender. In fact, more than just forgiving the offender, you need to...

- **Repay them with kindness.**

This is what Joseph did for his brothers. He said...*(v. 9-11)* *"Come down to me; don't delay. You shall live in the region of Goshen and be near me...I will provide for you there..."*

In spite of the fact that he had been sold for 20 shekels many years before, Joseph repaid his brothers with kindness when had the opportunity. It seems outrageous to do good to someone who has gone out of their way to do harm to you, but that is exactly what God has called us to do. And in this he leads by example. Jesus was beaten, mocked, and spat upon, even though he had done nothing worthy of such treatment. And while he was hanging on a cross he didn't deserve to bear, he said, "Father forgive them." Each of us has gone through a time of rebellion when we have, so to speak, spat on the love of God, and still he offers us his unconditional love, his all-encompassing forgiveness. We rejected him, and he repaid us with kindness... *While we were still sinners, Christ died for us. (Romans 5:8)*

If you've been mistreated, look for the opportunity to repay the mistreater with kindness. Your parents may have mistreated you as a child, but don't withhold your kindness from them now. Your brother or sister may have hurt you in the past, but if you can do good for them now, do it. Your neighbor may have taken advantage of you, but if you now have the chance do him a favor, do it. Repay them with kindness. Finally...

- **Re-invent the relationship.**

*(v. 14-15) Then he threw his arms around his brother Benjamin and wept, and Benjamin embraced him, weeping. And he kissed all his brothers and wept over them. Afterwards his brothers talked with him.* It's as if Joseph was saying, "Let's start over, and let's do it right this time."

Some of you are probably asking, "Does this mean I should let my abusive husband back in the house, as if nothing has happened? Are you saying I should re-hire a dishonest employee and make my business vulnerable again?" I didn't say "resume the relationship", I said "re-invent" it. Make it the way it should have been all along, with the proper boundaries and the proper understanding of each other.

Joseph re-invented his relationship with his brothers—with new boundaries. He didn't invite them into his life so that things could go back to being the way they were; he wasn't about to give them a chance to sell him back into slavery. So, in that sense, he didn't resume the relationship—he re-invented it. Reconciling with someone who has hurt you in the past doesn't mean that you're setting yourself up to be hurt all over again. Change the terms of the relationship. Make it the way it should have been all along. This is what Joseph did with his brothers.

## CONCLUSION

It's inevitable that you will be mistreated. Mistreatment can be the catalyst for God doing something great, or it can be the catalyst of your undoing. How you respond to mistreatment will determine whether or not you experience God's peace and joy. The sooner you begin living by these principles, the sooner you'll overcome the effects of mistreatment. Recognize God's hand, and trust him to turn the curse into a blessing. Release the offender, because in doing so you release yourself. Repay them with kindness when the opportunity presents itself. Finally, re-invent the relationship to make it what it should have been all along.

## ELIMINATING ENVY
PSALM 37

In the mid-seventies country music made some changes. The old Nashville style of slicked back hair, rhinestone suits, and songs about trains, trucks, and cheating was replaced by a new breed of country artist with shaggy hair and bell-bottom jeans, and songs about sunshine, love, and peaceful easy feelings. John Denver led the pack. He was more successful than any "country" singer had ever been. Before 1975, only a handful of country artists had a gold record (i.e. sold 500,000 copies). Denver's records, however, went platinum—selling more than a million copies. He was phenomenally successful; his huge crossover audience blurred the lines between country and pop—and many, many people in the country music industry hated him. At the 1975 Country Music Awards show, singer Charlie Rich was asked to present the award for "Country Artist of the Year". When he opened the envelope and saw John Denver's name, rather than announcing the winner, he took out a cigarette lighter, set fire to the paper, and walked off stage.

I don't know what motivated Mr. Rich to do what he did, but I know what was behind much of the music industry-related resentment directed at John Denver in those days. Envy. Many artists had spent decades to achieve modest success; he came on the scene and in just a few short years was the best selling "country" artist of his day. Besides, he had long hair and said things like "Far out." In their opinion, it just wasn't right. He didn't deserve it.

Fair or not, when some people succeed, others become envious. For every successful person on the planet, there are hundreds (or thousands) who say, "He doesn't deserve it. It should have been me." One of my favorite Dik Lapine cartoons is of a Promise Keeper's Pastor's Convention. There's a man on stage speaking before thousands, his image projected onto a jumbo screen. The caption shows most of the audience thinking to themselves: "I could do better than this guy."

Envy. It's that voice that tells us "He doesn't deserve to succeed. It should have been me." In the workplace, it has sidelined more careers, stalled more projects and, most likely, bankrupted more companies than we'll ever know. When envy and petty jealousy overtake a person's heart, that person becomes ineffective in all they do. Their productivity gives way to self-pity. They become consumed with a victim's mentality, saying "Why me? Why me? It's not fair!"

A friend took his family out to eat. They all love Mexican food—especially his son—so he took them to an upscale, expensive Mexican restaurant. His daughter got to bring a friend along, and the son didn't. Dad wasn't playing favorites; the daughter just happened to have a friend visiting at the time, and she was invited to come along. This made the son unhappy, and he pouted through most of the meal. When he was asked what was wrong, he finally said, "Why did she get to bring a friend tonight, and I didn't? She always gets special treatment. I get nothing." So the boy sat there, not eating, just poking his food and pouting. Instead of enjoying a meal at his favorite restaurant, he wallowed in misery. Sound familiar, anyone?

It happens in families, it happens at work, it happens in the ministry, it happens among friends. When people become envious, they lose their ability to enjoy life. They don't have the capacity to appreciate what they have, because they're too focused on keeping tabs on everyone else.

We feed our two cats in separate dishes. Kipper can't bear the thought that Sassy is allowed to eat, too. If Sassy approaches his own dish while Kipper is eating, Kipper hisses and chases him off. (Maybe we should have named him *Sissy*) While Kipper is hissing, you can take her food away and she won't notice. She isn't nearly as concerned about her food as she is about making sure that the other cat doesn't get to eat.

That's what envy does to you. It prevents you from enjoying life. It prevents you from enjoying your own success, and it causes you to resent everyone else's. That's the why the Bible says...*(v. 8) Do not envy others – it only leads to harm.*

David wrote Psalm 37 to encourage us not to become envious when other people succeed—especially the undeserving, the wicked. He says if their success isn't deserved, it will not last. He begins the Psalm by saying, *(v. 1-2) Don't worry about the wicked. Don't' envy those who do wrong. For like the grass, they soon fade away. Like springtime flowers, they soon wither.*

Whether the person we envy deserves their success or not— whether they're good or bad, wicked or evil, right or wrong—our feelings of envy have the same debilitating effect on us. So, the question is not "Does John Denver deserve to be Country Artist of the Year; does your sister deserve to bring a friend along for a meal; does the other cat deserve to eat?" The question is: "How will I deal with my feelings of envy, resentment, and jealousy?" For those who struggle with envy, David lists four words that will help get your mind focused on what God wants to be doing in your life. The first word is...

- **Trust**

When it comes to measuring our success against the success of others, we need to put our trust completely in God, because he is faithful and just.

One Christmas when I was a teenager, my Dad had been out of town for an extended period and didn't have the chance to buy my sisters and I individual Christmas presents. So, on Christmas Eve he held a book up and said to my sister, "Kathy, your gift is on page 50. Now, go into the next room, open the book and take your gift." She disappeared for a moment, and came back with a big smile. He said to my other sister, "Your gift is on page 100. Go into the next room, open the book and take your gift." She did, and came back with a big smile. Then he said to me, "Stephen, your gift is on page 150. Take the book into the next room and get your gift." I went into the next room, opened the book to page 150, and there was nothing there except a bunch of words. I scratched my head and took a long look at that page. I remember the book very well; it was called, *101 Games of Solitaire*. I thought, Maybe there's a clue in the words of this page that will tell me what my gift is. Maybe it will make reference to a new car! I read the entire page. Nothing. Finally my dad said, "Hey, hurry up in there!" I came back, handed him the book and said, "Thanks"—still just a little bewildered. I knew he wouldn't merely pretend to give me a gift, so I assumed he would spring it on me eventually.

While we talking later, he absent-mindedly reached his hand in his pocket and took something out, and suddenly got a confused look on his face. In his hand was a $100 bill. He stared at it for a minute, then said, "Did everyone get their Christmas gift out of the book?" When both sisters said, "Yes," he looked at me. I said, "You told me turn to page 150, and there was nothing there but words." He said, "How long did you expect to wait before you said something?" I said, " I just thought you were planning to give me something later, so I wasn't worried."

When it comes to our own success and our own blessings in life, that's the way we need to trust God—with one small difference: God doesn't make mistakes. He doesn't absent-mindedly misplace anything he has for us. If it seems that others are getting more than they deserve and you are getting less than you should, just trust God. He hasn't forgotten you. He won't overlook you, and he won't short change you. David said...*(v. 3) Trust in the Lord and do good. Then you will live safely in the land and prosper.*

The gospel of John records a conversation that took place between Jesus and Peter after the resurrection. Jesus told Peter that he would die the death of a martyr. Peter pointed at John and said, "What about him?" Jesus said...*"If I want him to remain alive until I return, what is that to you? You follow me."* (John 21:22)

Jesus was saying to Peter, and he's saying to us today, "Don't look at them, look at me. Follow me. Trust me." If you struggle with envy, begin to put your trust in God. He will take care of you. The second word to remember is...

- **Delight**

    *(v. 4) Take delight in the Lord...* What brings out envy in you? Someone driving a better car? Earning more money? Getting more recognition? Having a bigger office with a better view? Traveling to places you've never been? More often than not, the things that make us envious are things that shouldn't be important to us anyway. Think about it. In 10,000 years will it matter how big your office was? Will it matter whether or not you were the one the company sent to Orlando? When jealousy and resentment flare up like this, it tells us that we are delighting in the wrong things. Our delight must be in the Lord, not in the trappings of success.

    We need to say, "Lord, I choose you over all those things. Rather than pursuing them, I will pursue you." That's what it means to delight in the Lord: to put him first; to choose him over everything else. When you do it, guess what happens? David tells us...*(v. 4) Take delight in the Lord, and he will give you your heart's desires.*

    It's a matter of the cart and the horse, and which will come first. When God has first place, you're in a position to be blessed. Here's how it works. When God is first, your priorities begin to fall into place. You discover that what once seemed so important is now suddenly insignificant. When God is first, your heart's desires become more holy, and less self-serving.

    For example, your desires will change from "I want a magnificent house" to "I want a magnificent home." See the difference? A magnificent house is pretty much determined by the price tag; a magnificent home is filled with happiness, with love and laughter bouncing off the walls. Regardless of the value of your house, if you delight in the Lord, he'll increase the value of your home—he'll give you home of the dreams. *(v. 4) Take delight in the Lord, and he will give you your heart's desires.*

    Do you struggle with envy? Let go of your desire for things, and begin to desire God above all else. Take delight in him. The third word I want you to remember is...

- **Commit**

*(v. 5) Commit everything you do to the Lord. Trust him, and he will help you.* This reminds me of Proverbs 16:3. *Commit your work to the Lord, and then your plans will succeed.* Committing your work to Lord means that you're willing to do the work that success requires, even if you don't get credit for the results—because you're working to please God, not impress the world.

One of the best fathers I know is a man named William. His two sons are grown now, and they've become everything a father could hope for: they're successful, they married well, and they're both committed Christians. And they are where they are today because for the last 32 years William has been willing to pay whatever price he had to pay in order to give his sons a good life. He could have been more successful in business if he had been willing to spend more time at the office—but Little League games and fishing with his sons mattered more than money. You could say he was a purpose-driven parent. Whether he was disciplining them, or playing a game, or checking their homework, he did everything with the intention of building character into his boys. And it worked.

Not everybody realizes that, though. William's sister (who had all kinds of trouble with her children) said, "William doesn't know how good he has it. He never had to deal with rebellious children like we did. He's lucky that his boys turned out so well." She doesn't get it. Luck has nothing to do with it. William's sons are who they are because William vowed to be a great father, and he gave it all his heart. Do you think that bothers him that some say he's lucky? Not at all. He doesn't care who gets the credit. His concern from the start has been that his sons become Godly men.

It doesn't matter who gets the credit. More important is, "What is the end result?" When you commit your success, your job, your family, your ministry, and anything else to God, you let go of your need for recognition. Instead, you give all the glory to God. Trust. Delight. Commit. Here's the fourth word...

- **Wait**

Does it sometimes seem like you're floundering while everyone around you succeeds? Don't be envious. Just wait. Your time will come.

Do you know what NFL players Trent Dilfer, Kurt Warner and Jake Delhomme have in common? In the last few years, they've all taken their teams to the Super Bowl. And each of them rose from virtual obscurity to do it. Two years before appearing in the championship game, none of them looked like championship-caliber quarterbacks. They worked odd jobs in the off-season and were shuffled around NFL Europe. No doubt each knew he was good enough to play at the NFL level, and I'm sure each wondered if his time would ever come. There was nothing to do but wait—each staying faithful to his game, striving to get better, and waiting for his time to come.

For each one, his time came. Your time will come, too, if you're willing to wait. Don't let other's success today destroy your chance for success tomorrow. Be willing to wait. David said...(v. 7) *Be still in the presence of the Lord, and wait patiently for him to act.*

Waiting is not passive. It's not about doing nothing until you get your "lucky" break. Waiting on God means that we keep doing what we know we should be doing, leaving the timing of the results in his hands. Just because you don't have success today doesn't mean that you'll never succeed. Wait on God. Keep studying the playbook; keep making sales calls; keep doing your job the way it should be done. And remain faithful to God. It's worth the wait. It's always worth the wait.

In fact, after his Super Bowl victory with the Ravens, Dilfer told Christianity Today that his professional struggles gave him spiritual insight he might never have gotten otherwise. He said they taught him to be still; they taught him to wait on God.

## CONCLUSION

Don't let yourself be sidelined by envy. Don't let it eat away at your effectiveness. Whether or not others succeed and whether or not they deserve it is not your concern. Your concern is to keep pursuing the path God has called you to take.

Trust him; he'll take care of you. Delight yourself in him; he'll give you your heart's desire. Commit yourself to him; forget about taking the credit and focus on giving him the glory. And wait on him; your time will come. God has given us an alternative to envy. Trust. Delight. Commit. Wait.

# PEACE FOR A TROUBLED HEART
PSALM 4

One day I was having lunch with the president of a software company. He said, "I woke up in the middle of the night and couldn't get back to sleep. I'm having trouble with an employee and it's got me so worried I can't sleep." The following week a woman in Sunday School said, "I feel awful today. I woke up in the middle of the night last night and started fretting about my problems at work, and I couldn't get back to sleep."

Have you ever noticed there's something about the middle of the night that makes our problems seem bigger than life? It's strange how, at a time of day when we are least likely to be able to do something about our problems, they have the greatest ability to keep us awake.

This happens to everyone. There have also been times in my life when I couldn't sleep because my troubles just wouldn't leave me alone. Worry keeps us awake. Fear keeps us awake. Anger keeps us awake. Resentment keeps us awake. Guilt keeps us awake. Regrets keep us awake. When this happens at night we feel more helpless than ever, because there's nothing we can do about it right then, we can only rehash the past or dread the future.

In contrast, David said in Psalm 4, *(v. 8) I will lie down and sleep in peace, for you alone, O Lord, make me dwell in safety.* If your troubles are keeping you awake...if peace of mind eludes you, then today's message is for you. Today we will see in Psalm 4 how you can have a heart full of peace, even when you have a head full of troubles. Here are three things that will help you find peace.

- **Pour out your heart.**

When we're called on to pray out loud in church, we tend to pray King James prayers. We pray them with a stained glass voice; Charles Spurgeon referred to it as "a steeple in the throat."

You know what I mean: "Dear Lord, we thanketh thee today for thine abundant blessings which Thou hath manifested to us in thine great providence...."

I'm not ridiculing the way anyone prays, but I'm saying this: If that's not how you talk in everyday life, you don't have to talk like that when you pray. There's nothing holy about Elizabethan English. In fact, in Elizabethan times, some thought it was a sin to pray in any language other than Latin. You don't have to learn a new language or speak in a funny voice to pray. You can pour out your heart to God as if you're speaking to your best friend — because you are.

In a theology course my professor said, "I have a problem with people who pray 'chummy' prayers. When you approach the Almighty, it should be done with a sense of reverence and awe." A student raised her hand and said, "Does this mean you have a problem with the book of Psalms?" She said this because the Psalms contain that very kind of prayer: David pours out his heart like he's talking to his closest friend. These aren't stained glass prayers. He cries, he complains, he expresses his fears and his frustrations and his doubts. He says things like...

• *(Psalm 10:1) Why, O Lord, do you stand far off? Why do you hide yourself in times of trouble?*

•*(Psalm 89:46) How long, O Lord? Will you hide yourself forever? How long will your wrath burn like fire?*

•*(Psalm 38:4) I am feeble and utterly crushed; I groan in anguish of heart.*

•*(Psalm 88) My soul is full of trouble...You have put me in the lowest pit...you have taken me from my closest friends...Why, O Lord, do you reject me?*

David isn't speaking theology here; God didn't reject him. David is pouring out his heart. He's telling God how he feels. It's a shame you didn't know me when I was teenager, because in those days I had all the answers. I never had a doubt, I saw everything in terms of black and white, and if anyone ever accused me of being narrow minded, my typical response was, "I can afford to be narrow minded; I'm right." In those days I was never comfortable reading the Psalms. I didn't understand how David, this giant of faith, could have doubts and struggles. I'm older now. I've taken some beatings and lost some battles—and I find solace and strength in the Psalms. I identify with David. His prayers become my prayers. And I find comfort in the fact that, through David, we learn that we can be absolutely honest with God about our hurts and doubts and fears. In Psalm 4, David says...*(v. 1) Answer me when I call to you, O my righteous God. Give me relief from my distress; be merciful to me and hear my prayer. (v. 3) Know that the Lord has set apart the godly for himself; the Lord will hear when I call to him.*

When your heart is troubled, pour it out to God. Tell him how you feel. Express your fears, your doubts, your worries. He will listen. And he will understand. This Psalm also teaches that when you are troubled you should...

- **Examine your heart.**

*(v. 4) In your anger do not sin; when you are on your beds, search your hearts and be silent.* About a year ago I made a business contract with a man, and he eventually broke the contract. It ended up costing me tens of thousands of dollars, and frankly, I'm not in a position to lose that much money. It created hardship for my business and for my family. When I would think about it, I would become angry. And guess when it happened? Usually at night, when I couldn't sleep.

On one restless night I read this verse and thought of my former business associate. I realized I had a right to be angry, but anger alone wouldn't solve the problem. So, in the solitude of a sleepless night, I searched my heart. I began asking myself questions, such as "What did I do wrong in this situation?...What could I have done differently?...What can I do now?" In searching my heart, I began to find answers. I learned how to make sure this never happens again. It taught me to be more sensitive to others. And searching my heart also gave God the opportunity to convict me of the sin in my life. When you're troubled, search your heart for answers. If you find yourself in the same mess again and again, search your heart for the reasons. Ask God to reveal whatever it is that you need to change, and ask for the strength to do it.

When you find yourself alone and troubled, instead of rehashing the past, search your heart for answers about your future. Ask yourself, "How do I want to be remembered in this life?...What can I do that will be of eternal value?...What is most important to me in my life?...What is the most important thing I can do tomorrow?...What kind of person would I like to become, and what would I have to change in order to be that person?" As you ask these questions, realize that God is right there with you. His Spirit is whispering in your ear, offering you encouragement and comfort.. When you're troubled, search your heart in silence, and listen to God.

- **Offer your heart.**

    Do you remember the Christmas song:
    *What can I give him, poor as I am*
    *If I were a shepherd, I would give a lamb*
    *If I were a wiseman, I would do my part.*
    *Yet what I can, I give him. Give my heart.*

That's what God wants more than anything else. *The sacrifices of God are a broken spirit; a broken and contrite heart, O God, you will not despise. (Psalm 51:17) I live in a high and holy place, but also with him who is contrite and lowly in spirit." (Isaiah 57:15)*

This helps us understand what David means in today's psalm when he says, *(v. 5) Offer right sacrifices and trust in the Lord.* The only right sacrifice you can offer God is your heart. Even if it's broken, troubled and weary, God will accept it. In fact, the only heart God won't accept is a proud one. He said, *Whoever has a haughty eyes and a proud heart, him will I not endure. (Psalm 101:5)*

After you have poured out your heart to God, after you have examined your heart in his presence, you can offer your heart to him as a sacrifice. Offering your heart to God means offering yourself to God—giving yourself completely to him. Put your hope in him, put your trust in him, put your life in his hands. It means living with an attitude that says, *(v. 6) Let the light of your face shine upon us, O Lord.*

When we offer ourselves to God, do you know what the result is? He puts joy back into our hearts. David said, *(v. 7) You have filled my heart with greater joy...*

## CONCLUSION

Every heart is sometimes troubled; we all go through times of despair. But God offers peace for troubled hearts. David said, *(v. 8) I will lie down and sleep in peace, for you alone, O Lord, make me dwell in safety.* That's the key to a heart full of peace—having a heart completely surrendered to God. The process of getting to that point is one of pouring your heart out to God, examining your heart before God, and offering your heart to God.

# THE ANSWER TO WORRY
PHILIPPIANS 4:4-7

As we approach Christmas, it occurs to me that a message on worry, stress and anxiety might be in order. People are more susceptible to stress during this season than any other. Primarily, this is because we become so much busier this time of year. We have parties to go to and shopping to get done. For many businesses the December workload increases substantially. On top of that, visiting relatives and financial pressures add to our stress. Plus, there is something about the holiday season that makes difficult times seem even more difficult. We have such high expectations for this time of year. We want peace, happiness, joy and good will; if things aren't right in our lives, we feel especially let down.

With this in mind, today we'll look at Paul's advice on how to eliminate anxiety. Some counselors talk about "how to cope with stress." I'll be honest with you: I'm not interested in "coping" with stress. I want to eliminate it. I don't want to get used to it, I want to get rid of it. In Philippians 4, Paul shows us how we can do just that. He begins by saying...*(v. 6) Do not worry about anything.*

As you probably know, this is easier said than done. Everyone knows that worry isn't good, yet everyone does it. The only thing more futile than worry is telling someone not to worry. But Paul does much more than just say "Don't worry." He tells us how to stop worrying. Do you have worries? Here's how to get rid of them. First of all...

- **Make everything a matter of prayer.**

*(v. 6) Do not be anxious about anything, but in everything, by prayer and petition, with thanksgiving, present your requests to God.* When I read the writings of Paul, I come to the conclusion that I do not pray enough. Again and again Paul commands us to pray about everything. We have a tendency to want to handle the little

things ourselves and only "bother" God with the big stuff. There are two problems with this type of thinking. First, it's all small stuff as far as God is concerned. Secondly, if we don't let God help us through the day-to-day problems, how can we trust him to help us tackle the toughies? When you pray about everything, you will begin to see God's power at work—in little inconveniences and in major crises. The Bible tells us to...*Cast all your anxiety on him because he cares for you. (1 Peter 5:7)*

In fact, Paul takes it a step further. He said, "Present your requests to God." That means that in any problem you have, or in any situation you encounter, you have permission—to be exact, you have a direct order—to make a request to God, telling him exactly what you want to happen.

That's quite a privilege, isn't it? What if you request something that isn't in line with God's will? Don't worry about that. God will take care of it. He won't give you something that he knows isn't best for you. Besides, the more you pray about something the more you will learn to discern the difference (when there is one) between God's will and your desires.

Don't be afraid to ask God for help. Twenty times in the New Testament we are commanded to "Ask God." Also, the book of James tells us, *You do not have because you do not ask God. (James 4:2)*

A professional political fund-raiser recently told me that the number one reason people do not give to a political campaign is because they are never asked to give. This is obvious: if a person is never given the opportunity to give, they cannot give!

Could it be that the reason God hasn't helped you is because you have never given him the opportunity? Think about the biggest problem you're facing today. Have you asked for God's help? Now, think about the smallest problem you are facing. Have you asked for God's help? It's okay to pray for parking spaces and laundry stains and runny noses and late appointments and broken water heaters and office conflicts and financial problems and marital problems and rebellious children and...cancer. If it concerns you, it concerns God. Bring your requests to him. The first step to getting rid of worry is pray like you ought to pray—make everything a matter of prayer.

- **Point your thoughts in the right direction.**

Our thoughts control us. Emerson said, "You become what you think about all day long." In the Bible, King Solomon said...
*As a man thinks in his heart, so is he. (Proverbs 23:7)*

What do you think about all day? When you wake up in the morning, what thoughts go through your mind? How you think during the first few minutes of the day can set the pace for the entire day. The *Casoslav* (the daily prayer book used in Russian Orthodox monastic communities) gives the following instruction for the beginning of each day:

Upon rising from sleep, pray "In the name of the Father, and of the Son, and of the Holy Spirit, Amen." Then, stand for a few moments in silence until you have achieved interior calm and you are recollected. Then, with three reverences, begin your prayers.

Norman Vincent Peale says to begin each day by boldly stating "I Believe! I Believe! I Believe!" Of course, this begs the question: "I Believe What?!" That's a good question. What do you believe? And how are you going to let it affect your life? Most people's lives are not governed by their beliefs, they're governed by their emotions. Most people allow their feelings, not their faith, to dictate the direction of their thoughts. How much more effective would you be if you began every day by thinking through your personal statement of faith—and let your beliefs control the way you think?

You could begin each day by saying, "This is the day that Lord has made! I'm above ground and my heart is beating, so it's a great day! I've got many things to look forward to. Today, I'm going to make progress on my problems. Today, God will be with me every step of the way. Today, God will cause all things to work together for good. Today, God will give me the opportunity to serve him. Today, I will encourage my family. Today, I will show God's love to everyone I meet."

Do you see how empowering this can be? If you point your thoughts in the right direction at the beginning of each day, your worries will not have room to squeeze in. This is why Paul says...*(v. 8) Whatever is true, whatever is noble, whatever is right, whatever is pure, whatever is lovely, whatever is admirable — if anything is excellent or praiseworthy — think about such things.*

These 8 things serve as filters that help us reject certain thoughts and prevent us from putting garbage into our minds. For example, much of what is offered on TV and in the theater simply cannot pass through these filters. Much of the music that gets played over the airwaves will not pass through these filters. You don't have to throw your TV in the trash, but you do need to be selective about what you put into your mind.

Paul teaches that a crucial step in eliminating worry or anxiety is to think the way you ought to think — point your thoughts in the right direction. Thirdly...

- **Take action against your worries.**

Many people resign themselves to their worries and do nothing. They tell themselves nothing can be done except to wait for the worst to happen. As a result, their worries get bigger and bigger, and things get worse and worse. Doing nothing fertilizes anxiety — it causes your worry to spread out of control. Taking action is a weed-killer. It removes worry once and for all. Paul said, *(v. 9) Whatever you have learned or received or heard from me, or seen in me — put it into practice. And the God of peace will be with you.*

Paul goes out on a limb with this statement. He's speaking to a church that knows him well. He had lived with them and served with them. If he said, "Do not worry" but was himself always stressed out and full of anxiety, they wouldn't have bought what he was saying. However, Paul's life matched his message, and he could say with confidence, "Follow my example. Do what I do, and you'll have God's peace."

There is a principle to learn here. Do you know someone who has a handle on worry? Follow their example. Do you know someone who can go through stressful situations without coming unglued? Then handle your problems the way they handle their problems. I've noticed that people who don't worry have committed themselves taking responsible action. Doers aren't worriers, and worriers aren't doers. If you take action in the direction of whatever worries you, your worries will fade away. Paul said, in effect, "You've heard me say it, you've seen me do it, now put it into practice: take action."

What kind of action should you take? Well, what are you worried about? Is it your marriage? Then do something that will strengthen the bond or open the lines of communication. Are you worried about losing your job? Make an effort to protect yourself and get your resume ready. Are you worried about your health? Take steps to become more healthy. It's a simple as this: Taking action eliminates worry.

## CONCLUSION

This all seems so obvious and elementary now...during the light of the day...on a pleasant Sunday morning. But what about later this week, when you wake up in the middle of the night and your worries refuse to let you get back to sleep? That's when you'll have a chance to put this into practice. Try it, and you'll see how quickly your worry and anxiety disappear. When your worries keep you awake, pray. Give your troubles to God, make your requests, and ask for his wisdom. Pray like you ought to pray. Then think about the problem in light of your faith, not your feelings, knowing that God will take care of you. Point your thoughts in God's direction, and think like you ought to think. Then, make a list of things you can do. Maybe you can't solve the problem completely on your own, but do what you can. Take action; act like you ought to act.

It comes down to this. The cure for worry and anxiety is to pray like you ought to pray, think like you ought to think, and act like you ought to act. Your worries will fade away, and the peace of God which passes all understanding will guard your heart and mind.

## HOW TO ATTACK PANIC
PSALM 31

A *National Geographic* photographer was assigned to get photos of a forest fire. There was too much smoke at the scene, so he called a local airport and asked to hire a plane. "No problem," they said. "Come here and we'll have one waiting for you." When he arrived at the airport, a plane was warming up near the runway. He jumped in and said, "Let's go! Let's go!" The pilot swung the plane into the wind and soon they were in the air.

The photographer looked out the window and said, "Fly over the north side of the fire and make three or four low level passes." The pilot said, "Why do you want to do that?" The photographer said, "Because I'm going to take pictures. That's what I do—I'm a photographer." The pilot gulped. "You mean, you're not the flight instructor?"

These guys know what it means to have a panic attack. And, no doubt, so do you. We've all been in situations that caused us to panic. When you find out you won't be able to meet an important deadline at work. Or when you discover you don't have the money to pay a bill. Or when you wake up in the middle of the night and your left arm is numb. Or when you feel a lump under your skin. Or when your teenage son or daughter storms out of the house in an act of rebellion, and doesn't come home for hours. When some people panic, they become unglued. Others face panic more stoically in an attempt to mask the fear. Regardless of how we handle panic externally, the internal result is the same: we become immobilized and powerless.

Today we'll look at a Psalm that David wrote after he had endured a fit of panic. It almost got the best of him, but he overcame it through the power of God. Afterwards, as he reflected on the experience, he wrote this Psalm. We're not sure exactly what David was going through at the time, though a couple of verses give us a clue. He says...

*(v. 21-22) Praise be to the Lord, for he showed his wonderful love to me when I was in a besieged city. In my alarm I said, "I am cut off from your sight!"* David was under attack, either figuratively or literally, but he got over it. And this Psalm shows us how. So, if you're under attack — if you're tempted to give in to panic — here are three things you should keep in mind. When panic attacks...

- **Don't trust your feelings.**

*(v. 22) In my alarm I said, "I am cut off from your sight!"* David thought God had abandoned him. He was convinced that he was all alone and God could do nothing to help, and so he became alarmed. But guess what? His alarm was wrong.

Have you seen the movie *"War Games"*? It takes place during the Cold War and Matthew Broderick plays a teenage kid who hacks into a computer and plays a game — Global Thermonuclear War. He takes the side of the USSR and launches an attack on the United States. Of course, he thinks it's just a game, but he doesn't realize that the computer he hacked into is part of our National Defense System.

And the National Defense computer doesn't realize it's just a game. The computer "thinks" we really are under attack from the Soviets, so it prepares a very real automatic counter attack. Nothing can be done to change the computer's programming; it is convinced the attack is real, and it responds the way it was programmed to respond. So, it's up to Matthew Broderick to teach the computer that it's only a game.

In the same way, when we are under attack, some of us are programmed to look at the circumstances, listen to our feelings, and base our beliefs on what appears to be true, rather than on the promise of God's Word. Your feelings may tell you that God has deserted you, but Jesus promised specifically *"I will never leave you or forsake you."* [Hebrews 13:5] Your feelings may tell you that something is more than you can bear, but the Bible tells us that we will never face a situation that is more than we can bear and that God will give us strength to face anything that comes our way. [1 Corinthians 10:13; Philippians 4:13] Your feelings may tell you to give up because God has more important things to worry about than you, but the Bible says God watches over you because you are important to him. [Luke 12:24]

When that feeling of panic sets in—that feeling that tells you the worst is about to happen—don't listen to it. When you're overwhelmed with the feeling that you're on your own and God is nowhere to be found, don't believe it. Don't trust your feelings. Some might say, "But I can't help the way I feel, and I certainly can't change the way I feel." That may be true. I'm not telling you to change the way you feel; I'm telling you not to trust your feelings. If you trust your feelings you'll become powerless and immobilized, or you'll be tempted to fall apart, or you'll withdraw and try to run from the situation, or you'll lose your temper, or you'll drown your sorrows with alcohol or food or drugs, or you'll give in to despair and give up completely.

You may not be able to change your feelings, but you don't have to trust them. Instead, when you're tempted to panic, ask God for help—in spite of how you feel. That is exactly what David did...*(v. 22) In my alarm I said, "I am cut off from your sight!" Yet you heard my cry for mercy when I called to you for help.*

Did you get that? Even when alarms were going off telling David that God had abandoned him, he prayed anyway—and the prayer worked. Don't trust your feelings, trust God. When your feelings run out of control, cry out to God for help. He will hear you. Secondly, when you're tempted to panic...

- **Put other people out of your mind.**

Remember when *Who Wants To Be A Millionaire?* was all the rage? A friend of mine auditioned for the show. When he qualified for the next level of the screening process, he decided not to continue. He said, "What if I make it to 'the chair' and miss an easy question? I would be humiliated. Everyone would laugh at me." I said, "Your friends wouldn't laugh at you." He said, "My friends wouldn't, but everyone else would." My response was, "Who cares what everyone else thinks?" This guy panicked about not answering a question he hadn't even been asked!

One thing that makes a panicky situation go from bad to worse is allowing yourself to be too concerned about other people. Don't worry about what "they" think. Don't worry about whether "they" like you or not. Don't worry that "they" might laugh at you, or take pleasure in your tragedies. I hate to say this, but it's a sad truth: no matter who you are, there are people who don't like you. They probably don't have a good reason, but some folks are so bitter and angry that they don't have it in them to be your friend, they would rather be your enemy. This kind of person would be happy to hear that you're having business problems, or marital problems, or health problems. It's an unfortunate fact, there are people like that. When you face a difficult situation, if you start worrying about they think, you'll have a hard time focusing on the solution.

David knew about this type of person; he had more than his share of opposition. Listen to what he says...*(v. 11-13)...because of all my enemies, I am the utter contempt of my neighbors; I am a dread to my friends – those who see me on the street flee from me. I am forgotten by them as though I were dead...I have become the slander of many; there is terror on every side; they conspire against me and plot to take my life.*

Most of us don't have it that bad, but we all have to deal with difficult people. Maybe the difficult people are the reason for your problems, or maybe they're just breathing down your neck and making your problems more difficult to manage – either way, you have to learn to ignore them. Do you know how David dealt with his enemies? He began by turning himself over to God. He said...*(v. 14) But I trust in you, O Lord; I say You are my God. My times are in your hands; deliver me from my enemies and from those who pursue me.*

David didn't try to fight his own battles; he asked God to fight his battles for him. He asked God to deal with his enemies as well. You can feel the intensity of his words when he says...

*(v. 17-18) Let the wicked be put to shame and lie silent in the grave. Let their lying lips be silenced, for with pride and contempt they speak arrogantly against the righteous.*

Don't worry about what other people think, or say, or do. Give yourself to God and let him deal with them.

The first year that I played football, I was a wide receiver. In practice, we ran a play that worked like a charm—I went downfield 10 yards, cut inside and caught the ball. However, when we played our first scrimmage game, it didn't work as well. The first time we ran the play, the defensive back was covering me so I knocked him down and got flagged for interference. The next play he was on my back again, so I fooled him, instead of cutting inside, I cut outside. It worked to an extent—I was open—but unfortunately the quarterback threw the ball to where I was supposed to be, and the pass was intercepted. My coach yelled, "May, you idiot! What are you doing?" I said, "That defensive back is all over me! I'm trying to get open." The coach said, "You run the route you're supposed to run whether there's a defender there or not."

That's good advice for life. Don't panic when someone is standing in your way, just run the route you're supposed to run. Don't get off course, don't get sidetracked into fighting a battle God doesn't want you to fight, don't let criticism hold you back. Just run the route you're supposed to run. Speaking of running, that brings us to the third point. When you're tempted to panic...

- **Run straight into the arms of God.**

When you read this Psalm, you see how this situation had affected David. It really knocked him off his feet. Listen to what he says...*(v. 9-10) Be merciful to me, O Lord, for I am in distress; my eyes grow weak with sorrow, my soul and body with grief. My life is consumed by anguish and my years by groaning; my strength fails because of my affliction.*

By the way, the word affliction can also be translated guilt. David was saying, "I'm in a mess, Lord, and it's all my fault." No wonder he panicked. No wonder he thought God had deserted him. It would have been easy for David to think "There's no way God will have anything to do with me now." But instead of running *from* God, David ran *to* God, because he knew God's love was bigger than any mistake he would ever make. Listen again...*(v. 7) I will be glad and rejoice in your love, for you saw my affliction, and you knew the anguish of my soul.*

God knows what you're going through. More than that, he understands. If you're tempted to panic, he understands. Even if you brought it all on yourself, he understands. It's not too late. You can still turn it over to him and he will help you out. The situation may seem hopeless to you but it's not hopeless for God. If you feel like a deer caught in the headlights there is only one thing you can do. Listen closely. If you've got nowhere to run, you've got to know where to run. Run to God. Before you panic, run to him, as you fast as you can. What do I mean when I say run to God? What does that entail?

**Ask God for help.** David said...*(v. 2) Turn your ear to me, come quickly to my rescue; be my rock of refuge, a strong fortress to save me.* Have you ever heard someone criticize those who turn to God only because things are bad? So have I. But remember, we don't listen to other people. And God never criticizes those who turn to him, no matter what the circumstances are that drove them there. Don't be afraid to ask God for help. Next...

**Give everything you have to God.** David said...*(v. 5) Into your hands I commit my spirit.* You're saying to God, "God. You're my only hope. I have no 'Plan B' to fall back on. I'm putting all my trust in you." Next...

**Let God lead you.** David said...*(v. 3) For the sake of your name, lead me and guide me. Free me from the trap that is set for me.* Whether you set the trap yourself or someone else set it for you, God will set you free. He will show you a way out. Quit looking at the trap, and start looking to him. Let him lead you.

## CONCLUSION

We panic when we feel powerless. Thanks to God, we're never powerless—we have his power to help us out. When you're tempted to panic, you don't have to face the situation on your own. When you've got nowhere to run, you've got to know where to run. Run to God, and let him save you.

# GETTING A HANDLE ON HAPPINESS
ISAIAH 55:1-5

Everyone in the world shares one basic desire: we all want to be happy. Different people define happiness different ways, but it boils down to the same basic human desire: we all want to be happy. Have you ever noticed that no one ever says, "I wish I weren't so happy all the time!"? Some people may not care about being successful, or rich, or good-looking. It doesn't matter to some if they're married or single, or whether or not they have a family, or whether or not they have friends. Some people don't care about material possessions, or being able to travel, or having enough time and money to do whatever they want whenever they want. None of these things may make a difference to some people, but regardless of the "things" people want in life, I am sure that everyone here wants to be happy. It is an intrinsic human desire—we're built that way.

However, I have learned through three decades of ministry that even though everyone wants to be happy—even though God wants everyone to be happy—many people aren't. They often think happiness is just around the corner—just a few dollars away, a new relationship away, or one career achievement away. And as they go through life accumulating these things, they never are quite able to get a lasting grip on happiness.

Madonna has made a career of self-indulgent behavior and is one of the wealthiest people in show business. In an interview a couple of years ago, she was asked if she was happy and her response was: "I don't even know anyone who is happy!"

An entire episode of Frasier was built around his brother Niles asking him the question, "Are you happy?" It took Frasier 28 minutes and two commercial breaks (and getting his latte prepared exactly the way he likes it) before he could finally say, with reservation, "Yes, in the grand scheme of things, I guess you could say that I'm happy."

True happiness—the kind that lasts through all of life's ups and downs—eludes most people. If it eludes you, then this passage from the book of Isaiah will give you a handle on how to find the kind of happiness that isn't dependent on situations and circumstances, or what people say or do, or whether or not your coffee has the right amount of cream in it. Isaiah shows us how to find lasting happiness. Simply put, happiness comes from experiencing the fullness of God. Nothing else can bring the joy that a personal relationship with God can bring, and once you learn to base your happiness on your relationship with God, nothing in the world can take it away from you. Here are three things from Isaiah 55 that will help you get a handle on happiness. First of all, if you want to be happy...

- **Stop making excuses and start making an effort.**

Most people who are unhappy can give a list of reasons why. "How can I be happy when I'm so deeply in debt? How can I be happy when I have to work for my boss? How can I be happy when I'm so busy? How can I be happy when my spouse is so uncaring?..." and on and on. The first step to finding happiness is to realize that your excuses about why you're unhappy are no longer valid. There are people whose problems are the same as yours, but they're happy. There are people with cancer who are happy, divorced people who are happy, singles who are happy, poor people who are happy, and on and on. You can be happy, too, but you must stop making excuses. Isaiah said...(v. 1) *Come, all you who are thirsty, come to the waters; and you who have no money, come, buy and eat!*

Isaiah is saying: Stop making excuses. Whatever you think is holding you back, isn't holding you back. God has eliminated all the barriers to fulfillment, peace and contentment. Even if you have no money, he says, don't use it as an excuse. Make an effort. Come, buy and eat. Don't let what you don't have prevent from experiencing the fullness of God. Come to Christ. If you turn to him as your source of happiness, he can fill you with joy you never imagined possible.

Stop making excuses. In the fifth chapter of John there is a story of a man who spent 38 years of his life lying beside the Pool of Bethesda, hoping to be healed. There was a belief that occasionally an angel would come to the pool and stir the waters, and the first one in the pool when the water was stirred would be healed. Jesus approached this man and said to him, "Do you want to get well?" Now, this is a simple, yes-or-no question, but instead of answering, the man made an excuse. He said, "I have no one to help me into the pool when the water is stirred." Jesus didn't ask him if he wanted to get in the pool, he asked him if he wanted to be healed. The man wasn't really thinking about getting healed, he was just thinking of all the reasons he couldn't get in the pool. Jesus said, in effect, "Forget about the pool. Get up, pick up your mat, and walk." And the man was healed that very moment.

Today, many of you are sitting beside some pool thinking, "If I could just get in...if I could just have this thing, or do this thing, or experience this thing then everything would be wonderful." Jesus is saying, "Forget about the pool. Your happiness isn't in the pool, it's in me. Stop making excuses and start making an effort. Come to me."

Later in the book of John Jesus said..."*If anyone is thirsty, let him come to me and drink. Whoever believes in me, as the Scripture has said, streams of living water will flow from within him." (John 7:37-38)*

Becoming happy requires effort on your part. You won't wake up one day to discover that all the pieces have come together and all your problems have gone away. You can't depend on your spouse or your children or your friends to see to it that your life works the way you want it to work. If you want to be happy, you're going to have to stop making excuses and start making an effort to find happiness in Christ. Secondly, if you want to be happy you will have to...

- **Eliminate some things from your life.**

*(v. 2) Why spend money on what is not bread, and your labor on what does not satisfy?* There are many people whose strategy for

finding happiness is to do things that can only make them miserable. It's like they say, "I want to see the sunset, and I'm going to look to the east until it happens." You will never see the sunset if look only to the east, and you will never find happiness if you look for it in those things which cannot give it. Yet this is exactly what many people do—day after day, year after year. This is what Isaiah refers to. Many people live their lives just the way Isaiah described—spending money on that which is not bread and spending their labor on that which does not satisfy. There are two ways that people do this.

### a. Destructive behavior

Some people fill their lives with self-destructive activities that are guaranteed to bring misery—such as abusing alcohol, spending too much money, being promiscuous, taking drugs, and on and on. They do this thinking it will bring them happiness, but it doesn't. It can't. It is "spending money on what is not bread" — and it leads only to emptiness and isolation. Frustratingly, those caught up in a lifestyle of destructive behavior are often blind to the consequences of their actions.

I spoke to a woman once who was anorexic, but she hadn't yet gotten to the point to where she was ready to deal with it. She weighed about 80 pounds, with dark circles under her eyes and skin the color of paste. She said, "People keep telling me that I have a problem with food, but they don't understand that the only thing that makes me happy is my ability to not eat." She didn't realize—though it was obvious to everyone else—that she was looking for happiness in something that could eventually kill her.

In the same way, alcoholics think they need a drink to be happy; in reality their drinking ultimately makes them miserable. Some people go from affair to affair thinking it will make them happy; in reality affairs lead only to misery. In order to get a handle on happiness we need to learn to identify self-destructive behavior, so that we can eliminate it from our lives.

Overcoming compulsive behavior is a complicated matter; it involves more than just turning over a new leaf and saying, "I won't do that anymore." If you are unhappy because you are caught up in some kind of addictive, compulsive behavior, I want you to know that God has the power to set you free. Your part in this process is to identify the destructive behavior, recognize that it is ruining your life, and do whatever you have to do to eliminate it. You can never experience the fullness of God until you eliminate destructive behavior, and God has the power to help you do it. Just as bad as making yourself miserable with destructive behavior is the tendency to make yourself miserable with...

**b. Futile behavior**

There are certain things we do that are not bad in and of themselves, but it is futile to expect them to make us happy. Most people who are unhappy fall into this category.

For example, a career is good—and necessary—but no career can bring ultimate happiness. Yet many pour themselves into a search for success, only to discover that success doesn't make anyone happy. Being married is good, but no relationship can provide the inner peace and contentment that we all need. Many people think, "If I could just meet the right person, everything would be fine." And many unhappily married couples think, "If we have a baby, maybe that will bring us the happiness we're looking for."

A job is good, and marriage is good, and children are wonderful—but why look to these things to give you more than they can possibly give? These can only add to your happiness, they cannot create your happiness for you. The only way to find happiness is to experience the fullness of God through a personal relationship with Jesus Christ. If you're not happy right now, then stop making excuses for your unhappiness and make an effort to get to closer to God, decide once and for all to eliminate everything that is keeping you from him, and thirdly...

- **Embrace your relationship with God.**

I don't know where you are spiritually right now. Maybe you have never made an effort to know Christ. Maybe your religion consists of nothing more than attending church on Sunday morning. I want you to know there is much more to having a relationship with God than being here on Sunday. You can have a life-changing spiritual connection to him that empowers you twenty four hours a day, seven days a week.

George Gallup conducted a survey that concluded that fewer than 10 percent of Americans are deeply-committed Christians. But the people who make up this group, according to Gallup, can be categorized as particularly influential and happy. He called them, "a breed apart." He said they are more tolerant of people of diverse backgrounds, they are more involved in charitable activities, they are more involved in practical Christianity, they are absolutely committed to prayer, and he said, "They are far, far happier than the rest of the population."

We all know church goers who are perpetually grumpy. We all know religious people who are always mad about something. There's an old joke about a guy who went to heaven and as St. Peter let him through the gates the first thing he saw was a complaint box. He said, "If everyone is so happy in heaven, why is there a complaint box?" St. Peter said, "We learned a long time ago the only way some people can be happy is if they have something to complain about."

We've all known people like that, but don't mistake what they have for the kind of happiness God offers to you. God offers happiness that is so deep and so dynamic that the Apostle Peter referred to it as "joy unspeakable" — joy beyond words [1 Peter 1:8]. That's what God wants each one of us to have. Through Isaiah, he said...(v. 2-3) *Listen, listen to me, and eat what is good, and your soul will delight in the richest of fare. Give ear and come to me; hear me, that your soul may live.*

You need not look any further. You don't need anyone else. You don't need anything else. All you need is God. Come to Christ and your soul will delight in the richest of fare. He can give you happiness above and beyond anything the world has to offer. God wants to fill your life with good things. He wants you to live—not just survive. Jesus said, "I have come that you might have life to the fullest." (John 10:10) And he means it. Embrace your relationship with God. Follow Jesus. Talk to him. Listen to what he says to you through his word. And put your hope for happiness in nothing but him—and he will give you happiness that cannot be put into words.

## CONCLUSION

The only way to get a handle on happiness is to experience the fullness of God, through a personal relationship with Jesus Christ. Stop making excuses for being unhappy, and start making an effort to experience the joy that God has in store for you. Ask him to help you eliminate everything that is keeping you from experiencing his fullness, and embrace your relationship with God. Cling to him as if he is your only hope for happiness in this world—because he is.

## BECOMING A TEAM PLAYER
EPHESIANS 4:2

Every sports team has its superstars—players like Derek Jeter, Peyton Manning, Michael Jordan. They're the reason millions watch the games, and they often find themselves in the center of the spotlight, overcome with adulation. The fans may not grasp this, but the players themselves understand one basic truth about team sports: stars wouldn't be stars without the support of the team.

For years at Christmas time Dan Marino did a commercial for Isotoner Gloves—"take care of the hands that take care of you." The point of the commercial (beyond selling gloves) is that Dan Marino wouldn't have been able to pull off all of those incredible fourth quarter comebacks without the assistance of his front line. That's because even though the stars get much of the glory, football is a team sport.

It's the same in other areas of life. Whenever movie stars win an Oscar, they give the same basic speech: "I would like to thank all the people who helped make this night possible—my agent, my manager, my director, my producer, the writers, the members of the cast..." and on and on. Most people who have succeeded in the film industry will tell you that it takes a whole lot of help from a whole lot of people to make it big.

On July 20, 1969, when Neil Armstrong walked on the moon, he was the focus of attention for the entire planet. Even today, his is the name most associated with the moon voyage. His statement "One small step for man..." will never be forgotten. What often is forgotten, however, is that the Apollo expedition succeeded because a large and committed team of individuals sacrificed day and night for years to make it happen. Neil Armstrong was only one of 218,000 people involved. He may have gotten most of the recognition, but he would be the first to tell you that it was a team effort.

That's the way it is with every area of life. Life is a team sport. God intends for us to work together in order to achieve success. One person cannot do it alone.

It's the same at church. Church is a team sport. In order to do the work that God has called us to do, we must work together as a team — though that has not been the strategy many churches have employed. Too often, the strategy is to hire a "professional" (or group of professionals) to do the work of the ministry for the people, who are the recipients of ministry. That's not the Biblical model. The Bible tells us God's method in Ephesians 4.*(v. 11-12) It was he who gave some to be apostles, some to be prophets, some to evangelists, and some to be pastors and teachers, to prepare God's people for works of service, so that the body of Christ may be built up...*

God's plan for evangelism is teamwork, but it's not always easy. Missionaries will tell you that their greatest obstacle is not loneliness, culture shock, or finances. The biggest problem missionaries face, according to missionaries, is the struggle to get along with other missionaries. After leaving behind family, friends, and financial security, it seems like getting along with other equally-committed people would be a snap — but it isn't always the case. In fact, a missions organization administrator once told me that he sends workers out in groups of two or four, but never three. He has learned from experience that in a three person team, on member inevitably feels picked on by the other two.

Evangelism and church growth, just like all of life, is a team sport. In order to succeed as a church and as individuals, we must develop a Team Player mentality. In Ephesians 4 Paul shows us how to do this. He says...*(v. 2-3) Be completely humble and gentle; be patient, bearing with one another in love.*

Three key words in this passage are the basis for developing an attitude of a team player. Paul said, "Be humble...be gentle...be patient." Today we're going to look more closely at these three attitudes, and consider how we can further develop them in our own lives. First of all, Paul said, "Be humble." That means having an attitude that says...

- **The team is more important than me.**

When Lou Holtz began his coaching career at the University of Minnesota he gave every player on his team at T-shirt. Printed across the chest in large block letters was the word "TEAM." Beneath TEAM, in tiny letters, was the word "me." Holtz told his team, "This T-shirt serves to remind you that the team is more important than you are, and you should always put the team above you." e should ask ourselves an important question: Am I willing to put the team above me? Am I willing to take a low-profile, low-glamour job that benefits others more than me?

In the past I have served churches where certain members expected to be given certain offices regardless of their ability to do the job. I've seen musicians unwilling to share musical responsibilities, teachers unwilling to give others a chance to teach, and leaders who insisted on being in control of areas they knew little about. Obviously, these weren't team players, and the churches suffered as a result. Paul said...*Do nothing out of selfish ambition or vain conceit, but in humility consider others better than yourselves. (Philippians 2:3)*

Every baseball fan remembers Kirk Gibson's game-winning homerun in the first game of the 1988 World Series. Kirk was more than a star, however; he was the ultimate team player. Dodger coach Tommy Lasorda said that the great thing about having him on his team was that Kirk was willing to do anything to win—bunt, sacrifice, walk, whatever—because the team's win/loss record was always more important than his own batting average. This is the attitude of a team player.

When you enter a room, your attitude can say one of two things: either "Here I am!" or "There you are!" One is humble, the other is proud. A team player projects a "there you are" attitude, because his attitude is that the team is more important than me. Secondly, Paul said, "Be Gentle." That means having an attitude that says...

- **My job is to encourage others.**

When Don Shula first began coaching the Miami Dolphins,

they were ranked at the bottom of the AFC. Long before the season began, Shula showed his new Dolphin team film of the previous season's championship team, the Baltimore Colts. He told the Dolphin players to focus not on each play, but on what happened after each play.

The Colt players helped each other up, high-fived one another, and shouted encouraging things to one another. In contrast, he showed the Dolphin players film from their previous season. These elements were missing. He challenged his players to get in the habit of encouraging one another on the field — because that's how champions play. As you probably know, Don Shula went on to become the winningest coach in the history of the NFL, and the Dolphins soon became the only team in history to post a perfect season.

My friend Jim, who owns a software business, was shocked (and irritated) one day when an incompetent employee asked for a raise. Of course, as far as most employers are concerned, there's never a good time to ask for a raise, but this request couldn't have come at a worse time. Jim was swamped, working 18 hour days, and this particular employee was habitually late and had recently blown a key assignment. In fact, Jim had decided earlier that he would have to let the man go — he was just waiting for the right time to do it.

When the man came in asking for more money, Jim said he was tempted to chase him out with a stick. However, he realized there might be a better way to handle the situation. He said, "I'm afraid you haven't yet earned a raise. But let's talk about what you can do to make it possible for me to pay you more money. If you will strengthen your performance in a few areas, I will pay you what you are asking." Together they outlined a more detailed job description for the "incompetent" employee — a description that included punctuality as well as increased responsibilities. Within a few months he had earned his pay increase. It was Jim's decision to be gentle that helped this employee improve his performance — and as a result they both became better team players.

I heard a saying once: "It's true man doesn't live by bread alone. Sometimes he needs buttering up." We all do. This is why Paul challenges us to treat one another with gentleness, with an attitude that says, "Your feelings matter." People who work together sometimes have to correct one another. When you have to do it, go about it gently. The purpose of correction is to inspire your teammate to do better. When someone is struggling at home or at work, that is when they most need encouragement. A team player's job is to be gentle; offer them encouragement.

Millions of golf fans watched as Greg Norman blew a huge lead in the Masters golf tournament in the spring of 1995, losing to Nick Faldo. After the debacle, the golf star says he experienced "the most touching few days" of his life. People from all over the world contacted him with words of encouragement. He received four times as much mail as when he won the British Open in 1993. This experience changed Norman's attitude towards people. He said, "There's no need for me to be cynical anymore. I never thought I could reach out and touch people like that. And the extraordinary thing is that I did it by losing."

Life is a team sport, and our job is to encourage everyone on the team—when they hit a homerun and when they strike out with the bases loaded. Paul said...*Therefore, encourage one another and build up one another, just as you also are doing. (1 Thessalonians 5:11)* Next, Paul said, "Be Patient." That's the attitude that says...

- **I will not give up on anyone.**

Have you ever thought about how optimistic the word patience is? It implies that the final result will be good, even if the process takes long. When I was a kid I used to say my parents, "I can't wait until I can drive a car." They'd say, "Be patient; someday you'll be able to." But when I would say, "What I really want is a motorcycle." They'd say, "Forget about it. It'll never happen." When it came to a motorcycle, they never told me to be patient, because patience wouldn't have done me any good. As far as they were concerned, my hope of riding a motorcycle was a lost cause.

Paul tells us to be patient with one another for the simple reason that no person is a lost cause. We are to keep believing in them and continue encouraging them until they come around. Paul expressed this same attitude in the book of Philippians...*I am confident of this, that he who began a good work in your will carry it on to completion until the day of Christ Jesus. (Philippians 1:6)*

When you read the gospels it doesn't take long to realize how fallible the disciples of Jesus were. James and John were overly ambitious, Peter was impulsive, Simon the Zealot was impatient, all of the others at one time or another showed cowardice, lack of faith, jealousy, and spiritual thick-headedness. Yet, Jesus kept them all (with the obvious exception of Judas, who betrayed Christ and then killed himself without seeking forgiveness). In spite of their faults, these men eventually were instrumental in changing the world.

Over the course of a few years, they went from being weak and afraid to being bold and strong. They took the gospel of Christ to ends of the earth, and in the process were all martyred — except for John, who was tortured and exiled in Patmos. What would have happened if Jesus had given up on them in the early days? Who would have fulfilled his Great Commission? Who would have carried on the work that he began? Jesus refused to give up on his disciples, in spite of all their mistakes, because he knew that eventually they would become the men they were capable of being. He saw them in terms of their potential, not their past. And as history proves, his patience paid off.

If God refuses to give up on others, what gives us the right to? When you show patience to your family, co-workers, fellow church-members, you are saying "I believe in you. I believe in what God can do in your life. I believe that your short-comings are short-term; if you can overlook mine for a little while longer, I can overlook yours."

A guest on The Tonight Show told a story about being caught at a red light when his engine stalled and the car wouldn't start. While he turned the key and the engine turned over and over, the guy behind him honked his horn non-stop. Finally, the driver got out, walked to the car behind him and said, "I'm having some trouble here and maybe you can help. If you'll go try to start my car, I'll stay back here and lay on your horn for you." It's hard to work as a team when you have to listen to honking criticism. We need to be patient with the other players on our team.

**CONCLUSION**

There's a story about a county fair that held a horse-pulling contest to see whose horse could pull the most weight. The second place winner pulled a sled of about 3500 pounds. The first place winner pulled a sled of about 4000 pounds. Then the administrators of the contest tried something different. They attached both horses to a sled to see what they could do. Combined, the horses pulled almost 10,000 pounds of weight.

This is true in all areas of life. Together, we can do far more than we can as individuals. In life, at home, in the church, we must develop an attitude that says, "Life is a team sport, and I'm going to be a team player."

## LIVING IN THE ZONE
JOHN 15:1-8

There's a popular phrase used mostly in sports and business. It's called being in "the zone." The Zone refers to that state when everything is clicking and you're doing everything right. You can't miss a shot, you anticipate what the opposition is doing, you have a quick answer for every question. Anyone who has ever played sports or performed in public knows what it's like to be in the zone. Also, anyone who has ever played sports or performed in public knows what it's like to be out of the zone—there are days when you can't think straight, can't perform well, and nothing seems to go your way.

When it comes to living the Christian life, there's a zone we can be in—a zone that makes it easier to walk in faith, live in obedience, see our prayers answered, experience joy, and handle adversity. It is a zone that Jesus challenges us all to live in. What is this zone? Jesus said...*(v. 4) Abide in me, and I will abide in you. (NASV)*

What does Jesus mean by, *Abide in me*? Where you abide is where you dwell, or (as this Greek word can be translated) where you *stay*. The NIV translates this verse *Remain in me*... Abiding in Jesus means remaining in the presence of Jesus throughout the day. Of course, if you are believer, you are always in the presence of Jesus, because he is with you every minute of every day. The problem is that sometimes we forget to acknowledge his presence. Too often we begin our days in a mad rush, blazing about at breakneck speed, moving from one crisis to the next, draining ourselves of all peace and joy, until finally at the end of the day we collapse in exhaustion. Jesus is telling us we don't have to live that way. We can experience an abundance of life and a fullness of joy—if we learn to abide in him.

One reason Celtic Christianity has experienced a resurgence of popularity in recent years is that many have discovered their lifestyles were in many ways similar to our own, and yet, as a culture they learned to incorporate Christ into their daily lives. Since Celtic communities were primarily agricultural, everyone—moms, dads, children, worked hard from sunrise to sunset. They didn't have an abundance of free time. They faced the challenges of harsh weather. They endured the stress of living in a predominantly non-Christian society. They lived with the risk of being raided by Romans, Irish, and Vikings. Life was hard, yet the writings from this era reveal a people who had discovered the joy of abiding in Christ. They incorporated their Christian faith into every area of life. Every daily activity became a ceremony of celebration for the presence of God.

For example, most people wash their face first thing in the morning, but the Celts made a religious ceremony of it. They would splash their face with water three times and pray...

*The palmful of the God of Life*
*The palmful of the Christ of Love*
*The palmful of the Spirit of Peace*
*Trinity of grace.*

As they clothed their children, the children prayed...

*Even as I clothe my body with wool*
*Cover Thou my soul with the shadow of Thy wing.*

Their lives were hectic; they didn't have time for long prayers. Throughout the day each event became an opportunity for prayer. As they kindled the fire, as they made the bed, as the baked bread or scattered seed—everything was offered in the name of God.

Do you know what that is? It's abiding in Jesus. It's remaining in his presence throughout the hours of the day. Imagine how much different our lives could be if we included Christ in every activity of the day. Every event would become sacred. There's nothing spiritual about washing your face or making a bed or building a fire or driving to work or turning on a computer or crunching numbers or waiting on customers—but these can become sacred events when you perform them in the presence of Christ.

An old friend of mine worked for years on an assembly line at General Motors. He said, "At first the job would be dull, but I learned that there is a rhythm to it—throughout the day I would pray, review the scripture I had memorized, and sing hymns. I knew God was with me all day long."

Another friend of mine who is a letter carrier would say a prayer for the family as he drops mail into their box. He knows most of them only by name, but he prays for them—house after house, day after day. He says, "I go home so full of Christ I can hardly contain my joy."

Jesus said, *"Abide in me and I will abide in you."* He is saying, "Include me in the details of your day, and I will fill your life with my presence." When we do that, we enter into "the zone" of Christian living, and our lives begin to work more effectively and more efficiently than ever before. In John 15:1-8 Jesus mentions three ways you will benefit from living in the zone of his presence. Here they are. First of all...

- **Your life will become more productive.**

*(v. 5) He who abides in me, and I in him, bears much fruit.* What fruit is Jesus talking about? He's talking about the fruit of your labors. He's saying that your work will become more productive. You'll do your job better, and you'll get better results.

When Orel Hershiser pitched the Los Angeles Dodgers through the 1988 World Series, the camera kept focusing on him between innings. He was in the most important game of his life, yet he appeared to be completely relaxed as he sat on the bench, his head leaned back, his eyes closed. No one realized it at the time, but later he explained to everyone that he was praying and singing hymns. In fact, on the Tonight Show he told Johnny Carson that praying in the dugout helped him stay focused during the game. Forget for a minute that he was a sports celebrity playing for millions of people and millions of dollars. In reality, he was an employee working for a business, getting paid to do a job. While he was at work, he remained in the presence of Jesus. As a result, he was better at his job.

Abiding in Jesus will help you be more productive in your job, as well. You'll bear more fruit as an employee, as a parent, as a spouse, as a friend, as a servant of God. When you abide in Christ, you put yourself in a position for God to bless the work you do.

When Jesus said you will bear fruit, he was also talking about the fruit of the Spirit—love, joy, peace, patience, kindness, goodness, faithfulness, gentleness, and self-control. Abiding in Jesus—living in his presence throughout the day—causes these qualities to bloom and grow within you. When you abide in Christ, he promises that you will bear much fruit; you will become more productive. Secondly...

- **You'll learn to be more selective.**

*(v. 1-2) My father is the gardener...every branch that bears fruit he prunes, that it may bear more fruit.* I know very little about gardening, and even less about how to prune. We used to live in a house that had some rose bushes in the front. Each year they produced beautiful flowers. One year a neighbor offered to prune the bushes for me. I agreed, so she went to work, clipping away at each bush. When she was finished they looked completely barren—like sticks in the ground. It appeared to me like she had completely scalped them. Later that year the bushes produced roses bigger and better and more beautiful than ever before, simply because my neighbor understand the principle of pruning.

Life is a process of pruning in which we learn to separate the good from the bad...and the good from the best. It's a process in which we learn to weed out those things that prevent us from maximizing our lives. As we get busier and our plates become fuller, we have to learn what to keep and what to toss. We have to determine which things are worth our time and which things aren't. The process isn't always easy. In fact, if a tree could talk, what do you imagine it would say when it gets pruned? Probably "ouch", because pruning can be painful. But it is necessary. And in the long run, it pays off.

When you live in the zone of abiding in Christ, God does the pruning for you. He helps you to prioritize and focus on that which is worth the most and eliminate the rest. What kinds of things does he prune away? Here are some examples.

**Time wasting activities:** I don't mean leisure activities, because play has its place in our lives. But God helps us get rid of those things that are not beneficial to us and do not give glory to him. It is too easy to over-commit yourself into a dozen projects that, in the long run, simply are not the best use of your time. God helps you weed those out, so that you can focus on what is best. Another area he prunes is...

**Destructive relationships:** When a relationship isn't good for you, God will prune it away. I'm not referring to friendships with non-Christians; I'm referring to relationships in which you don't have the amount of influence you should have—relationships in which God isn't given his proper place. If the relationship or friendship doesn't build both of you up, expect to God to prune it. Another area in which God prunes us is...

**Sinful behavior:** He will not allow sin to reign in your life. When you begin to abide in Christ, sin becomes an unwelcome guest. We're all vulnerable to sin in one way or another. Maybe it's anger, or self-control, or laziness, or lust, or gossip—whatever it is, God wants it out. When you give him a chance, he'll snip it away.

Learning to abide in Christ takes practice and patience, but remember, he is there with you every step of the way. The third way you'll benefit from living in the zone is...

- **Your prayers will become more effective.**

*(v. 7) If you abide in me, and my words in abide in you, you will ask what you desire, and it shall be done for you.* Some parents left their child with a baby sitter for the evening. When they got home, the sitter said, "Billy had trouble getting to sleep, but I talked to him for awhile, and he finally drifted off." The parents were pleased until the sitter said, "Oh, and by the way, I promised him you would buy him a pony tomorrow."

Some people think God's promises are like the baby-sitters': Comforting words spoken with no intention of being fulfilled. Too often, we preachers are guilty of trying to explain away the words of Christ—"This is what he said... but *this* is what he meant."

Today, I'm going to tell you exactly what Jesus meant when he made this promise. He meant: *If you abide in me, and my words in abide in you, you will ask what you desire, and it shall be done for you.* In other words, he meant what he said. How could he make such a promise? How could he say unequivocally that you will get whatever you desire?

It's simple. When you abide in Christ, your desires become what they should be. When Christ is not the center of our lives, we live in constant conflict with our desires. We want what we shouldn't want; we don't want what we should want. When we're not abiding in Christ, we don't know what to ask for—we're not sure what we should and shouldn't have.

However, abiding in Christ causes you to experience change from within. Your desires are completely overhauled, so that when you pray for material things (for example), you pray out of need, not out of greed—and you can therefore pray with confidence. Also, your prayers become less self-serving since you know that you will use his gifts for his glory. Also, you learn to see the world with the perspective of a mature believer. A child might ask for candy at every meal, but a grownup knows better. Abiding in Christ gives you the wisdom to know what to want. So...abide in Christ, and ask for whatever you desire. It will be given to you. The miracle is not only in the answered prayer, it is in the change that God will work in the desires of your heart.

## CONCLUSION

If you want your life to flow more smoothly—if you want to be more productive, more selective, and more effective—learn to live in the zone. Abide in Christ. Acknowledge his presence in each event. Recognize that he is with you every step of the way. Abide in him, and you will never be the same.

## SIX THINGS EVERY LEADER MUST FORGET
NUMBERS 11:4-34

I love reading about Moses. He's one of us: frail and fallible, prone to mistakes—nothing at all like Charlton Heston's larger-than-life portrayal in *The Ten Commandments*. In scripture we meet a Moses who struggles with sin, who sometimes lacks self-confidence, and is often unsure of how to go about the task of being a leader. In spite of it all, Moses was a great man and a great leader—and God used him in a great way. We can take some comfort in the fact that leadership didn't come naturally—or easily—to Moses. He had to learn it one step at a time, just like us. Today, we'll take a look at one scene in Moses' life that teaches us *Six Things Every Leader Must Forget*.

The story takes place in Numbers 11. Moses has successfully led God's people out of Egypt, and they're journeying now through the wilderness. In Egypt they had been slaves, but Moses brought them out of captivity and was in the process of leading them to their own land—a land flowing with milk and honey—where they could live in freedom and prosperity. This story takes place after Egypt and before the Promised Land.

In the wilderness, God provided for them every day by raining down Manna, literally "bread from heaven." Each morning the people of Israel would gather the manna and eat it. They made Manna Stew, and Manna Cakes, and probably Manna Burgers and Manna Casserole and Manna Surprise and on and on. And guess what? The people got tired of Manna. They began to complain: "If only we had meat! In Egypt we had cucumbers and garlic and onions and melons. Now we get nothing but manna!" Moses became frustrated with their attitude and went to God and said, in effect, "Why are you doing this to me? I can't make these people happy! Why don't you just kill me and put me out my misery?" God said, "Moses, you need to change your style of leadership. Choose 70 men; they will help you carry the burdens you're trying to carry on your own. And trust me, because I will help you get through this." Through the course of this story Moses learned to forget six things that every effective leader, coach, boss, parent, pastor, teacher, and manager must forget. Let's take a look at each one. First of all, if you want to be an effective leader you must...

- **Forget about winning a popularity contest.**

In spite of the great things Moses had done, there were still disgruntled people in the camp. They were no longer impressed with the parting of the Red Sea; they were annoyed because they had to live on manna. The Bible says...(v. 4-6) *The rabble with them began to crave other food, and again the Israelites began wailing and said, "If only we had meat to eat! We remember the fish we ate in Egypt at no cost — also the cucumbers, melons, leeks, onions and garlic. But now we have lost our appetite; we never see anything but this manna!"*

While they remembered fondly the food from Egypt, they conveniently forgot how inhumanely they had been treated as slaves...how they were forced to do back-breaking work in the scorching sun while the Egyptians sat in the shade enjoying the benefits of slave labor. Instead of thanking Moses, they made him the target of their anger. That's the way it is for leaders. Forget about winning a popularity contest; there will always be disgruntled people to contend with.

In 1998 coach Phillip Fulmer led the Tennessee Volunteers to an undefeated season and a National Championship. When visiting my brother-in-law, who works for the university, I heard about a small but vocal group of fans who were "anti-Fulmer." They didn't like him and they wanted him fired. Can you imagine that? What could they possibly not like about him? How do you improve on a 12-0 record and a National Title?

That's just the point. No matter how well you do your job, there will be people who complain. And if, in your area of leadership, you begin to go through a stretch of wilderness, these people will turn up the volume and do all they can to make you miserable. If you want everyone's approval, forget about being a leader. A leader can't be concerned with winning a popularity contest. And while we're on the subject of disgruntled people, I'll point something out. God said to Moses in verses 18-20: "They're tired of Manna, so I will give them quail to eat. Before too long they'll be sick and tired of quail, too." That's the way it is with disgruntled people. No matter what you do, they'll find something to gripe about. So, forget about winning a popularity contest. Secondly...

- **Forget about doing it on your own.**

When the rabble began to complain to Moses, Moses began to complain to God. After he poured out his heart he finally made the realization...*(v. 14) "I cannot carry all these people by myself; the burden is too heavy for me."* Every leader must eventually understand that he or she has been called to be a leader, not a savior. There's a difference.

Jesus Christ came to earth and single-handedly paid the price for the sins of the world. He alone carried our sins to the cross. He alone died so that we could live. He carried the weight of the world on his shoulders, and he's the only one who can do that. You can't. You might be called to be a leader, but you're not called to a savior—so forget about doing it on your own without anyone's help.

Leaders must learn to develop a team mentality; only a team can get the job done right. That's why we have a church board. That's why we have committees. That's why we have leadership teams. One person can't carry, for example, the burden of youth ministry all alone. The youth pastor provides leadership for this area of ministry, but he needs a team of volunteers working with him to keep things in balance.*(v. 16) The Lord said to Moses: "Bring me 70 of Israel's elders who are known to you as leaders and officials among the people...I will come down and speak to you there and I will take of the Spirit that is on you and put the Spirit on them. They will help you carry the burden of the people so that you will not have to carry it alone."* A leader needs a team. Forget about doing it on your own.

- **Forget About Giving Up**

As Moses poured out his heart, he said something interesting...*(v. 15) "If this is how you are going to treat me, put me to death right now...and do not let me face my own ruin."* Do you see what Moses is saying? "Lord, I would rather die than fail. If this is how it's going to be, put me out of my misery—because I don't want to give up and I don't want to witness my own ruin."

Robert Schuller is pastor of one of the largest churches in North America, but for most of the early years his ministry teetered on the brink of failure. At one point (while still in his thirties) he prayed, "Lord, let me die of a heart attack, so I can fail with dignity." Like all great leaders, he would rather die than give up.

Lou Holtz is a college football coaching phenomenon. He took the Arkansas football program to a new level. He turned around the Minnesota program. He led Notre Dame to a National Championship. He created a winning tradition in South Carolina. He took them each to a bowl game in his second season—an impressive (and unmatched) accomplishment. But did you know that Lou Holtz was once the head coach of the New York Jets, and he failed miserably? In fact, he quit his job only 8 months into his contract. What made the difference in the New York job and all his other jobs? He said it was because he didn't go to New York with a "do or die" attitude. He took the job with Jets thinking that failure was a possibility. When things got rough, he bailed. In the process, he learned something about the need for commitment in a position of leadership.

Leaders are committed to the point of saying, "I would rather die than fail." Every leader eventually faces a situation in which walking away is the most attractive option. You catch yourself thinking, "If I could just wash my hands of this mess and get away from it once and for all, my life would be so easy." That may be true, but walking away isn't worth it. If God has called you to a task, forget about giving up. Stick with it. It's easier to do this when you...

- **Forget the meaning of the word "impossible."**

When God told Moses that the people of Israel would be eating meat until they were more than satisfied, Moses said...
*(v. 21-22) "Here I am among 600,000 men on foot, and you say, 'I will give them meat to eat for a whole month!' Would they have enough if flocks and herds were slaughtered for them? Would they have enough if all the fish in the sea were caught for them?" (v. 23) The Lord answered Moses, "Is the Lord's arm too short? You will now see whether or not what I say will come true for you."*

Moses was saying, "Lord, there's not enough meat in the camp to feed these people." This was probably a true statement, but then Moses did what many leaders do when they're stressed out. In his mind, he began making the situation worse than it really was. He said, "There's not even enough fish in the whole sea to satisfy them!"

God's response was simple and straight to the point: "My arm isn't short!" God is saying, "When you work for me, the word 'impossible' doesn't exist. There isn't anything I can't do." A few verses later, the Bible tells us that God sent a great wind and drove quail in from the sea, and the people gathered all they wanted.

It's amazing that Moses had to be reminded. After all, he witnessed the burning bush. He had witnessed the plagues of Egypt. He had witnessed the parting of the Red Sea. And now he said, "God, what you're saying is impossible!"

How quickly we forget! Instead, we need to learn to forget the meaning of "impossible" — because when God is involved, the word doesn't exist. This is what Jesus said to his disciples...
*"With God all things are possible." (Matthew 19:26)*

Do you remember that great line from *Star Trek 2*, when James Kirk says, "I don't believe in the no-win scenario"? Christians can say that, too. With God, there is no such a thing as a "no win scenario." With God, there is no such thing as an impossible situation. Forget the meaning of the word. Fifthly, as a leader, you must...

- **Forget about settling your own scores.**

When the rabble rose up and complained about the food, God became angry. They weren't merely rebelling against Moses, they were rebelling against God. He, not Moses, got them out of Egypt. He, not Moses, led them toward the Promised Land. He, not Moses, provided for their needs along the way. When they complained, they incurred his wrath. The people of Israel went out to gather quail, and began to eat, and the Bible says...*(v. 33-34) But while the meat was still between their teeth and before it could be consumed, the anger of the Lord burned against the people, and he struck them with a severe plague. Therefore, the place was named Kibroth Hattaavah [which means 'graves of craving'], because there they buried the people who had craved other food.* By the way, I recommend that you mark these verses and read them to your children next time they complain about what's for dinner.)

What do these verses teach about leadership? That God will kill off the complainers? Not exactly. The more important lesson is that God will settle his own scores. It's not a leader's job to get revenge. When people try to undermine you, God will take care of them. You don't have to do it. Moses didn't seek revenge; he let God handle it. This is why the Apostle Paul says...*Do not take revenge, my friends, but leave room for God's wrath, for it is written, "It is mine to avenge; I will repay," says the Lord. (Romans 12:19)*

Paul goes on to say, *"If your enemy is hungry, feed him; if he is thirsty, give him something to drink." (Romans 12:20)* He's saying that you've got to be big enough to treat your critics with kindness. So forget about settling the score—that's God's job. He'll take care of it. Lastly...

- **Forget about being a control freak.**

In the seminars held at Saddleback Church, pastor Rick Warren often says, "You may not agree with everything that's going on at Saddleback, and that's OK. To tell you the truth, I don't agree with everything that's goes on at Saddleback." Rick Warren's style of leadership is not about keeping everyone under his thumb, it's about letting the Holy Spirit move according to

God's will and purpose. When you approach leadership with that attitude, you can't always control everything that happens. That's the way God wants it to be.

A pastor once told me that he didn't want his church of 200 to get any bigger. Two hundred, he said, was the most he could handle and still keep order. He told me how a handful in his congregation had decided to start a Home Bible Study on their own, without the church's involvement. He informed them that he would have to be included if they wanted to continue. He said to me, "If I'm not involved, there's no telling what kind of doctrinal error might disseminate from that group." This is not the attitude of a leader; it's the attitude of a dictator. Most pastors are thrilled when their members have the initiative to study the Bible on their own.

Conscientious leaders strive to maintain the balance between giving direction and taking control. On the one hand, you don't want your people to stumble without your help; on the other hand you don't want to be a tyrant. It's a fine line. You walk it by the grace of God.

Moses faced this situation. After he had appointed the 70 leaders, he learned that there were two others, named Medad and Eldad, who also had received God's spirit and were prophesying among the people. Joshua came to Moses and said, "Moses, stop them!" Moses revealed his wisdom when he said...
(v. 29) *"Are you jealous for my sake? I wish that all the Lord's people were prophets and that the Lord would put his spirit on them."*

Moses was saying, "My job isn't to keep these people under my thumb. My job is to lead so they remain safely in God's hands."

## CONCLUSION

Being an effective leader comes down to recognizing that you are involved in God's project, not your own...recognizing that you have the responsibility to lead his way, not your way. This is why there are so many things a leader must forget. Forget about being popular, because it is God you are trying to please.

Forget about doing it on our own, because God has called you to build a team. Forget giving up, because great leaders don't quit. Forget about impossibilities, because with God all things are possible. Forget about getting revenge, because God will defend you and he will defend himself. And forget about being a control freak, because God is in control, and he will do things his way. Effective leadership is a matter of forgetting those things that hold us back, and remembering that God has called us, as leaders, to move forward in his name.

# THE SEARCH FOR SIGNIFICANCE
1 CORINTHIANS 9:24-27

Have you ever noticed that during the eulogy of any funeral, the minister talks about how the deceased person's life impacted those around him? We have a tremendous need to assign significance to a person's life at this point; nothing worse can be said than, "This person's life had no meaning whatsoever." Everybody wants—and needs—to achieve significance in life. Some go about it the wrong way. Others, for different reasons, may give up on trying to attain it. But it remains a basic human need and desire, nonetheless.

God intends for us to live meaningful lives. Jesus said, "*I have come that you may have life, and have it abundantly.*" (*John 10:10*) However, the search for significance requires some effort on our part. It doesn't happen by accident.

The Apostle Paul wrote a great deal about the search for significance. In 1 Corinthians 9:24-27 he describes his philosophy of life, and in his words we see how we, too, can find meaning in our existence. First of all, the person who wants to live a meaningful life must have...

- **Drive**

(*v. 24*) *Do you not know that in a race all the runners run, but only one gets the prize? Run in such a way as to get the prize.* Many years ago Auburn played Syracuse in the Sugar Bowl. Late in the game, with Syracuse leading 17-14, Auburn was driving downfield. With 7 seconds remaining, it was 3rd down for Auburn on the Syracuse 12. Auburn coach Pay Dye was faced with a decision: go for the touchdown to win the game, or kick the field goal and settle for a tie (This was before the "overtime" rule was implemented in college games; games could end in a tie.) Pat Dye played it safe. Auburn kicked a field goal.

They didn't lose, but neither did they did win. Amazing, after investing blood, sweat and tears to make it to a nationally televised bowl game, when they had their chance for glory—they settled for a tie. In this passage, Paul is telling us: "Don't settle for a tie." Give every day all that you have to give. God has given you one life to live—live it for him. Paul said...*I press on toward the goal to win the prize for which God has called me heavenward in Christ Jesus. (Philippians 3:14)...Let us throw off everything that hinders and the sin that so easily entangles, and let us run with perseverance the race marked out for us. (Hebrews 12:1)*

It's a tragedy when someone with talent drifts through life, settling for mediocrity. It's like the guy who was asked, "How long does it take you to get to work in the morning?" and he replied, "About an hour after I get to the office."

If any word described the Apostle Paul, it would be *drive*. He didn't live life, he attacked it. In Acts 14, Paul was preaching to a crowd in Lystra. Some of his enemies were able to turn the crowd against him, and they stoned him, dragged him outside the city and left him for dead. As soon as Paul came to, the Bible says "...he got up and went back into the city." He had such a burning desire to preach the gospel that even the threat of physical violence couldn't keep him away. Talk about drive! No wonder Paul could say at the end of his life...*I have fought the good fight, I have finished the race, I have kept the faith. (2 Timothy 4:7)*

He was running his race in such a way as to win. And he encourages us to do the same. Secondly, the person who wants to live a meaningful life must have:

- **Direction**

*(v. 26) Therefore, I do not run like a man running aimlessly; I do not fight like a man beating the air.* In Alice in Wonderland, Alice asks Cheshire Cat, "Would you tell me, please, which way I ought to go from here?" The cat replies "That depends a good deal on where you want to get to." Alice says, "I don't much care where..." and the cat replies, "Then it doesn't matter which way you go." Alice says that she just wants to get somewhere, and Cheshire Cat tells her, "Oh, you're sure to do that if you only walk long enough."

We are certain to end up somewhere. The question you must ask is "Where am I going?" Having direction in life means that...
**a. You must have a plan.**

(*v. 25*) *Everyone who competes in the games goes into strict training.* Every coach enters the game with a plan designed to help his team win. When decisions have to be made, the plan provides the foundation for the team's strategy. In the same way, we can't blueprint our lives — and God doesn't expect us to. But it is crucial for each of us to develop a plan by which we can accomplish the most with our lives. Paul said, *"To this end I labor, struggling with all his energy, which so powerfully works in me."*

A man driving through Nebraska stopped his car to ask an old man on the side of the road how far it was to Omaha. The man said, "Well, sonny, if you keep the going the way you're headed, it's about 25,000 miles. But if you turn around, it's about ten." Having direction in life means having a plan. Also...
**b. You must be persistent.**

A well-known insurance salesman was asked how many times he will call on a prospect before giving up. His answer was: "It depends on which one of us dies first!" You cannot accomplish anything in life without persistence. Heisman trophy winner Herschel Walker once said, "My God-given talent is my ability to stick with something longer than anyone else."

*Therefore, my dear brothers, stand firm. Let nothing move you. always give yourselves fully to the work of the Lord, because you know that your labor in the Lord is not in vain. (1 Corinthians 15:58)*

It's been said that success is just getting up one more time than you fall down. There is truth to that. Fred Smith, founder of Federal Express experienced setback after setback during the early days of his enterprise, and he had many opportunities to quit. But he would not turn back. His persistence paid off; the success of Fed Ex is business legend.

Jesus told the story in Luke 11 of the man who comes to his friend's door asking for 3 loaves of bread. The man inside tries to send the visitor away, but he will not leave. Finally, Jesus says, "I tell you, though he will not get up and give him the bread because he is his friend, yet because of the man's persistence he will get up and give him as much as he needs." Jesus finishes the story by saying..."*Ask and it will be given to you; seek and you will find; knock and the door will be opened to you*". (Luke 11:9)

Persistence is the key to finding significance in life. The last thing a person who wants to live a meaningful must have is...

- **Discipline**

*(v. 25, 27) Everyone who competes in the games goes into strict training...I beat my body and make it my slave...* At 27, Benjamin Franklin decided to take control of his life. He selected 12 virtues to master, and kept a daily chart of his progress. Whenever he missed the mark, he put a black dot beside that virtue. His goal was to ultimately have no dots on the chart. This method contributed to Franklin's success as an inventor, publisher and statesman.

We will not experience holiness without some effort on our part. Though it is wrong for us to think that we can achieve holiness on our own strength and by our own goodness, it is also wrong for us to neglect a disciplined approach. After all, disciple means "disciplined learner." Paul said...*If anyone competes as an athlete, he does not receive the victor's crown unless he competes according to the rules. (2 Timothy 2:5) For if you live according to the sinful nature, you will die; but if by the Spirit you put to death the misdeeds of the body, you will live. (Romans 8:13)*

## CONCLUSION

God's plan is for us to lead a life full of meaning and purpose. Our search for significance ends when we commit ourselves to following Jesus. A life full of meaning and purpose does not happen by accident; it is the result of living life on purpose. This is what Paul challenges us to do. The end result is that we hear the Father tell us, "Well done, good and faithful servant."

## DEALING WITH DOUBTS
JOHN 20:19-31

I asked our bible study group, made up of new and veteran believers, to tell me what doubts they struggle with. Submitted anonymously on folded sheets of paper, some of the responses I received were...
- *Does God exist?*
- *Will Christianity ever work for me?*
- *Will my life ever make sense?*
- *Is everything in the Bible true?*
- *Does God really care about me?*
- *Is Jesus the only way – is Christianity the only true religion?*
- *Can God forgive me for all the sins I have committed?*

At some time or another, most people have doubts about the Christian faith. This may surprise you, but doubt can be a good thing. Doubt can motivate you to nail down what you believe. The Bible teaches that your faith must be YOURS; it must be a personal faith, and it must be a real faith. It's not something you can inherit from your parents. True, they can help guide you in the right direction—and if you have Christian parents you have much to be thankful for—but they can't do your believing for you. You have to nail it down for yourself.

If you grew up in a non-Christian home, and your parents always told you that spiritual things are not important, that all religions are basically the same, that Christianity is no better than any other, and you begin to doubt what you've been told and decide to examine these matters on your own—that's a good thing. Your search will lead you to the truth. How do I know that? Because God made a promise: *You will seek me and you will find me when you seek me with all your heart. (Jeremiah 29:13)*

On the other hand, if you grew up in a Christian home, hearing that the Bible is God's word, Jesus is the son of God, and so on—and you begin to doubt what you've been told and examine these matters on your own, that's good, too. Why?

Because examining your doubts can help you nail down the truth and help you make the transition from having a faith that is based on hearsay to having a faith that goes deep into your heart.

Today we'll look at the story of a man who became famous for his doubts. In fact, he's called Doubting Thomas. This label is a little unfair when you consider the totality of his life. He followed Jesus faithfully for three years as his disciple. He didn't betray Jesus as Judas did, or deny knowing Jesus as Peter did — he just had some doubts about the reality of the resurrection of Christ. After those doubts were resolved, he became a leader in the early church, and (according to tradition) was a missionary in India before being martyred. He believed in Jesus to the point that it cost him his life, and yet, when we refer to him today, we call him *Doubting Thomas*.

Here's the story. After the resurrection, Jesus appeared to his disciples, showing them his wounds to prove he really was alive. Thomas wasn't there, and when the other disciples told him about it, he just couldn't believe them. He said...*(v. 25) "Unless I see the nail marks in his hands and put my finger where the nails were, and put my hand into his side, I will not believe it."*

A week later, when the disciples were together (including Thomas), Jesus appeared to them. Before Thomas could say anything, Jesus spoke. *(v. 27) "Put your finger here; see my hands. Reach out your hand and put it into my side. Stop doubting and believe."* Thomas's response was, *(v. 28) "My Lord, and my God!"* Jesus said, *(v. 29) "Because you have seen me, you have believed; blessed are those who have not seen and yet have believed."*

The story of Doubting Thomas reveals how God responds to our doubts, and it teaches us how to deal with our doubts. If you've ever doubted the validity of the Christian faith today's message is for you. There are three things I want to point out that will help you deal with your doubts. First of all, realize...

- **God doesn't abandon you when you have doubts.**

Doubt is not the same as disbelief. It's simply seeking further evidence to confirm the validity of what appears to be (and professes to be) true. There are some organizations that simply will not tolerate doubt on any level. A article in *Christianity Today* a few years ago addressed the lack of tolerance some academicians have for differing views regarding the subject of evolution. CT told about Anna Harvey, a straight-A sophomore in Lawrence, Kansas, who raised her hand in biology class one day in 1999 and asked, "When are we going to learn about creationism?" Her teacher exploded, "When are you going to stop believing that [nonsense] your parents teach you?" The fact is, if you doubt the veracity of some scientific *theories* in certain intellectual circles, get ready to be raked over the coals—because doubts are not allowed.

Sadly, some Christians act this way, too. Their attitude is *Just believe what I tell you to believe. When I want your opinion, I'll give it to you* — as if a simple doubt means you're not really sincere in your desire to know God.

People may act this way, but God doesn't. Don't get the impression that God expects you to take everything at surface level without any effort of examination on your part. Nothing could be further from the truth. God won't abandon you just because you have doubts. In fact, if you have doubts, he'll help you in your search for answers.

Keep in mind, there's a difference between doubt and close-mindedness. Some people reject Christianity without ever examining it. For whatever reason, they decide that it isn't true and they never take a closer look. If you talk to them about faith, they won't hear you; their mind is made up. This is not doubt, it's close-mindedness. It is not the attitude Thomas had. He didn't say, "Nothing will change my mind." He said, "I need more evidence before I believe. I want to see the same thing you've seen; I want to see his hands and side." It's obvious Thomas *wanted* to believe; a week later he was still hanging out with the disciples. If his mind was already closed he would have left the others long before.

Jesus didn't punish Thomas for having doubts. He didn't say, "OK Doubting Thomas, from now on I'll only meet with my disciples when you're not here. If you doubt my word then I want nothing to do with you." He didn't say that. Instead, he appeared specifically to Thomas, called him out the group, and answered his doubts. As a result, Thomas believed.

If you have doubts, don't use them as an excuse to avoid seeking God. Instead, let your doubts drive you deeper into a search for truth. And keep searching until you're convinced, one way or the other. I don't hesitate to say this because...

- **The Christian faith can withstand intense scrutiny.**

When a business claims that their financial status is solid, you have to ask: What is the basis of this claim? If they say, "We still have lots of checks in our checkbook, so that means we must have lots of money," then you know the business is in trouble. Or, if they say, "According to our records we have 'x' number of dollars. The bank says we have less than that, but we figure we're right more often than the bank, so we'll go by our records, not theirs." — then you know the business is in trouble.

But if they say, "We have three full-time accountants on staff who track every penny each department spends, plus each year we're audited by an independent firm, and they give us a top rating." — then you know that this company can back up their claims. They can endure an IRS audit or any other kind of challenge that comes along.

Some religions are based on a foundation about as flimsy as the guy who thinks he still has money because he still has checks. But Christianity isn't that way. Christianity is like the company whose books balance to the penny. No matter how closely you examine the claims of Christ, he always passes the test. He can endure intense scrutiny, because he is God. His kingdom isn't built on half-baked ideas that fall apart under inspection. It's built on truth. It can withstand any challenge that comes its way.

Over the years a number of theories have been suggested as alternatives to the idea of the physical, bodily, death-defying resurrection of Christ. One theory is that the disciples didn't really see the physical Jesus, they saw the ghost of Jesus. It was a spiritual resurrection. A second theory is that disciples didn't see Jesus, but an imposter. The body of Jesus was stolen and another man pretended to be him—and this imposter was able to fool Christ's closest followers and even Christ's own mother.

Another theory (my "favorite") is the *swoon* theory. The idea is that Jesus didn't really die on the cross, he just passed out. Even though the Romans were quite skilled in the art of crucifixion, they mistakenly took him down from the cross while he was still barely alive. In the coolness of the tomb he regained consciousness, and on Easter morning—in spite of the fact that 36 hours earlier he had been beaten, stabbed, pierced with nails, stuck with thorns, and hung on a cross—he had the strength to roll away a one ton boulder, sneak past the soldiers guarding his tomb, and (most amazingly) convince everyone that they were looking at a glorious, perfect, eternal, resurrected body. This is the weakest link in the swoon theory. Even if the other aspects of this theory were true (already quite a stretch), it would have been impossible for Jesus to pull off a convincing resurrection while hobbling around on his wounded feet, weak from the loss of blood, with wounds in his body that had not had time to heal.

When Jesus appeared before Thomas, he eliminated—from Thomas's mind, at least—each of these three possibilities. He said, "Touch me....See, I am real, I'm not a ghost. The wounds are real, but they no longer hurt. I truly am resurrected." Jesus' physical body was evidence of the truth of his resurrection; he didn't hesitate to allow Thomas to examine the evidence in order to know the truth. The Christian faith can endure whatever scrutiny you subject it to. Don't hesitate to put it under the microscope. This foundation is rock solid. It can take it.

This is exactly what Vic Olsen did. Olsen was a surgeon who had dismissed Christianity as irrelevant. He was convinced science had proved it to be nothing but myth. But he and his wife became curious, and began to put Christianity to the test. They examined it from a scientific perspective, reading a book by 13 members of the American Scientific Affiliation who showed that the Bible and science really aren't in conflict. They examined it from a legal perspective by reading a book by a well-known D.C. attorney who demonstrated how the Bible's credibility withstands grueling cross-examination.

They looked at it from an archaeological, medical, and even a detective's perspective. They let their doubts propel them to the truth, and they discovered the Christian faith stands up under rigorous examination. Ultimately, they gave their lives to Christ and began serving him. [adapted from *Inside the Mind of Unchurched Harry and Mary* by Lee Strobel.]

The Christian faith can withstand scrutiny. You cannot prove it wrong. But suppose for a moment you could. Suppose your investigation of the Christian faith revealed that it is nothing but a farce. Wouldn't you rather know now? Don't run from your doubts. Examine them. Look for the answers. You have nothing to fear from the truth.

- **After all the evidence is in, it still requires faith.**

When Thomas touched Jesus, Jesus said, *(v. 27) Stop doubting and believe.* The implication is that Thomas, even after touching the resurrected Christ, could have continued to doubt. He could have continued to find reasons not to believe. When it comes things of a spiritual nature, there's always room for doubt, because there must be room for faith. The question is, which of these will you accommodate?

If you're inclined not to believe, many of Jesus' miracles can be explained away. When Jesus fed the 5000 with a small portion of fish and bread, some say it really didn't happen that way. They say that many in the crowd had brought their lunch with them that day. When they saw a little boy share his food with others, they felt guilty about being selfish and began sharing with others. So, what appeared to be a miracle was really just an example of what happens when people share.

Also, some say that the resurrection of Lazarus could have been staged. Jesus and Lazarus were long-time friends. Maybe he persuaded Lazarus to pretend to die, and lay in the tomb for a few days until Jesus arrived, so Jesus could pretend to bring him back to life in front of a large crowd of mourners. Another miracle I have heard explained away—and it's difficult to get through this one without laughing—was about Jesus walking on the water. Someone suggested to me that Jesus wasn't really walking, he was surfing. (Not surprisingly, this conversation took place in California.) I said, "Do you mean to tell me, with a straight face, that you think Jesus was riding a surfboard?" He said, "Well...he could have been body-surfing."

There's always room for doubt because there must be room for faith. When you examine the Christian faith, you will significantly narrow the gap between doubt and certainty, but you won't close the gap completely. There will always be an element of faith involved. Why? Because our relationship with God is based on faith. We are saved by faith. [Ephesians 2:8] Without faith it is impossible to please God. [Hebrews 11:6] Following Christ requires a step of faith, but understand this: it is not a step into the dark. It is a step into the light. And it is not a step we take without supporting evidence.

## CONCLUSION

I became a Christian when I was 15, after seeing the difference Jesus made in the life of a friend. For years I accepted without question everything I was taught. In my early twenties, however, doubts began to emerge. I didn't reject Christ or Christianity, but I wanted to nail down some answers. I studied church history, I listened to countless sermons and lectures on tape, and I drove my pastor to madness with thousands of questions. Ultimately I came to this conclusion: The evidence proves that Jesus is who he claimed to be. And yet, knowing this doesn't take away our need for faith. At some point, you must take that step where you stop doubting and start believing.

Thomas took that step. He had to discover the truth for himself, and when he did—when he recognized that Jesus was in fact risen from the dead—he put his faith completely in him. He said to Jesus, "You are my Lord and my God!" One final thought. When Thomas said that, Jesus responded by saying...

*(v. 29) "Because you have seen me, you have believed; blessed are those who have not seen and yet have believed."* Was Jesus scolding Thomas for a lack of faith? Not really. In fact, I don't think Jesus was speaking directly to Thomas. He was speaking to you. You don't have the opportunity Thomas had. You can't see the wounds in his hands and touch his side. You can narrow the gap between doubt and certainty, but never to the point that you will eliminate the need for faith. However, after you examine all the evidence, if you take that step of faith by trusting Christ completely as your Lord and your God, you will be blessed. It is the best decision you'll ever make, and you'll never be the same.

If you have doubts, I hope you won't ignore them. I hope you examine them. Read books, ask questions, study the Bible, seek the truth. And more than anything else, after you've weighed the evidence, I hope and pray you will allow yourself to reach the point where, like Thomas, you can stop doubting and believe.

## LIVING IN A MATERIAL WORLD
LUKE 12:13-21

A Southern Californian was on his way to work in his brand new SUV when the Big One hit. The ground began to tremble, the earth began to separate, and his vehicle was swallowed up. As he crawled from the wreckage he didn't notice that his left arm had been severed above the elbow. He just stood by the side of the road, staring into the abyss, crying out "Oh no, my Hummer, my Hummer!" One who had witnessed the disaster said, "How can you be crying about your truck? Don't you realize that your arm has been cut off?" The man looked down in horror at his missing limb and said, "Oh no! My Rolex!"

There is no question that we live in a materialistic society, and that money is the driving force behind much of what happens in our daily lives. People who want to live a life based on spiritual values often find themselves struggling with the issue of money. They ask "How much is enough? What should I do with my money? Does God want me to have money? Can you be affluent and still be spiritual? Should I give all my money to the poor? Should I give any of my money to the poor? What would Jesus have me do with my money?"

When you read the gospels you may be surprised to find that Jesus spoke often about this topic often. 16 of the 38 parables deal with how to handle money and possessions, and 10% of the verses (288 in all) deal with the subject of money. The Bible offers 500 verses on prayer, less than 500 verses on faith, but more than 2000 verses on money and possessions.

Since the Bible has so much to say about money, why are there so many misconceptions about it? Some of them are based on misinterpretation of scripture, others come from our culture. Let's quickly examine a few of them.

**Money is the root of all evil.** This has been attributed to the Bible, but it's a misquote. Actually, the Bible says *"The love of* *money is a root of all kinds of evil.*" (1 Timothy 6:10) There's a big difference. Money, by itself, is neither good nor bad—it is our attitude toward money that determines its usefulness.

**God needs my money or the church will fail.** God is not poor. He owns it all. When you give to God, you are not "helping him out of a jam." In the book of Psalms, David quotes God as saying, *I have no need of a bull from your stall or of goats from your pens, for every animal of the forest is mine, and the cattle on a thousand hills. (Psalm 50:10)*

**Having enough money will make me happy.** The problem is that the target for "enough" keeps moving. Financial guru Ken Roberts said that when he first began building his fortune, he thought one million dollars was the magic number that would make him happy and eliminate his worries. When he became a millionaire, he realized that he needed $5 million to be happy and at peace. Then the target moved to $10 million. He finally realized that no amount would ever be enough—his peace of mind would have to come from something other than his bank account.

**If I had enough money, I could do a lot of good.** In a survey asking, "How would you spend a million dollars?" nearly everyone's answer included giving money to charity. While it is true that most charities and churches are not in a position to turn down a donation, it is also true that, as a church, we have needs superseding our financial obligations. Money doesn't solve social problems, people do. Money doesn't spread the gospel, people do. Giving is good, but please understand: the ability to change the world requires something more valuable than money. It requires your time.

**God doesn't want me to have money.** Some people teach there is a certain spirituality in being poor. They refer to Jesus' command to the rich young ruler that he sell all he owned and give it to the poor. But remember, Jesus said this only once—to a man who was obsessed with money. He had other followers who appear to have been affluent. In the Old Testament, David, Solomon, Job, and Abraham were all wealthy. God doesn't insist that you become poor, but he does insist that you have the right attitude toward money. So what is the right attitude about money? Jesus said...*(v. 15) Watch out. Be on your guard against all kinds of greed; a man's life does not consist in the abundance of his possessions.* Jesus said our greatest danger is to become greedy. If you think only of stockpiling things for yourself, and neglect your relationship with God and your obligation to others, you will ultimately self-destruct. Today we'll look at three things you can do to guard against greed and develop the attitude toward money that Jesus would want you to have. First of all...

- **Realize that money isn't the most important thing in life.**

Universities are full of students who are pre-med, or pre-law, or working toward an MBA, not because they have a passion for their field, but because they believe their degree will enable them to earn a good living. You know what happens to many of these students — years later they find themselves earning an enviable salary, yet completely dissatisfied and too trapped to make a change.

When Peyton Manning decided to delay entering the NFL draft so that he could play his senior year at the University of Tennessee, many said he was crazy to let the chance slip through his fingers. There are so many uncertainties in football — what if he was injured? What if he had a bad season and lost his superstar status? What then? On ESPN, one "expert" said this decision could cost Peyton millions of dollars and cause him to drop several positions in the draft. Manning's response was, "These people don't get it. I wouldn't trade playing my senior year at Tennessee for anything in the world." (By the way, the expert was wrong; Peyton went first in the draft his rookie year, and he's done all right financially, too.)

People who make career choices — or any other choice — based solely on financial priorities often find these decisions come back to haunt them. Money is a miserable master. When you let it decide for you, you discover that it leads inevitably to loneliness and isolation. Jesus said, "A man's life does not consist in the abundance of his possessions." There is more to life than making money. To the extent that we remember this, we can safeguard ourselves against greed.

- **Learn to enjoy the financial blessings in your life.**

No matter where you fall on the socio-economic scale, there are some people above you and some below you. Many people can't appreciate what they have because they're focused on what they don't have. True, there are people in this world who do not have the financial pressures you have, and from your point of view, their life may appear carefree, and maybe you think that's unfair. At the same time, there are those who do not have it as easy as you do. Instead of thinking about what is missing, be grateful for all you have.

Orange County California is the most affluent county in the nation. According to Money Magazine, the median income in Orange County is 80% above the rest of the country. Yet, a few years ago when Orange County residents were surveyed about their financial status, the overwhelming response was "I need a little bit more." Here are tens of thousands of the richest people in the world who, instead of enjoying their wealth with a sense of gratitude, are convinced they need more. But I'm not picking on Californians. I see this attitude every where I go. Solomon warned against it...*It is better to see what you have than to want more. Wanting more is useless – like chasing the wind. (Ecclesiastes 6:9 NCV)*

Do you want to get rid of the "never enough" mentality? Do you want to enjoy your financial blessings? Do you want to experience financial freedom? There's a way to do it. It's simple, but it's not easy. It takes a little effort at first. Here it is: Live within your means. Spend less than you earn, and don't buy anything you can't pay for with cash. Some of you may respond "That's impossible!" The truth is, it's possible. The key to financial freedom is not to increase your income, it is to decrease your wants. The wealthiest person is the one who is satisfied with the least number of things.

At a goal-setting seminar we were encouraged to write down everything we want out of life: accomplishments, travel, relationships, income projections, and on and on. We were also encouraged to list the possessions we wanted to accumulate: cars, homes, boats, planes, electronics. The idea was to help us develop a burning desire for these things, motivating us to earn the money to buy them. We were given ten minutes to record our list of material wants.

My co-worker who attended the seminar with me finished in about a minute. He told me, "I couldn't think of anything I really want." I looked at his list. It contained a half a dozen items, the most extravagant being a Sony Discman. All six items combined would have easily cost less than $1000. I said to him, "Why don't you just go buy these things? You have the money." He said, "I suppose I could. Before today I didn't realize I wanted them." When he said that, I began crossing things off my list. Being goal-driven doesn't mean you have to be possession-driven. I decided that I didn't want the driving force of my life to be the accumulation of possessions.

Jesus said, "Be on guard against all kinds of greed." This means that we should strive to enjoy the things we have. Third...

- **Practice giving to others.**

In today's parable, this man's sin was not that he was successful. His sin was that he was selfish. He produced a good crop and thought only of himself. He neglected spiritual priorities. As a result, his soul was required of him that very night, and he never received any of what he had prepared for himself. Then Jesus said...*(v. 21) This is how it will be with anyone who stores up things for himself but is not rich toward God.*

It's no coincidence that the words miser and miserable come from the same root. God didn't bless you financially so you could keep it to yourself. When you try to hang on to everything, you lose the joy of abundance. You also miss out on the joy of being a blessing to others.

The only way to release the grip of materialism is to learn to give. Most people intend to be generous eventually...when they can afford it. And for most people, that day never comes. Expenses tend to rise with income, and it is easy for your entire paycheck to be consumed by "necessities." If we don't make a concentrated effort to give, we'll procrastinate forever. Solomon warned of this...

*The more you have, the more you spend, right up to the limits of your income, so what is the advantage of wealth—except perhaps to watch it as it runs through your fingers! (Ecclesiastes 5:11 TLB)* This is why Solomon recommends that we become generous...*Give generously, for your gifts will return to you later. (Ecclesiastes 11:1) He who is kind to the poor lends to the Lord, and he will reward him for what he has done. (Proverbs 19:17) Do not store up for yourselves treasures on earth, where moth and rust destroy, and where thieves break in and steal. But store up for yourselves treasures in heaven, where moth and rust do not destroy, and where thieves do not break in and steal. For where your treasure is, there your heart will be also. (Matthew 6:19)*

Jesus is teaching a basic life principle: *The secret to living is giving.* Sometimes we're reluctant to give because we don't have much to give. Big givers tend to attract attention. Sometimes their magnanimous gifts make ours seem insignificant in comparison.

For example, a few years ago, Ted Turner made the cover of Newsweek with a pledge to contribute $1,000,000,000 to the UN. While I don't want to negate the value of his generosity, due to the tax benefits and the ten year distribution schedule, the donation didn't affect his 3+ billion dollar net worth. But he certainly reaped a public relations windfall from the donation.

Jesus recommended another way of giving. One day, when donations at the temple were being collected, many wealthy individuals were "throwing in" large amounts to much fanfare. Along came a poor widow who gave two small copper coins—barely worth a penny. Jesus said to his disciples..."*This poor widow has put more into the treasury than all the others. They all gave out of their wealth; but she, out of her poverty, put in everything—all she had to live on."* (Mark 12:43-44) Jesus is not saying that we should turn our backs on our responsibility to our children and give all of our money away. He is saying that we should be willing to give until it hurts. On the subject of giving, C.S. Lewis said, "The only safe rule is to give more than we can spare...If our charities do not at all pinch or hamper us, I should say they are too small." (*Mere Christianity*, Book 3, Chapter 3) On this subject, John Wesley said, "Earn all you can, save all you can, give all you can." Both of these great men understood this basic life principle: the secret to living is giving.

## CONCLUSION

What would Jesus do about money? It's plain that his attitude is different than ours. He is not against you having money; he just doesn't want money to have you. He warns us to be on guard against greed—to watch out for the mentality of "more more more." The best way to combat this is to recognize that money isn't everything, and to recognize that we already have much to be thankful for, and to discover that the secret of living is giving. This loosens materialism's grip. It enables you to have money, without money having you.

# THE STATE OF THE HEART
JEREMIAH 17:9-10

When the Bible talks of the heart, it is referring to the center of our emotions, the center of our desires. In fact, you could say that when the Bible refers to our heart, it is referring to our deepest motives. The Bible teaches that when it comes to our heart—when it comes to the very essence of our motives—we are complicated beings, indeed. In the passage that we will examine today, Jeremiah says...(v. 9) *The heart is deceitful above all things and beyond cure. Who can understand it?*

The answer to Jeremiah's question is, of course, God, and only God. The next verse says that God knows our hearts and judges us accordingly. According to what? We'll get into that in a few minutes.

The word "heart" appears in the Bible more than 100 times. Most often it refers not to the organ that circulates blood throughout your body, but to your innermost being—your psychological core, so to speak. Again, we can say it refers to your deepest motives.

The Bible has much to say about our heart. Leviticus says do not hate your brother in your heart (19:7). Deuteronomy says to carefully follow God's laws with all your heart (26:16). First Samuel says...*The Lord does not look at the things man looks at. Man looks at the outward appearance, but the Lord looks at the heart. (1 Samuel 16:7)*

The book of Psalms repeatedly refers to loving and praising God with a pure heart, with a whole heart. In Psalm 51:10 David says, *Create in me a clean heart...* In Jeremiah we are told to seek God with our whole heart [29:13]. In Ezekiel we are commanded to receive a new heart [18:31].

In the New Testament, Jesus said that what's in your heart will be reflected in what comes out of your mouth [Matthew 12:34], and he said that where you put your money, your heart is sure to follow [Matthew 6:21]. In Ephesians Paul prays that the eyes of your heart might be enlightened [1:18]. Colossians says to set your heart on things above [3:1] And First John reminds us that "God is greater than our hearts." [3:20]

Your heart—your innermost being, your deepest motives—is the most important part of who you are. Therefore, it is absolutely crucial that your heart be right with God. We often refer to "asking Jesus into your heart as your personal Lord and Savior." Even though that actual phrase doesn't appear in the Bible, the idea can be found on virtually every page. God's purpose for us is that we give our hearts completely to him.

The state of your heart is the most important thing—it's more important than the state of your marriage, the state of your business, the state of your portfolio, the state of your health, or the state of anything else. So, today we'll discuss *The State of Your Heart*, and we'll see what the Bible says about getting your heart in shape, making it the kind of heart God wants it to be. Jeremiah 17:9-10 says three things about your heart that I want you to notice. First of all,

- **Don't try to judge your own heart.**

*(v. 9) The heart is deceitful above all things and beyond cure. Who can understand it?* You cannot know your own heart. And, I should also say, you can't know the heart of anyone else. So don't waste time trying to judge your heart, or the hearts of others. It's a call that you simply aren't equipped to make. You can't see your heart as it really is.

In the NFL there is a "review policy" which allows coaches to challenge an official's call they think might be incorrect. When that happens, the official goes to the sidelines, views the playback on a special monitor, and decides whether or not the call should be overturned. While he's reviewing the play, those of us watching on TV also see the replay, and sometimes we come to a completely different conclusion than the official—even though we have been reviewing the same footage. It doesn't make sense, but that's the way it is. In the NFL there are some plays that are simply too close to call. You can run the play in super slow motion, but you still can't tell: Was his foot in bounds? Did he have control of the ball? Is it a legal catch?

That's the way it is with your heart. You can't review it. You can't examine it. You can't judge it. You can't make this call, only God can. When we try, we inevitably make one of two mistakes: we judge ourselves too harshly, or we give ourselves too much credit. We beat ourselves up when we deserve a break, and we try to justify ourselves when we're clearly in the wrong.

That's what Jeremiah is warning us about. He's saying your heart will play tricks on you. Sometimes it will accuse you, sometimes it will excuse you, and you can't count on it being accurate. That's because it has the capacity to be deceptive above all things. Don't judge yourself. Don't judge your heart. Don't judge your motives. It's not your call. Also, don't let others judge your heart and your motives. They will certainly try, but you can't let them.

I hate to tell stories that cast my parents in a less-than-favorable light, but here goes. One day our family was traveling in our brand new 1965 lemon-yellow Cadillac convertible. We stopped at Stuckey's, and my folks decided to buy us all milk shakes. While mom was inside paying, my dad and my sisters and I waited in the car. It was a windy day in Oklahoma—if you've ever been there you know how redundant that statement is—and as Mom approached the car with our shakes, a huge gust of wind blew by and ice cream went everywhere—all over mom, all over the outside of the car, and all over the ground.

Needless to say, this made my mom mad. She got in the car and said, "Forget the shakes. Let's go." Dad roared out of the parking lot and I burst into tears. I felt sorry for my mom. She looked helpless and rather pitiful, sitting there with ice cream all over her. And our beautiful new car—I thought it was ruined; I didn't realize the ice cream would wash right off. And, of course, I was also disappointed because I didn't get my chocolate shake. So, I continued to cry. After a couple of miles my dad said, (using a phrase he got out of the *Dad Handbook*) "Stop crying, Stephen, or I'll give you something to cry about." That didn't make sense to me, because I already had something to cry about. Then he said, "You're just crying because you didn't get your milk shake." I said through my tears, "No. I'm crying because I feel sorry for mom, and because our car is ruined." Dad said, "Don't give me that. I know why you're crying."

But, do you know what? He didn't know why I was crying. He didn't know what was in my heart. And even then, my five year old mind wouldn't accept his judgment. I didn't believe it was completely true.

People may try to tell you what your motives are, but that's something they have no way of knowing. It's not their call to make. It's something only God can know. You can't read someone else's heart.

In the story of David and Goliath, when David approached the battlefield, his brother became angry and said..."*I know how conceited you are and how wicked your heart is; you came down only to watch the battle.*" (1 Samuel 17:28)

David's brother had it all wrong. David was a man after God's own heart, according to God. David's heart was right; David's brother was wrong. If David had believed his brother, he would have gone home and the Philistines would have won the battle. Don't try to judge your own heart and motives, and don't let others judge your heart and motives. Instead—and this is the second thing I want you to notice from Jeremiah...

- **Place your heart in God's care.**

Instead of judging your own heart, let God take care of it. *(v. 10)* "*I the Lord search the heart and examine the mind...*" God knows you inside out. If your heart isn't what it should be, he can fix it. You can't change your heart, but God can. And he will, if you offer it up to him. Listen to these words from Ezekiel. This is God speaking..."*I will sprinkle clean water on you, and you will be clean; I will cleanse you from all your impurities and from all your idols. I will give you a new heart and put a new spirit in you; I will remove from you your heart of stone and give you a heart of flesh*".*(Ezekiel 36:25-27)*

All we can do is offer ourselves to God, saying, "Lord, I don't always know the state of my heart. It seems to be a mixture of good thoughts and bad thoughts, of pure motives and self-serving motives. I can only offer it up to you, and ask you to give me a heart that is pleasing to you—a pure heart, a clean heart." This is what David was saying in Psalm 51, when he said...*Create in me a clean heart, O God, and renew a steadfast spirit within me. (Psalm 51:10)*

The only way you can be sure your heart is right is to yield it completely to God. You can analyze it to death and you'll only deceive yourself. You can listen to the opinions of others, and they'll lead you astray. But if you give your heart to God, and trust him with it, he will remove that which is made of stone, and replace it with a heart of flesh—a heart that beats only for him.

- **Your actions reveal the state of your heart.**

*(v. 10) I the Lord search the heart and examine the mind, to reward a man according to his conduct, according to what his deeds deserve.* When all is said and done, your actions and your conduct—more than anything else—reveal the state of your heart. Therefore, the Bible says that God doesn't reward us according to our feelings; he reward us according to our actions.

Your actions count. There's no such thing as a good-hearted person who refuses to do right. Once on *Law & Order* there was a story about an 18 year old boy who had committed cold-blooded murder. His mother didn't want her son to go to jail, and she said something along the lines of, "My son is really a good boy." Of course, you knew it wasn't true. If he was a good boy, he wouldn't have committed murder.

This show may be fiction, but how many times have you heard someone say something like that? "I know he's constantly screaming at his employees, but I think he means well." "My husband is sometimes cruel, but he's really got a good heart." "I realize she said some awful things about other people, but she's really a good person." It doesn't work that way. Your actions reveal the state of your heart. You can't take refuge in the idea that deep down inside you really mean well, because God is saying, "If deep down inside you really mean well, then your actions will reveal it."

Don't let your heart accuse you, and don't let it excuse you, either. Put your heart in God's care, and focus on doing what you know is right. It is by your actions that you will be judged.

Years ago I was involved in a ministry project, and a crucial member of our team suddenly decided to drop out. When I asked him about it, he said, "Well, my heart wasn't in it. If I had continued, I wouldn't have had the right attitude, and I would have been there for all the wrong reasons, so I decided to beg off." Basically, he was saying "I didn't feel all warm and gooey inside, so I decided not to serve God, because if I don't feel warm and gooey my motives might be not be right. So I'll use that as an excuse to quit." Where do these crazy ideas come from?

Well, to some extent, I'm afraid they come from preachers. We're constantly challenging people to not go through the motions, to not play church, to not do the right thing for all the wrong reasons.

As a result, people are constantly second-guessing themselves—"Is my heart really pure? Do I really mean it when I say I love God? Am I really, truly thankful?" And if they don't have this certain feeling inside, they start judging themselves, saying, "I must be a hypocrite, or else I wouldn't feel this way." According to the Bible, it's not our feelings that reveal the state of our heart. It's our actions.

Don't get me wrong. I don't want anyone here to play church. But if you *are* playing church—if you're just going through the motions of a religious life—the solution is not to stay home and do nothing. The solution is to keep doing what is right—keep coming to church, keep making an effort—and along the way ask God to cleanse your heart and purify your motives. It's something only he can do. And it's his job, not yours. Your job is to do what you know is the right thing to do. Leave your heart in his hands, and let him reward you according to your actions.

## CONCLUSION

We're not saved by good works. We're not saved by good feelings. We're not saved by good motives. We're not saved by anything we do on our own. We're saved by one thing only: the blood of Christ, which cleanses us from all sin. There is only one way to receive it: through faith in him.

You may not always know the state of your heart, because your heart can sometimes play tricks on you. But you can know the state of God's heart. It is beating with mercy for you. Put your life in his hands. Let him take your heart of stone and replace it with a heart of flesh. Let him give you what you cannot give yourself: a pure heart, a clean heart, a whole heart. Stop worrying about your feelings, and forget about second guessing yourself. Give him your heart, and let your actions follow.

*SERIES: PRAYER: THE ULTIMATE LIFESTYLE*
**HOW TO DEVELOP A PRAYER LIFESTYLE**
1 THESSALONIANS 5:17

Today we begin a new series called *Prayer: The Ultimate Lifestyle*. For the next few weeks this will be our focus: prayer as a lifestyle. Paul said, *Pray without ceasing (1 Thessalonians 5:17)* How do we do that? If prayer was just an exercise that we go through that required us to assume a certain posture and recite certain phrases, then following Paul's commandment would be impossible. But prayer is much more than that. It's not just something you do occasionally, or even for a few minutes every day. Prayer, when applied to your life the way God intended it to be, is a 24 hour a day, 7 day a week conversation with God. It's a lifestyle.

Today we're going to talk about how to put Paul's commandment in Thessalonians into practice: how to pray without ceasing...how to develop a prayer lifestyle. Richard Foster wrote a book called *Prayer: Finding the Heart's True Home*. In the first chapter of this book he teaches the most powerful principle on prayer that I have ever learned. Here it is:

**We learn to pray by praying.**

All of my life I have been taught that I should pray. I grew up in a church where we recited the Lord's Prayer every week; I went to a school where we said a prayer together each day before the noon meal; when I was young I was told to say my prayers each night before bedtime. Today, I have on my bookshelf probably one dozen books on the subject of prayer. I've attended numerous seminars on the subject and have listened to countless sermons about it. But I learned how to pray by praying.

You'll find this is true in your own life. You can come to church for the next six weeks and listen to these messages about prayer, but you'll learn the most about prayer in the privacy of your own prayer life. You learn to pray by praying.

Today, we'll look at three prayer related principles that will help you develop a prayer lifestyle. First of all...

- **Begin where you are.**

Don't try to clean your life up first. Don't try to make yourself "worthy" to be heard in prayer. It doesn't work that way. You don't clean yourself up for God, you come to him to as you are and he does the cleaning.

Most of us understand this principle at salvation — that we could never earn or deserve his forgiveness, and it is only through his grace and mercy that we are saved. But after experiencing his grace at salvation, we often try to earn his continued acceptance through our own good works.

I don't know if this has ever happened to you, but it's happened to me. There have been times in my life when I've fallen out of fellowship with God and have become just to a little too familiar with sin. At those times, when the subject of prayer comes up, my first reaction is: "I can't even think about praying right now...I've got to get my life straightened up. I doubt God would even want to listen to me right now, and he's certainly not going to answer any of my prayers."

The part about needing to clean our lives up is correct, but there's a crucial distinction to be made here. We cannot get the cart before the horse. We don't clean ourselves up so that we can come to God, we come to God so that he can clean us up. When your life isn't where it should be, the first step toward getting things back on track is prayer.

There's a great example of this in Luke 18. Jesus told the story of two men who came into the temple to pray. The story:

*Two men went up to the temple to pray, one a Pharisee and the other a tax collector. The Pharisee stood up and prayed about himself: 'God, I thank you that I am not like other men — robbers, evildoers, adulterers — or even this tax collector. I fast twice a week and give a tenth of all I get.' But the tax collector stood at a distance. He would not even look up to heaven, but beat his breast and said, 'God, have mercy on me, a sinner.' I tell you that this man, rather than the other, went home justified before God. For everyone who exalts himself will be humbled, and he who humbles himself will be exalted." (Luke 18:10-14)*

This tax collector understood the principle of beginning where you are in prayer. He was a sinner and he knew it, so he came to God confessing it. Too often we find ourselves in the tax collector's shoes, and instead of turning to God right then, we start thinking of things we can do that will enable us to pray the Pharisees prayer next Sunday...or next month...or next year. That's not the kind of prayer life God wants from us. He doesn't want (or need) us to recite to our spiritual resume to him. He wants us to begin right where we are, and to be absolutely honest with him, and with ourselves in the process.

That's the second key to developing a prayer lifestyle. First, begin today, right this moment, where you are; and second...

- **Be absolutely honest with God in your prayers.**

In the Chevy Chase movie *Vacation*, the Griswold's Aunt Edna dies, so Ellen Griswold (Beverly D'Angelo) decides to say a prayer for her. Now, everyone disliked Aunt Edna because she was harsh and abrasive, and she contributed to making their vacation miserable. However, when Ellen prays she adopts a voice filled with fabricated emotion and says something along the lines of..."Dear Lord, Aunt Edna was such a dear, sweet woman, whom we loved with all our hearts, and we will miss her terribly..." and so on.

It's funny because it's so realistic. That's how we often approach prayer. We say things that we know aren't true, and that we know that God knows aren't true...but we say them anyway. That's because we think of prayer as a Polite Ritual in which we whitewash our words in order to make them socially acceptable to God.

In contrast, I am shocked at the brutal honesty of some of the prayers that are recorded in the Bible. Some of the great men of God said things in prayer that most of us would never dream of saying. And yet, God responded to their prayers. For example, Jeremiah once prayed, *O Lord, you deceived me, and I was deceived;*

*you overpowered me and prevailed. I am ridiculed all day long; everyone mocks me. (Jeremiah 20:7)* Can you imagine daring to say such a thing to Almighty God? "Lord, you lied to me!"

There are many such examples in the book of Psalms; one can be found in Psalm 73, in which David cries out, *In vain I have kept my heart pure; in vain have I washed my hands in innocence. All day long I have been plagued; I have been punished every morning. (Psalm 73:13-14)*

Can you imagine saying something like that to God? David was saying: "Lord, I have been good, and it has been a total waste of effort. You bless everyone but me."

Or how about Job? Talk about brutal honesty! When Job went through his time of trial, in which he lost his family, his fortune, and his health, he cried out to God...

*The arrows of the Almighty are in me, my spirit drinks their poison; God's terrors are marshaled against me. (Job 6:4)*

*Does it please you to oppress me, to spurn the work of your hands, while you smile on the schemes of the wicked? (10:3)*

*Why then did you bring me out of the womb? I wish I had died before any eye saw me. If only I had never come into being...(10:18)*

*Surely, O God, you have worn me out; you have devastated my entire household. (16:7)*

*Then know that God has wronged me and drawn his net around me. (19:6)*

*I cry out to you God, O God, but you do not answer; I stand up, but you merely look at me. You turn on me ruthlessly; with the might of your hand you attack me. You snatch me up and drive me before the wind; you toss me about in the storm. I know you will bring me down to death, to the place appointed for all the living. (30:20-23)*

When I read these words spoken by a mere mortal to the God of the universe, I can only say: Wow! Do we dare be that honest in our prayers to him?

The answer is Yes. You can be absolutely honest with God in your prayers, and for a very obvious reason: He already knows what's going through your mind anyway. It's not as if your honesty will take him by surprise, and he'll say, "My goodness! I never knew you felt this way!" He knows. You know that he knows. He knows that you know that he knows. So be honest with him about what you're going through, so that he can help you deal with it. In each of the cases mentioned above—Jeremiah, David, and Job—these men were restored to a right relationship with God and their situation improved.

The strength of this kind of prayer is not only its honesty, but its tenacity. Even if your prayers are full of misconceptions and self-pity and bad theology, as long as you're crying out to God he can reach you...he can help you get to where you need to be. It's when you *stop* crying out to God...it's when you turn your back on him and reject him...it's when you give up on him that the doors of possibility close in your life.

It's not unlike a marriage. As long as a married couple are willing to communicate with one another, talk through their problems, and listen to one another, there is hope for the marriage to survive. But when a couple stops working at the marriage, stops talking to one another, stops living together, the chances for the survival of that marriage become nil.

Ted Turner (the founder of CNN and TBS, among others) is one of the most vocal non-Christians in America. He has made headlines (and drawn criticism) for calling Christians "losers"; for saying that he doesn't need someone to die on the cross for his sins; for saying the 10 Commandments are obsolete, for making fun of the Pope, and for ridiculing some Christians who worked for him as a "bunch of Jesus freaks." Why is Mr. Turner so adamantly non-Christian? Because many years ago his sister died. At the time, Ted considered himself a Christian, but God didn't answer his prayer. So Mr. Turner made a life-altering decision. He turned away from God. Instead of pouring out his heart to God in absolute honesty, he ended the conversation altogether and walked away. When he did, he closed the door of possibility in his life; it will remain closed until the day he decides to open it again.

Jesus is waiting outside the door of your heart; it is up to you to keep that door open through prayer. He said...

*Here I am! I stand at the door and knock. If anyone hears my voice and opens the door I will come in and eat with him and he with me. (Revelation 3:20)*

It is up to you to keep the lines of communication open with God. As long as those lines are open, God can continue to work in your life. If your attitude is wrong, he can help you correct it. If you have sin, he can help you overcome it. If you're feeling sorry for yourself, he can help you develop a more accurate perspective on life.

As long as you're willing to communicate with him, he can communicate with you. So, don't play games. Be absolutely honest with him about what you're going through, and let him do his work.

It is all right to say, "God, I'm lonely, and I feel like no one cares about me...God, I'm desperate, and I don't see a light at the end of the tunnel...God, I want to sin more than I want to please you...I want to take a drink more than I want to stay sober...I want to live by my rules instead of your rules...I want out of the mess that my life has become!"

Those attitudes may not be right, but if that's what you're going through right now you've got to choose between one of three options. You can be like Ellen Griswold and pray shallow, meaningless prayers that don't contain a word of truth to them. Or you can be like others, and end the conversation completely and live your life without God. Or, you can be like David, Jeremiah, and Job, and be absolutely honest in your prayers. I think it's obvious which of these options works best!

C.S Lewis said that when we pray we should "lay before him what is in us, not what ought to be in us." [From the book *Letters to Malcolm, Chiefly on Prayer*] He's saying that we should be absolutely honest with God in our prayer life.

Developing a prayer lifestyle requires that we begin right now, right this minute, right where we are; it requires that we be absolutely honest with God in our prayers, and the third thing is something I hinted at earlier: tenacity. We need to...

- **Continue the conversation all day long.**

Have you seen *Fiddler on the Roof*? In this story the main character, Tevye, has an on-going conversation with God. He doesn't pray fancy prayers; he just talks to God.

This is a good example for us to follow. We need to develop the habit of talking to God all day long. I mean, he is right there with you; why ignore him?

I was visiting a man's home one evening, as I was getting ready to leave, I said, "Let's go to the Lord in prayer." He looked a little confused and said (with a straight face), "Where do we need to go? Can't we just pray right here?"

Even though it was just a cliché, he had a point. We don't have to "go" anywhere to be in the Lord's presence. He is already here.

I remind myself of this often. When I'm in my office, or driving my car, or taking a walk, or talking on the phone, God is here with me. I don't have to "enter in" to his presence; he is already present. I just need to remember to acknowledge it all day long.

Nehemiah needed a big favor from the king. The king asked Nehemiah what he wanted and Nehemiah said, *Then I prayed to the God of heaven and I answered the king...(Nehemiah 2:4-5)* He didn't have time to put this item on his prayer list and pray about it the next day. And he knew better than to ask a favor of the king without seeking God's help, so he prayed a "bullet" prayer: "God help me right now as I talk to the king."

The more we become aware of God's presence in our lives throughout the day, the more common these kinds of prayers become, and the more of God's power we experience.

This is why Paul said, *"Pray without ceasing."* You can't spend the day in ceaseless prayer if your concept of prayer is limited to kneeling with your head bowed and your eyes closed and hands folded in front of you. But you can, if you choose to, carry on an endless conversation with the one who is your constant companion.

## CONCLUSION

There's no trick to developing a prayer life, unless you consider opening your mouth and letting words come out a trick. Or unless you consider directing your thoughts to God to be a trick. *You learn to pray by praying.*

Do you want to develop a prayer life? Then begin today, right where you are. Be absolutely honest about what's going on in your life, so that he can do his work in you—so that he can purify your heart, cleanse your motives, remove your sinful attitudes. And keep the doors of communication open. Keep the conversation going on, all day long. Pray without ceasing.

*SERIES: PRAYER: THE ULTIMATE LIFESTYLE*
**GUIDELINES TO ANSWERED PRAYER**
VARIOUS TEXTS

One phenomenon about prayer is that it is answered. Prayer is not just talking things over with God — though that certainly is part of it — but it's also entreating God to act on your behalf. And the amazing thing is that he has promised to do this: he has promised to act on our behalf when we bring our requests to him. In other words, he has promised to answer our prayers.

So, does God answer every prayer that is submitted to him? On the surface, it appears that the answer is "No." It appears that many prayers go up, but only a few answers come down. However, the problem with unanswered prayer is not in prayer itself, but in the way many prayers are offered. Today we're going to talk about three guidelines for answered prayer.

Before we get to them, though, I want to mention a couple of things about prayer. First of all, asking and receiving is a primary part of prayer. I have heard some teachers on this subject imply that this kind of prayer is like elementary school for believers; as believers grow in their faith, their prayers will be less about asking and more about contemplation. This isn't exactly right. While it is true that as we grow in our faith our prayers will become deeper and more contemplative, it is also true that we will never get to the point in our lives where we surpass the asking-and-receiving aspect of prayer. This is how God wants it. He wants us dependant on him. He wants us to ask him for the things we need. Jesus urged his disciples to pray: *"Ask and it will be given to you; seek and you will find; knock and the door will be opened to you." (Matthew 7:7)*

This can also be seen the Lord's Prayer — it is essentially a prayer of petition. It begins and ends with adoration, but there are three personal requests in the middle: a request for our material needs to be met, for sins to be forgiven, and for deliverance from temptation. Whatever we need, God wants us to ask for. Another comment I hear goes along these lines: I shouldn't bother God with petty details...he has so many other things to worry about—things much more important than my silly little problems. Actually, most often I hear this comment made in criticism of someone else's prayers. One evening at church a lady talked about praying for a parking space and someone said, "Thousands are starving every day, and she's pestering God about a parking space!"

Yes, sometimes our requests are trivial, but don't ever make the mistake of thinking that God is so small he can listen to a limited number of requests at a time. Praying is not like calling technical support, you know, where they put you on hold and tell you that your call will be answered in the order it was received. It's not as if God was prevented from diverting a disaster halfway around the globe because he was distracted by your request to help you find your car keys. God can handle everyone's prayers. In fact, if every person on the planet were to pray about his or her problems at this very moment, God capacity to answer would not be pushed to the limit. He has the ability to give everyone's prayer the attention it needs.

In fact, to imply that God is not interested in hearing someone's prayer is to reveal a lack of understanding about who God is, and how powerful he is, and how much he cares for us.

I have three children. Imagine if one of them said to me, "Dad, I have a problem that you could help me with, but I'm not going to bother you with it. You have other children, and you probably care about their problems much more than mine." If that happened, I would be insulted! I would say to that child (in my best Marlon Brando voice): "What have I done that you should treat me with such disrespect?" I would say, "If you think that I favor one child over the other—that I care about their problems more than yours—then you must not know me very well."

The asking aspect of prayer is not optional for believers; it is the foundation of our prayer life. God wants you to ask and he's willing to answer—if we follow the Biblical guidelines for answered prayer. Let's take a look at them. The first guideline is:

- **Ask with a clean heart.**

David said, *If I had cherished sin in my heart, the Lord would not have listened. (Psalm 66:18)* A while back a man named Kenneth Bruner attempted to put prayer to work in his life. He and seven accomplices were preparing to hold up a jewelry store in Des Moines, Iowa. Bruner, being the stepson of a minister, asked God for his protection as they carried off the heist. As it turned out, the robbery wasn't successful and the would-be thieves were arrested. [*McHenry's Stories for the Soul*, page 222] This is an extreme example but it makes the point that David makes: if we cherish sin in our hearts, God will not hear us.

If we were to be honest with ourselves we would have to admit that sometimes we ask with less than good intentions. James made reference to this when he said... *You do not have, because you do not ask God. When you ask, you do not receive, because you ask with wrong motives, that you may spend what you get on your pleasures. (James 4:2-3)*

If you want your prayers to be answered, you have to ask yourself: Why am I asking for this? What is my motive? Is it to become a more effective follower of Christ, or is it just to serve my own agenda? If being a faithful follower of Jesus Christ isn't your top priority, you will discover there is a barrier between your prayers and heaven's throne; your prayers will go unanswered.

And the reverse is true. If you are walking in obedience to Christ, then your prayers will have power, and God will answer them in a mighty way. John said... *Dear friends, if our hearts do not condemn us, we have confidence before God and receive from him anything we ask, because we obey his commands and do what pleases him. (1 John 3:22)*

If you want the phenomenon of answered prayer to become part of your daily life, then make sure that you ask with a pure heart. Give Jesus Christ first place in your life. Secondly...

- **Ask in faith.**

Jesus said, *If you believe, you will receive whatever you ask for in prayer. (Matthew 21:22)* He also said, *Therefore I tell you, whatever you ask for in prayer, believe that you have received it, and it will be yours. (Mark 11:24)*

What does it mean to ask in faith? We'll look at this aspect of prayer more closely in a couple of weeks. An important key, however, is realizing that there is a difference between believing God *can* do something and believing God *will* do something. We all know that God *can* do anything, because he's all powerful, but the crucial question is: As you bring your requests to him, do you believe that God *will* do something about it?

There's an old story about a preacher who served a church in a farming community that had gone through a long drought. The preacher called a special prayer meeting for the members of the church to come and pray for rain. As he stood before his congregation that evening he said, "Folks, I see you brought your Bibles, but none of you brought your umbrellas!"

Asking in faith means that we take action in the direction of God's answer. If you're asking God for rain, then start carrying an umbrella. If you're asking God to bless your business, then begin making preparations to handle the increase. If you're asking God to restore your marriage, begin making plans for a second honeymoon. Take action in the direction of God's answer.

A few years ago a woman named Peggy who attended our church was diagnosed with cancer. She began praying that God would heal her—and not just heal her of cancer, but that he would make her completely healthy. Peggy had always had a bit of a weight problem and had never been very energetic, so she made some major changes in her lifestyle.

She started walking every day and she drastically changed her diet. Eventually the cancer went into remission and she discovered that she was healthier than she had ever been in her life. She said to me, "I asked God to restore my health, and he said to me, 'Then start living like a healthy person lives.' When I gave up those fatty foods, I knew it would be for 20 years, not just a few months." Peggy started taking action in the direction of God's answer; that's asking in faith.

- **Ask according to God's will.**

John said, *This is the confidence we have in approaching God: that if we ask anything according to his will, he hears us. And if we know that he hears us – whatever we ask – we know that we have what we asked of him. (1 John 5:14-15)* John is saying that in order for our prayers to be answered, we need to ask according to God's will.

Once I was leading a Bible study for new believers and as we began discussing prayer, I read this verse. One of the members of group said, "Aha! Now we're getting down to the small print! Here's the catch: If you don't ask according to God's will, he won't answer your prayer; if you do ask according to God's will, he would have done it anyway."

First of all, if you look closely at your Bible you'll notice the print of this verse in First John is the same size as the print elsewhere – this isn't God's escape clause. Secondly, let's not assume that just because something is God's will, it always gets done. In fact, God's will isn't always done. That's why Jesus added this line to the Lord's prayer: *Your kingdom come, your will be done on earth as it is in heaven. (Matthew 6:10)*

For example, we know that he does not want anyone to perish, but everyone to come to repentance. [2 Peter 3:9] God's will is that all should be saved, but everyone won't be. In the same way, he wants his children to experience the fullness of knowing him, but many miss out on his blessings. Why? Because he has left it up to us to get in tune with his will for our lives. There are many things God wants to give us that we don't receive – because we don't ask.

For example, he wants us to experience peace [John 16:33], yet I know many believers who have no peace in their life. He wants us to have joy [John 15:11], yet I know many believers who have no joy. He wants us to be fulfilled in our work, to accomplish great things, and to have enough to live on [Ecclesiastes 3:12-13], yet I know many believers who are frustrated in their jobs, who are wasting their potential, and who are living in a constant state of lack. Why? It goes back to the verse mentioned earlier: *You do not have because you do not ask.* *(James 4:2)*

There are so many things that we know are God's will, and yet we miss out on them because we fail to ask him — in spite of the fact that we have his promise that he will give anything we ask for according to his will. "His will" covers an enormous area — love, joy, peace, holiness, power over sin, fulfillment, strong family relationships, a satisfying career, abundant life, financial stability, discipline, good health, hope, happiness, forgiveness...and so much more. There are literally hundreds of promises in the Bible of blessings that God wants to give us...if we will only ask.

The phrase about asking "according to his will" is not God's escape clause, it's his seal of guarantee. If something is his will for you, there is no way he'll keep it from you. So ask for what you know he wants you to have. He will not hold back from answering.

## CONCLUSION

Finally, there's one more principle of answered prayer I want to mention. Someone here might say, "There's a promotion coming up at work. Should I ask God for it?" Yes, by all means. Someone here might say, "I've got some health problems. Should I ask to be healed?" Yes, by all means. Someone who is single might say, "I want to get married. Should I ask God for a wife or a husband?" Yes, by all means. Ask for these things, but ask with this understanding: God will give you whatever you ask for — or something better.

Several years ago I was working for a church that was meeting in a rented warehouse. We desperately needed a building of our own and when a building downtown became available, we began praying that God would make it possible for us to buy it. One night the leaders of the church gathered around the building at midnight (I have since forgotten the significance of meeting there in the middle of the night), and we sang songs and marched around the building and laid hands on it and claimed it for God's kingdom—and a restaurant bought it. We were so disappointed; we needed that building! Why didn't God answer our prayer? Because less than 3 months later, another building became available—in a better location, with more space, at a price we could afford. Suddenly it made sense. God didn't give us the downtown building—with its limited space, limited parking, and less-than-ideal location—because he had something better in mind. God will give you what you ask for—or something much, much better.

Jesus said... *Which of you, if his son asks for bread, will give him a stone? Or if he asks for a fish, will give him a snake? If you, then, though you are evil, know how to give good gifts to your children, how much more will your Father in heaven give good gifts to those who ask him! (Matthew 7:9-11)*

You've heard the saying, "It doesn't hurt to ask." In prayer, this is especially true. Don't hesitate to ask God for whatever you need, or whatever you want. And when you ask, ask with a pure heart. Ask in faith. Ask according to his will. He will give you what you ask for...or he will give you something better. That's his promise.

*SERIES: PRAYER: THE ULTIMATE LIFESTYLE*
**HOW TO PRAY FOR YOURSELF**
MATTHEW 6:10-12; JONAH 2:1-10

When you read prayers in the Bible, the overwhelming majority of them are prayed for the benefit of someone else. When Paul talks about prayer, he nearly always talks about the prayers he prays for others. This tells us something: Intercession is a crucial part of our prayer life.

Though there aren't many examples of prayers that people pray for themselves, there are a few—and this also teaches us something about prayer: We need to pray for ourselves. Not exclusively—we need to pray for others—but we also need to pray for ourselves.

The question is: When we pray for ourselves, what are we to pray? Is it right to pray for things—such as a new car, or a new house, or a diamond ring? Is it right to pray for success, to pray to make the sale? When you pray for yourself, what should you pray? There are some examples in scripture of people praying for themselves that offer a few guidelines. First of all...

- **Pray for God's mercy.**

This is where prayer begins. Jesus told a story about two men who went into the synagogue to pray. One was a Pharisee, and he prayed a self-righteous prayer. He thanked God that he was so good and righteous and so much better than other people. The other was a tax collector—considered a sinner by most religious people—and his prayer was simple and to the point: *God have mercy on me, a sinner. (Luke 18:13)*

Prayer is not a job interview. The purpose of prayer is not to sell God on the idea that, deep down inside, you really are a good person. Neither are you playing the role of an attorney, pleading your case before the judge. God already knows you inside out. He knows every good thing and every bad thing about you. You can't play games with God; neither can you negotiate with him. You can only come to him as you are, pleading mercy. And without exception, everyone in this room today needs God's mercy.

The good news is that when you come to God for mercy, he gives it to you. What does he expect in return? The same thing: mercy. He expects you to show mercy to others. Jesus said... *Blessed are the merciful, for they will be shown mercy. (Matthew 5:7)*

In the prayer that Jesus taught us to pray, known as the Lord's prayer, he said... *Forgive us our debts, as we have also forgiven our debtors. (Matthew 6:12)* Jesus then went on to say... *For if you forgive men when they sin against you, your heavenly father will also forgive you. (Matthew 6:14)*

We are all in need of God's mercy. Asking for mercy is where prayer begins. Showing mercy to others is how we ensure our prayers are answered. When you pray for yourself, pray for God's mercy, and be prepared to show mercy to others. Secondly...

- **Pray for God's help.**

A man who was facing death once said to me, "I've never been a praying man. I won't be a hypocrite and pray now just because I'm in trouble." I told him, "It's not hypocritical to start doing now what you should have been doing all along. Neither does it make sense to compound your mistakes by refusing to turn to God at this moment." When your life is in a mess—even if it's all your fault—you can still turn to God. Don't let pride or shame prevent you from seeking his help.

You know the story of Jonah. When God told him to go to Nineveh, he refused. He got in a boat and took off in the other direction. A big storm came up, and Jonah was tossed out of the boat and swallowed by a big fish. Through his disobedience, Jonah had made a mess of his life, and at that moment his future didn't look very bright. So, from the belly of the whale, Jonah began to pray.

At this point observers might have said to Jonah (if they had the opportunity), "You've got a lot of nerve asking God for help now! Do you really expect God to hear you? Do you really expect him to help when just a few days ago you were running as fast as you could to get away from him?"

You may have spoken similar words to yourself during a time of trouble. "How can I expect God to help me out when I've made such a mess of things?" Here's something to remember: When you've messed up, don't compound your mistakes by refusing to turn to God for help.

If Jonah had refused, he probably would have died in the belly of the whale, but instead he cried out to God. Listen to what he said... *In my distress I called to the Lord and he answered me. From the depths of the grave I called for help, and you listened to my cry. (Jonah 2:1-2) But you brought my life up from the pit, O Lord my God. When my life was ebbing away, I remembered you, Lord, and my prayer rose to you, to your holy temple. (Jonah 2:7)*

If you're in trouble, ask for help. Even if it's your fault, ask for help. Even if you brought it on yourself, ask for help. Even if you've neglected prayer in the past, ask for help. When you're ready to ask, God is ready to help. You don't have to wait till reach rock bottom; he will help at whichever point you turn to him. But even if you do wait till things are at their worst before you ask for his help, it's still not too late—he will help you.

I have a friend named Larry who is (was) an alcoholic. For years he lived the party lifestyle, and in the process he ruined his life. Some of the time he had fun; most of the time he was absolutely miserable. Finally, his wife divorced him. His children refused to see him. His employer fired him. The bank took his car and his house—and this was especially difficult for him because at one time he had been on the board of directors of that bank. He ran to Las Vegas with all the money he could scrape together—a few hundred dollars—hoping to win back the fortune he had lost. Needless to say, it wasn't long before he lost his money at the tables. One night, with only 14 cents in his pocket, Larry crawled into an alley off the Vegas strip, looking for a place to sleep. Someone was waiting in that alley, and Larry was beaten and robbed—the thief took his last 14 cents.

Larry had half-heartedly asked God for help before, but this time something was different. In the past he prayed along the lines, "Lord, change my wife's attitude; Lord, don't let my bosses find out about my drinking problem; Lord, help me win this roll of the dice." This time, however, his prayer was different. He said, "Lord, whatever it takes...whatever I have to do...I need your help."

God answered his prayer, and he was able to turn his life around. He said to me, "For years I resisted turning to God for help. I was afraid he would take all the fun out of my life. Then I finally realized that the fun I was living for wasn't very much fun. I was miserable. Thank God, now my life is worth living."

Larry could have asked for help at any other time in his life and God would have been there for him. He could have asked for help before he ran to Vegas. He could have asked for help before he got fired, or before he lost his house, or before his wife left him, or before he ever took his first drink. He could have asked for help at any time during this entire process, and God would have helped him. He could have saved himself a lot of misery. He didn't have to wait until he reached rock-bottom to cry out for help—but he did, and even at the very bottom God was there to help.

No matter what stage of turmoil your life may be in, ask God for help. The book of James says... *Is any one of you in trouble? He should pray. (James 5:13)*

When you pray to God for help, be ready to do whatever it takes to straighten things out. If your situation is impossible, God will take care of the impossible part—if you're willing to do your part. Notice what Jonah said... "*But I, with a song of thanksgiving, will sacrifice to you. What I have vowed I will make good. Salvation comes from the Lord." And the Lord commanded the fish, and it vomited Jonah onto dry ground. (Jonah 2:9-10)*

Jonah couldn't get himself out of the belly of the fish—he needed God's help for that to happen—but he could make good on his vows to God. Jonah asked God for help, and because this time he meant business, God helped him.

It works the same way in your life. Ask God for help now — and mean business. Ask him for help with your little problems before they become big problems. Ask him for help with the big problems before they kill you. And be ready to do whatever it takes. Thirdly...

- **Pray for God's strength.**

Here's a morning prayer someone emailed to me...

*"Dear God, so far today I've done alright. I haven't lost my temper, I haven't spread any gossip, I haven't been selfish or over-indulgent. But in a few minutes God, I'm going to get out of bed and from then on, I'm going to need all the strength I can get!"*

That's a good prayer, and it's a good way to start the day: ask God for his strength. You don't have enough of it to make it on your own, but he is willing to make his strength available to you. Listen to what King David said... *When I pray, you answer me; you encourage me by giving me the strength I need. (Psalm 138:3 NLT)* One of my favorite hymns is *I Need Thee Every Hour*. My favorite verse goes...

> *I need thee every hour, stay thou nearby*
> *Temptations lose their power when thou art nigh*
> *I need thee, oh I need thee; every hour I need thee*
> *Oh bless me now my savior, I come to thee.*

Pray for God's strength; he'll give it to you. Next...

- **Pray for God's blessing.**

No doubt you're familiar with *The Prayer of Jabez*. It sold somewhere in the neighborhood of 4 million copies, and has had a major impact on the way many people pray. The book has also attracted some criticism. One of my closest friends read it and said, "What a bunch of materialistic nonsense!" That is not the impression I got from the book—not at all. In fact, when I read it, I felt challenged to live a more holy, consecrated life. Let's take a quick look at this prayer...

*Oh that you would bless me and enlarge my territory! Let your hand be with me, and keep me from harm so that I will be free from pain. (1 Chronicles 4:9)*

The part of the prayer that most people take issue with is the part that suggests we follow the example of Jabez and pray "Oh that you would bless me..." Some say that such a prayer is selfish.

I disagree.

Asking to be blessed is not selfish—if your desire is to be a blessing to others. In fact, you can't be a blessing to others unless you yourself are blessed. I'm not referring specifically to material blessings; this applies to "spiritual" blessings as well. You can't share your joy with others if you have no joy to share. You can't give love to others if you have no love to give. You can't show patience if you don't have patience...and on and on. To minister to others, you first need to experience God's work in your life.

Pray to be blessed. Do you know what the word "blessed" means? The New Testament word for blessed is *makarios* (ma KAR ee os). There isn't a word in the English language that matches this word exactly. It is sometimes translated "happy", which is reasonably close to the original meaning. When you pray to be blessed you're praying, "Lord, help me be happy." The Greek word *makarios* was also used to describe the idea of contentment, fulfillment, and satisfaction. When you asked to be blessed, you're asking God: "Help me be content; help me be fulfilled; help me be satisfied." Is this a selfish prayer? Only if your plan to is withhold your happiness from everyone else—and I don't think that is your intention.

Here's another way to look at it. If God had only a limited number of blessings to give out, then asking for one of them might be considered selfish. If there are 500 people in this church and God could only bless 100, then asking for one of those blessings would be greedy. Of course, we know that God is not limited in the number of blessings he can give. If everyone on the planet asked for and received God's special blessing in their life, he would still have plenty left over. He wants to bless you, and he will—if you ask. A good verse to remember with this topic is found in the book of James: *You do not have, because you do not ask God. When you ask, you do not receive, because you ask with the wrong motives, that you may spend what you get on your pleasures. (James 4:2-3)* Don't hesitate to ask God to bless you. And when he does, be ready to share his blessings with others. Last...

- **Pray for God's will.**

In the Lord's Prayer, Jesus encouraged us to pray... *"Your kingdom come, your will be done, on earth as it is in heaven." (Matthew 6:10)* Later, when Jesus was facing death, he prayed..."*My Father, if it is possible, may this cup be taken from me. Yet not as I will, but as you will." (Matthew 26:39)*

This is the culmination of prayer. We ask for things along the way, but the underlying motive is "Not my will, Lord, but yours be done." You may ask God for a new job, for example, but the underlying motive behind your prayer is "Not my will, Lord, but yours." Pray for what you want, but also pray for God's will to be done in your life. And be willing to be obedient to do his will.

## CONCLUSION

When you pray for yourself, pray for God's mercy; pray for God's help; pray for God's strength; pray for God's blessings; and pray for God's will. But there's a fundamental theme to these guidelines: you must be willing to take action.

When you pray for God's mercy, be willing to show mercy. When you pray for God's help, be willing to do whatever it takes to make things right. When you pray for God's strength, be willing to rely on him throughout the day. When you pray for God's blessings, be willing to share his blessings with others. And when you pray for God's will, be prepared to be obedient to do his will. This is how you pray for yourself.

SERIES: PRAYER: THE ULTIMATE LIFESTYLE
**HOW TO PRAY FOR ANYONE AND EVERYONE**
PHILIPPIANS 1:3-11

When I became a Christian I was made aware of my responsibility to pray for the people in my life. So I put together a list, starting with everyone in my family—including aunts and uncles I hadn't seen since preschool and cousins so far removed that any genetic link between us was by now untraceable. I also included the name of every one in my youth group (about 150 students) and all the key people at church—my pastor, youth minister, Sunday school teacher, youth choir director, and so on. I included my friends at school, the people my mother worked with, my teachers, my coaches, the guys who worked with me at "Sonic", the two nuns who lived across the street from me, the paper boy, and a guy named Frank Lewis who was a missionary in Belize. Strategically, I divided my list into seven sections and made a commitment to pray over one section each day.

On day one I ran into a snag. The first name on the list was my cousin Margaret, whom I barely knew. I prayed, "Lord, bless Margaret. She's my cousin. Uh....I haven't seen her in a few years; please bless her. Also bless her mom and dad, whose names I forgot to put on this list. So...uh...please bless her."

Then I went to the next name on my list—a guy at work named Burt. I prayed, "Lord, please bless Burt....uh...I work with him...so...uh...please bless him." It soon became obvious that I desperately needed help developing my prayer life. In fact, if the word "bless" could have been surgically removed from my vocabulary, my career as a prayer warrior would have come to an abrupt halt.

I'm not the only one who has experienced this. Many people have said to me, "When I pray for someone, I don't know what to say, and I don't know what to pray." In the first chapter of Philippians, the apostle Paul offers a blueprint we can use when we pray for people. Whether the people on your list are friends, or enemies, or relatives, or strangers, or missionaries, or anything else, Paul shows us how to pray effectively for anyone and everyone. First of all...

- **Make it a positive prayer.**

Whether or not you have a positive relationship with the person you're praying for, you can still pray a positive prayer. Paul said...*(v. 3-4) I thank my God every time I remember you. In all my prayers for all of you, I always pray with joy....*

As you read Philippians, it becomes evident that Paul was close to the Philippian people. It also becomes evident that although they were a good church, they weren't a perfect church. They had their share of problems and conflicts. Still, Paul's prayers for them were positive—full of thanksgiving and joy.

Whenever you pray for someone, begin by thanking God for them. Thank God for the role they've played in your life, for all that they've done for you, for the good things they've done for others. Even if you're having conflict with this person, thank God that he or she is giving you the opportunity to grow spiritually, learn forgiveness, be more patient, and on and on. If you try, you can find something to be thankful for in just about anyone. Instead of focusing on everything negative about that person, focus on the good things.

Are you familiar with the 80/20 rule? Business consultants say 80% of your sales come from 20% of your customers; sociologists say that 80% of crime is committed by 20% of the population, and so on. I once pastored a church where the 80/20 rule was in effect. 80% of the church wanted to fire me, the other 20% wanted to kill me. (That's an exaggeration, though at the time I was sure it was the truth.) I knew I should pray for the "opposition"—but it wasn't easy. I saw how Paul prayed for the Philippian church, and I began thanking God for the people in my church—even the ones who were against me.

One person in particular comes to mind. He was a key person in the church, and he despised me. I knew it and he knew that I knew it. What he probably didn't know was that the feeling was mutual. I didn't want to be around him any more than he wanted to be around me. I wished he would move to another church as much as he wished I would move, too.

Every Sunday morning, as I began my message, he would put on his glasses, take out his Sunday School book, lean back comfortably in his pew, and begin to read. When I decided to pray for him, I sincerely looked for things to be thankful for. Though I didn't appreciate his attitude, there were some good things about him. He was in church every Sunday. He gave generously. He was always doing projects around the building—fixing this and that. He taught Sunday School—and I knew he was preparing his lessons each week because I watched him do it! His grown children were an active and vital part of the church. He was a good grandfather—his grandchildren loved to climb all over him. He had a great lawn. He was punctual. The list continued to grow.

After praying for him several times I discovered it was impossible not to like him a little bit, in spite of how he felt about me. Through prayer, our relationship changed. Did we become best friends? Not exactly. But we didn't kill each other.

One Sunday after church my car wouldn't start. He happened to be close by, and volunteered to give me a ride home. My immediate thought was "Oh no. What will we talk about for 10 miles?" On the way home I didn't say anything—I didn't have the chance. He talked the whole time. He said more to me that afternoon than he had said in three years previous. He told me about his wife's surprise birthday party, about the place where he used to work, about working on cars, and on and on. As I was getting out of the car, he said, "Good sermon, today. I wouldn't mind hearing that one again." I couldn't believe my ears. Prayer made the difference in our relationship.

The great preacher George Buttrick said when you pray for enemies you should begin the prayer this way, "Lord, bless so and so whom I foolishly regard as an enemy. Keep them in thy favor. Banish my resentment."

When you pray for someone, make it a positive prayer. The Bible gives you a good reason to do this. Paul said...*(v. 6) I am confident of this, that he who began a good work in you will carry it on to completion until the day of Christ Jesus.*

Paul reminds us that every person is God's project. He is at work in the life of every one in the world. Through the Holy Spirit, God is either drawing people into a personal relationship with Jesus Christ, or drawing them into a closer walk with Jesus. God considers everyone on the planet a pet project. The Bible says, *He is not willing that any should perish, but that all should come to repentance.* (2 Peter 3:18)

God doesn't give up on people. Ever. He doesn't reject people; people reject Him. As long as a person has breath, God's spirit continues to deal with them, calling them, convicting them. As long as there is a chance they will come around, he will not give up. The thief on the cross is a good example of this.

Since God doesn't give up on people, neither should we. In the sixties a button became popular that said PBPGIFWMY. It stood for "Please be patient. God isn't finished with me yet." When you pray for people, make it a positive prayer. God believes in people and so can you. When you pray, make it a positive prayer—not because you have faith in that person, but because you have faith in God who never gives up on us. Next...

- **Make it a personal prayer.**

*(v. 7) It is right for me to feel this way about all of you, since I have you in my heart...God can testify how I long for all of you with the affection of Christ Jesus.* When you pray for others, take time to reflect on how this person affects you personally, and what the relationship means to you. When you pray for your children, or your parents, or your friends, or your co-workers, or the people in church, say to yourself "What would I do without him, or without her? I am so lucky that this person is part of my life. They mean so much to me."

Think about all the good things they have done. That's exactly what Paul did...*(v. 4-5) I pray with joy because of your partnership in the gospel...(v. 7) All of you share in God's grace with me.* Prayer is not just a religious ritual. It is a matter of the heart. It touches our emotions. It is so much more than a daily routine where we recite a few words and read some names off of a list. When you pray for people, you share your heart with them. Make your prayer a personal prayer.

You can do this even for strangers. Every week I pray for pastors I do not know—many whose name I can't even pronounce! Yet, my prayer for them is personal. How? When I pray I think of all the good they are doing. Some of them are serving in third world countries where the people live in extreme poverty—poverty beyond our ability to comprehend. Some of them are serving parts of Asia or the former Soviet Union where Christianity is under attack by the government, and they have to meet in secret. I think of the emotional toll these hardships must take on the pastors. I think of how their children and wives must suffer as a result of their ministry. My heart goes out to these pastors—they are my heroes and my inspiration. When I pray for these pastors, it is so much more than just reading a name and saying a few words—it's a prayer from my heart.

Richard Foster, author of *Prayer: Finding the Heart's True Home* tells a story about a holy lady he met when he was teenager. She was sick and spent all of her time in bed. Once during a visit she showed him her "family album" containing 200 pictures of missionaries and others she prayed for. Every week, she flipped through the pages of that album, looking at the photographs and lifting each person in prayer. Her prayers were so much more than words. She was sharing her heart. When you pray for others make it a personal prayer. Also...

- **Make it a purpose-driven prayer.**

Remember when I said that my prayers consisted of only "Bless him...bless her" and that was it? At the time I had no idea what to say. Paul shows us exactly what to pray for...*(v. 9-11) And this is my prayer: that your love may abound more and more in knowledge and depth of insight, so that you may be able to discern what is best and may be pure and blameless until the day of Christ, fill with the fruit of righteousness that comes through Jesus Christ — to the glory and praise of God.*

Paul prayed three things for the Philippian people. He prayed that they would grow in love, wisdom and holiness. You can pray this for anyone, whether you know them well or hardly at all. When you pray for someone to grow in love, wisdom and holiness, you are giving them a very special gift.

A person whose *"love abounds more and more"* is a person who will be happy and have a rich, rewarding life. They will have strong, healthy relationships with others. They will be able to make friends and keep friends. They will be optimistic about the future. They will not find themselves being held back in life by fear because, as the Bible says, *Perfect love casts out fear. (1 John 4:18)* When you pray that a person grows in love, you are praying that they become happy, generous, friendly, and well-adjusted. Don't you want this for the people you pray for? Aren't these good qualities?

A person who is growing in *"knowledge and depth of insight"* and is *"able to discern what is best"* is a person who has the wisdom to make clearheaded decisions at crucial points in their life. This person isn't paralyzed by doubt and indecision. He or she will win the battle between right and wrong, as well as the battle between good and best. This person will be able make wise choices and act on them. When you pray for a person to grow in wisdom, you are praying that person becomes confident, focused, able to make tough decisions and stick with them. Don't you want this for the people on your prayer list? Isn't this a good thing to pray for someone?

A person who is *"pure and blameless until the day of Christ"* and is *"filled with the righteousness that comes through Christ"* is a person who is alive spiritually. This person's religion consists of more than just going to church on Sunday morning. They are involved in a dynamic day-to-day relationship with Jesus that permeates every area of life: their job, their marriage, their friendships, and all others. It goes beyond the externals and makes them good from the inside out, enabling them to live their lives with integrity. When you pray that a person grows in holiness, you are praying that person becomes completely good through and through, from the inside out. Isn't this a great prayer to pray for people? Don't you want everyone you know to grow in love, wisdom and holiness?

**CONCLUSION**

Prayer is not just a religious ritual. It is a matter of the heart. When you pray for someone, you do much more for them than you could do otherwise. I urge you to pray for the people around you—the people you like and the people you have difficulty getting along with. Pray a positive prayer for them. Make it personal. Pray with purpose. Pray God's best for them. You will find you're not just saying words, you're sharing your heart.

*SERIES: PRAYER: THE ULTIMATE LIFESTYLE*
**LEARNING HOW TO ASK IN FAITH**
MARK 10:46-52

One day Jesus was walking down the road with his disciples, on his way out of the city of Jericho, when a blind man named Bartimaeus began calling out to him, saying, "Jesus son of David, have mercy on me!" The people around him told him to be quiet, but he called out even louder, "Have mercy on me!"

Jesus stopped and said, "Call him." When Bartimaeus approached, he asked him one simple question: "What do you want me to do for you?" Bartimaeus replied "I want to see." Then Jesus said something that surprised me the first time I read this story: he said, "Go. Your faith has healed you."

Your faith has healed you? What did Bartimaeus do that showed such faith? He wasn't like the men who tore open the roof of the home where Jesus was teaching so they could lower their sick friend into his presence. He wasn't like the woman who fought through the crowd so she could touch the hem of his garment. He wasn't like the centurion who came to Jesus and said, "Just say the word from here and my servant will be healed." When you read this story, you can't help but wonder: What was this great demonstration of faith on the part of Bartimaeus? All he did was ask!

Hmmm. Maybe there's a lesson here. The story of Bartimaeus receiving his sight teaches us that the act of asking is an act of faith.

I was on an airplane once, and as I walked through the first class section I noticed five or six empty seats. I can't afford to fly first class so I kept walking toward the back of the plane, taking my place with the rest of the riffraff in coach. Before takeoff, as the flight attendant made sure we were all buckled in, the man across the aisle stopped her. I heard only part of what he said, something about "empty seats in first class...can I have a free upgrade?" She smiled and said, "Sure, I think we can do that." The man collected his belongings and walked through the curtain that separates the castes of American society, where I'm sure he was coddled for the duration of the flight.

Now, I knew there were still 4 or 5 empty seats remaining in first class, but I just couldn't bring myself to ask if I, too, could be upgraded for free. I could imagine the flight attendant saying, "Just because I did it for him doesn't mean that I will do it for you. Stay put." So, I didn't ask.

The book of James says, *You have not because you ask not.* (James 4:2) That was certainly true in my case that day. And it is true in many of our lives, day-in, day-out. We do not have because we do not ask.

All Bartimaeus could do was ask to be healed—and it was enough. It demonstrated faith on his part, and as a result, Jesus healed him. Just asking is, in itself, an act of faith. Today, as we take a closer look at this story, we'll see there is a right way to ask; we'll look at how to ask in a way that will open the door for God to reward us. There are three things this story teaches us about how to ask. First of all...

- **Ask immediately.**

When Bartimaeus heard that Jesus was passing by, he immediately began calling out: "Jesus, have mercy on me!" I don't know how much Bartimaeus knew about Jesus...what stories he had heard...but when Jesus came his way he made up his mind that he would not let this opportunity slip away. He immediately began to call on the name of Jesus, and he continued to call on the name of Jesus until Jesus heard him.

Here's the problem we have with prayer. Too often, it's not our first option. We try first to fix things ourselves, without getting God involved. We think that we can handle the situation more efficiently than he can. After all, he might make us wait. He'll expect us to repent. He'll cause us to re-evaluate and re-organize our priorities. It's easier to try to do things on our own. And as a last resort, if nothing else works, then we'll try prayer.

Of course, this kind of asking doesn't demonstrate faith. Asking in faith requires that we ask immediately, that we turn to God as a first resort, not a last resort. If you really believe God can help you, he'll be the one you'll call on first.

One day I was having computer trouble, and finally (as a last resort) I called my friend, Mike, to see if he could help. He couldn't, but he suggested I call our friend, Jim. I said, "I already called Jim, and he couldn't help." Mike then said I should try calling the company's technical support line. I said, "I did, and they couldn't figure it out either." Mike then said, "It sounds like I was your last resort. Why did you wait to call me last?" I said, "Because I didn't think you'd be any help...and I was right!" Obviously, if I thought Mike could help me, he would have been my first choice, not my last. The fact that I called everyone else first showed that I didn't have much faith in Mike's ability to help me solve my computer problem.

When we don't call on God first we're demonstrating the very same lack of faith. Only, it's a foolish lack of faith, because God *can* help you with any problem you face in life.

If you want to receive anything from God, the story of Bartimaeus teaches us to call on God immediately, and continue to call on him until he answers.

Jesus said, *Ask and it will be given to you; seek and you will find; knock and the door will be opened to you. (Matthew 7:7)* Those verbs—ask, seek, knock—can be translated from the original Greek as "Keep on asking; keep on seeking; keep on knocking." It's not a onetime request. It's a continual prayer. Bartimaeus asked immediately, and he kept on asking until Jesus answered him. The second thing this story teaches us about how to ask in faith is...

- **Ask defiantly.**

Defiantly? Yes. Here's what I mean. When Bartimaeus began calling out to Jesus, the Bible says... *(v. 48) Many rebuked him and told him to be quiet, but he shouted all the more, "Son of David, have mercy on me!"*

The people surrounding Bartimaeus decided it was their job to keep him in his place. After all, he's just a blind beggar. What right does he have to approach Jesus? He needs to keep his mouth shut—and that's what they tried to get him to do. But he didn't care what the crowd said or what the crowd thought. He defied them and called out to Jesus anyway.

I want you to realize there were some risks involved in this. First of all, Bartimaeus was a beggar. The people around him were the ones he begged from. If he antagonized them, they might decide not to give him anything ever again. Secondly, what if Jesus ignored him? What if he just walked by without acknowledging Bartimaeus? Wouldn't Bartimaeus have looked foolish? Wouldn't everyone had said, "See! I told you so! You're just a beggar! Why would Jesus pay attention to you?"

Bartimaeus decided it was worth the risk. It didn't matter what people said or thought, he wasn't about to let Jesus walk by without at least trying to get his attention. His attitude was, "Maybe you can stand there and let the King of Kings pass you by, but I can't! I want to experience God's power. This is my chance. I'm not letting it get away." Bartimaeus risked ridicule when he began calling the name of Jesus, and he also demonstrated his faith.

When you ask anything of God, you sometimes have to ask in defiance of popular opinion. Others may try to put you in your place, saying, "What gives you the right to think God will bless you? There are sick people everywhere, what gives you the right to think God will heal you? This world is in turmoil, what gives you the right to think God is concerned with your silly problems?"

Yogi Berra was a catcher for the New York Yankees. One afternoon during a game a batter stepped into the box and crossed himself. Yogi said, "Why don't we just play the game and leave God out of it? OK?" Now, I like Yogi Berra, but this was one time when he was wrong. Ball players have the right to ask God to help them do well. Sales people have the right to ask God to help them do well. Teachers have the right to ask God to help them do well. Everyone has the right to ask God to help them in their daily lives. I realize the world is in turmoil and there are many serious global issues to contend with, yet the God we serve is concerned with each and every one of us—even a blind beggar sitting on the side of the road.

If you want to experience God's power, you'll have to defy the critics and ask anyway...even if it puts you at risk of looking foolish. It's that kind of bold defiance that demonstrates faith.

- **Ask specifically.**

When Jesus heard Bartimaeus call him, he stopped and asked him directly, *(v. 51) What do you want me to do for you?* Bartimaeus didn't hesitate. He just said, *"Rabbi, I want to see." "Go," said Jesus. "Your faith has healed you."* There are two things I want you to notice about this exchange.

*a. Bartimaeus knew exactly what he wanted.* Jesus said, "What do you want me to do?" and Bartimaeus said, "I want to see." His request was specific. He didn't say, "Uh...I want to be helped. I want to get better. I want you to bless me." He said exactly what he wanted: "Lord, I want to see."

We've got to remember that God can't answer a prayer that we aren't willing to make. He can't give what you do not ask for. If you want something from God, you have to ask specifically for it. The act of asking is a demonstration of faith. It does no good to ride coach all your life and hope that the flight attendant will pick you out of the crowd and invite you to sit in first class. It won't happen. You have to ask, and you must be specific.

At a goal setting seminar, one attendee told the leader his goal was to have more money. The leader reached into his pocket, gave the man 50 cents and said, "There you are. You asked for more money, and now you have it. You've reached your goal." If you want to be on the receiving end of God's blessings, you must have enough faith to ask specifically for whatever it is you want. At this point some people say, "What if I'm asking for something that's against his will?" Don't worry. He'll let you know. But don't make the mistake of trying to edit in advance what God is willing to do for you. Ask specifically.

*b. Bartimaeus asked for it all.* He could have asked for a few coins and Jesus probably would have given them. If he asked for food, Jesus probably would have given him that as well. But Bartimaeus had the faith to ask for the impossible: he asked to be able to see. And he got what he asked for.

Bartimaeus wasn't afraid to ask for everything. He wasn't content just to say, "Lord give me a cabin in the corner of glory land." He said, "I want a mansion, Lord...I want the impossible."

The act of asking demonstrates your faith. The size of your faith is revealed by the size of your prayers. Do you have enough faith to ask for something big? Do you have enough faith to ask for it all? Do you have enough faith to ask for the impossible?

## CONCLUSION

Just as Jesus spoke to Bartimaeus on the Jericho Road 2000 years ago, he's standing before you today and asking, "What do you want me to do for you?" What is your answer? What are you willing to ask for? Are you willing to ask and keep on asking? Are you willing to ask even if it puts you at risk of looking foolish? Are you willing to ask for the impossible? When you ask God for anything at all, you demonstrate your faith. The size of your faith is revealed by the size of your prayers.

Be like Bartimaeus. Ask God immediately, and keep on asking. Forget about what the crowd may think or say. Ask anyway. And ask specifically for what you want, even if it seems impossible. That's the kind of faith God rewards. I love the way this story ends. It says...*(v. 52) Immediately he received his sight and followed Jesus along the road.*

Bartimaeus' greatest benefit was being able to follow Jesus. From that day on he witnessed Jesus performing miracles and touching people's lives. He heard him teach the crowds who surrounded him. Jesus performed the impossible for Bartimaeus, and Bartimaeus responded with greater love and devotion than he had ever known. God wants to make it possible for you to be a more devoted follower of Christ. Don't be afraid to ask.

*SERIES: PRAYER: THE ULTIMATE LIFESTYLE*
**THE KEY TO PRAYING WITH POWER**
LUKE 18:1-8

Today's story teaches a crucial principle regarding prayer. It's the key to praying with power. The story, from Luke 18, is about a ruthless judge who fears neither God or man, and a widow who comes to him repeatedly with the request, "Grant me justice." For a long he time he refuses to consider her request, but finally in exasperation he says...(v. 4-5) *"Even though I don't fear God or care about men, yet because this widow keeps bothering me, I will see that she gets justice, so that she won't eventually wear me out with her complaining!"*

Jesus said in the same way God will bring about justice for his chosen ones who cry out to him day and night. Here's the principle. The key to praying with power—the key to getting results in prayer—is to keep at it. Pray with persistence.

This is where we most often drop the ball when it comes to praying. Too often, we pray for awhile, but when we don't get an answer soon enough, we give up. We say "It must not have been God's will"...or we say, "Maybe this prayer thing doesn't work after all"...or we say, "Maybe God doesn't care enough about me to answer my prayers—he'll answer prayers for others, but not me." None of these are true—but we fool ourselves into believing them simply because it's easier to give up than it is to keep praying.

God answers prayer, but he doesn't answer every prayer immediately. There are some prayers that he answers only when we pray persistently. Why? Why does God want us to pray with persistence? Today we'll look at three reasons—three ways you benefit from persistent prayer. First of all...

• **Persistent prayer keeps you in God's presence.**

Just like the widow stood before the judge day after day seeking justice, persistent prayer places us in God's presence, day after day after day. There's something more important to God than answering your prayer: he wants a personal relationship with you. He wants you to know him intimately. He wants to be your best friend—your constant companion. Persistent prayer helps you develop and nurture your relationship with God.

One evening I was having dinner with a married couple, Kirk and Dianne, and they told me how they met. Diane was a realtor and Kirk was looking for a house. Diane said, "I had to show him more than a dozen houses before he found one he was willing to buy. We were looking at houses together 2 or 3 times a week, and we eventually fell in love. Fortunately for me, Kirk doesn't make quick decisions." Kirk said, "Fortunately for me, Diane doesn't give up on making a sale!" Looking at properties together kept them in each other's presence long enough for their relationship to develop.

It's the same with prayer. If you pray about something every day, that means you're spending time with God every day—and the more time you spend with God, the closer you get to God. That's why Jesus said in verse 6 that we're to cry out to God "day and night." It's why the Psalmist said...*Evening, morning and noon I cry out in distress, and he hears my voice. (Psalm 55:17)*

God wants to be the central focus of your life. The purpose of prayer is not to get God to do things for you, it is to teach you to depend on him as your only source. Persistent prayer keeps us in God's presence. Secondly...

- **Persistent prayer helps you define and refine your requests.**

I firmly believe that anything you want you should pray for first. Anything at all. Does that mean you'll get it? Of course not. This is what will happen. As you pray earnestly and persistently over a period of time, you'll refine and re-define your request according to God's will. At first you may ask for one thing, but as you continue to pray and seek God's will, your request will be transformed into one that is pleasing to him.

My friend Ken, tired of living hand-to-mouth, began to pray for a raise in salary or a better paying job. His employer said,

"You're doing good work, but there's no money for a raise this year." So, Ken sent dozens of resumes, and not a single decent offer came back. Meanwhile, God began to convict Ken about his spending habits. Over time, his request changed from "Give me more money" to "Make me a better steward."

He reduced his expenses $300 a month by cutting unnecessary items such as HBO, a gym membership (he rarely went), changed calling plans on his cell phone, ate out less, and so on. Also, Ken had always had a car payment; every couple of years he would trade in his "old" car for a new one. This year, he decided to pay off the car and keep it—freeing up another $400. He said, "My income hasn't changed, but it's like I got an $8000 a year raise!" It began with a request for more money. Ultimately, the request became "Lord, make me a better steward." If God had immediately answered Ken's original request it would have just been a matter of time before he was as over-committed as ever. Instead, because he prayed persistently, his request was refined into what he really need to pray for, and God was able to do a great work in his life.

When we begin praying for something, we might not be praying for all the right things for all the right reasons. Persistent prayer improves our prayers; it helps us get on the right track. It's difficult (if not impossible) to pray persistently for something frivolous. The longer you pray, the more you realize: "This is silly; this isn't God's will."

Persistent praying helps you define and refine your requests so that you're ultimately asking for something that is consistent with God's will. Thirdly...

- **Persistent prayer proves your faith.**

Jesus ended this parable by saying...*(v. 8) "When the Son of Man comes, will he find faith on the earth?"* In other words, will he find people praying persistently? Persistent prayers demonstrate faith. Earlier in the gospel of Luke, when Jesus was teaching on this very same subject, he said..."*Ask and it will be given to you; seek and you will find; knock and the door will be opened to you. For everyone who asks receives; he who seeks finds; and to him who knocks, the door will be opened". (Luke 11:9-10)* The verbs "ask", "seek" and "knock" are spoken in the present tense, indicating an on-going action. In other words, "Ask and keep on asking"; "Seek and keep on seeking"; "Knock and keep on knocking". You prove your faith by continuing to ask.

A friend dropped by my office yesterday. My truck was out front, so he knew that I was here. The outside entrance was locked, so he started pounding on the door. I was on the phone, and he kept pounding. This went on for at least five minutes — every 30 seconds or so he would pound on the door or tap on the glass or shake the door handle. When I finally made it downstairs I said, "Are you trying to drive me crazy?" He said, "I knew you were here, and I knew you would answer eventually. I just didn't want you to think that I had given up and gone away." That's how we need to pray.

When we have refined our requests and are asking for the right things, God will answer our prayers. Jesus said so. *(v. 7-8) "And will not God bring about justice for his chosen ones who cry out to him day and night? Will he keep putting them off? I tell you, he will see that they get justice, and quickly."*

Wait a minute. Does that say "quickly"? Then why do we have to pray and pray and pray and ask and ask and ask seemingly forever? Because "quickly" is determined by God's timetable, not ours. "Quickly" doesn't mean we can snap our fingers and God will speed up the process; it means that God will answer our prayers on time. He's always on time. He's never in a hurry, but he's never late, he always right on time.

## CONCLUSION

Power in prayer is found in persistence. It keeps you in the presence of God, it helps you define and refine your requests according to his will, and it proves your faith.

Persistent prayer takes prayer out of the "Plan B" category — the "last-ditch-effort" category — and puts it where it belongs: top priority in your life.

*SERIES: HANGING ON THROUGH HARD TIMES*
**IT'S A GOOD THING YOU'VE GOT PROBLEMS**
JOSHUA 3:7-17

A camp meeting evangelist was preaching full throttle when a big fly zoomed by him. He swatted at it and kept preaching. A moment later the fly came at him again. The preacher swatted again and kept preaching. He finally paused for a moment and said, "Did you ever think how much easier our lives would be if Noah had swatted those two flies?"

Most of the obstacles we face are like that fly—they don't make life impossible, just inconvenient. Of course, there are times when we face big challenges. Most of the time, however, it's not cancer holding us back—it's a cold.

Ninety percent of the problems we face aren't directly related to our purpose and mission in life—they're just inconveniences. They're not insurmountable; they just take up our time when we could be doing something more productive.

The Israelites faced this. God had promised them their very own land, and he had commanded Joshua to go in and take the land—but when they did, they ran into a minor obstacle: the Jordan River. It was full and they had no immediate way of getting across. Now, this was not the same type of problem that Moses faced at the Red Sea. The Red Sea was impossible to cross, the Jordan River wasn't. Moses had an army breathing down his neck, Joshua didn't. Moses faced a crisis; Joshua faced an inconvenience.

But, if we're not careful, it's the inconveniences that will do us in. Some couples never spend quality time together because they're just too busy—and their relationship slowly deteriorates. Some people don't get involved in church because the early service starts too early and the late service ends too late. It would be a grave mistake to miss out on life by trying to avoid the inconveniences that happen along the way. In fact, the inconveniences help us more than they hurt us. Today, we're going to look at three ways you can benefit from life's minor problems. First of all, they provide...

- **A lesson in leadership**

*(v. 7) And the Lord said to Joshua, "Today I will begin to exalt you in the eyes of all Israel, so they may know I am with you as I was with Moses."* This was Joshua's opportunity to prove himself to the people of Israel, and it was the Israelites chance to see Joshua's leadership skills in action. Soon, they would be facing real challenges—they would be in battle—and it was important for them to know now that Joshua could provide leadership.

In 1994 when Michael Jordan decided to play professional baseball there was some question about whether or not he could make it. After he was signed by the Chicago White Sox, he was sent to play Double A ball in Birmingham. Birmingham was a test; if Jordan could do well in the minors, he would be ready to play in the majors. Unfortunately, he wasn't good enough for minor league ball. This is nothing against Michael Jordan. He's the greatest to ever to play the game of basketball, no question. But, in baseball, he couldn't pass the minor league test.

The inconveniences that we face are our minor league test. If we can't handle them, we won't be able to handle the big league stuff that inevitably comes our way. Every little obstacle we face is a chance to grow...a chance for us to get a little stronger...a chance for us to become better. A second way we benefit from life's minor problems is that they...

- **Teach us to build our faith**

*(v. 10) This is how you will know that the living God is among you, and that he will certainly drive out before you the Canannites, Hittites, Hivites, Perizzites, Girgashites, Amorites, and the Jebusites.* The Jordan River was a metaphor for the future victory God had in store for Joshua and the people of Israel. Experiencing victory here increased their faith in what God could do in the future.

In Star Wars, as Luke Skywalker and his comrades are attempting to destroy the Deathstar, one of the other pilots tells

Luke he can't make a particular maneuver—it's too risky. Luke says, "It's just like Beggar's Canyon back home." And, of course, you know what happens next. Luke hits the target and the Deathstar is blown up. Being able to navigate through Beggar's Canyon as a boy gave Luke the confidence he needed later when he faced a bigger challenge.

It was the same way with David. When he was preparing to battle against Goliath, King Saul told him, "You are not able to go out against this Philistine. You are only a boy." David said, "When I used to keep my father's sheep and a lion or bear would attack the flock, I would kill it. If I can kill a lion or bear, I can kill Goliath." [1 Samuel 17]

Those small victories over minor problems build our faith for the big challenges that inevitably come our way. The third way we benefit from life's minor problems is they enable us to...

- **Experience god's power in the present**

    Keep in mind, the Jordan River did not present an insurmountable challenge for the Israelites. It wasn't a crisis; it was an inconvenience. It was nothing like the challenge Moses faced at the Red Sea. The Red Sea is a huge body of water; the Jordan River is much smaller. The Egyptian Army was in hot pursuit of Moses; no one was chasing Joshua. Crossing the Red Sea was impossible for Moses; for Joshua it was only difficult. For Moses the situation was do or die; Joshua had plenty of options. He could have waited until the water subsided to cross the river. He could have taken the time for people to build rafts. They could have trekked left or right until they came to a shallow part of the river and then waded across. Moses needed a miracle; Joshua could have handled things on his own. Note: he could have—but he didn't.

    Joshua didn't handle it on his own, because God made it clear to him that this was a chance to experience God's power. Joshua didn't have to have a miracle, but he got one. The Bible says that he had his priests carry the ark of the covenant into the water, and when their feet touched the water's edge...

*(v. 16) the water from upstream stopped flowing. It piled up in a heap a great distance away...So the people crossed over opposite Jericho.* What does this tell us? It reminds us that we don't have to handle life's minor problems all alone—God wants to be part of even the small details of life.

## CONCLUSION

I know a woman named Sue who became a Christian. Sue is a homemaker. Her husband, John, is a doctor. At first, John's attitude towards Sue's conversion was one of amusement and condescension. He was happy for her, in a patronizing way. Yet he couldn't ignore the impact that Sue's faith had on her daily life. She involved God in every detail. She even prayed over her laundry: "Lord help me get the stains out of these jeans." John's attitude had always been that you call on God for emergencies; the small stuff you handle yourself. In Sue he saw that God can be part of every detail of our lives. It was this one distinction that ultimately led to John's conversion.

We cannot escape life's little problems. They're inevitable. But they are not what they appear to be. They actually help us, if we use them to our advantage. Life's little problems make it possible for us to become better leaders and more powerful believers. For that reason, it's a good thing you've got problems.

SERIES: HANGING ON THROUGH HARD TIMES
**HOW TO AVOID BURNOUT**
EXODUS 20:9-11

The army conducted a study a few years ago in which they observed several soldiers in various conditions to determine at what stage these individuals achieved the maximum level of output. The Army discovered that after 7 consecutive days of hard work the soldiers' performance dropped. But the most interesting discovery was that even though the soldiers' performance dropped, the soldiers themselves were unaware of it. They thought they were still operating at peak level.

When people work day-in, day-out for weeks and months on end, their performance level continues to drop and the worker becomes emotionally burned-out. And the occasional day off doesn't help much. On our day off we're likely to get up early to mow the yard, go to the bank, go to the cleaners, drop the kids off somewhere, go to the grocery store, visit the mall, clean the house, wash the car, take the dog to the vet, go pick up the kids, go to Wal-Mart, run by the post office, fix the children's bicycle, and re-organize the storage room—and our boss wonders why we're so exhausted when we "just had a day off!"

God didn't intend for us to live like this. In the Old Testament, when God gave Moses the Ten Commandments, he said...*Six days you shall labor and do all your work, but the seventh day is a Sabbath to the Lord your God. On it you shall not do any work...(Exodus 20:9-10)*

God takes the idea of a day of rest as seriously as he takes "Do not steal, lie, or commit adultery," but we seem to think we can break this commandment without consequence. In fact, we often brag about how busy, how overworked, and how completely stressed we are.

I heard a preacher say once that he never takes a day off because the devil never takes a day off. "And besides," this preacher said, "I can rest when I get to heaven!" As we examine the life of Christ, however, we see that during his 3 year ministry he took 10 "vacations" or "retreats", and he always kept the Sabbath. So the question is: Whose example do we want to follow—Jesus or the devil?

As far as God is concerned, the fourth commandment (*"Remember the Sabbath"*) is just as important as the other nine. In fact, this commandment contains a total of 94 words, far more than any of the other commandments, as if God went into detail on this one so that we could get it right! It's unfortunate, then, that we have ignored or abused his exhortation for us to remember the Sabbath. As a result, our lives have become cluttered and hectic, and we have lost sight of our spiritual priorities. Jesus summed up the Sabbath by saying *"The Sabbath was made for man, not man for the Sabbath." (Mark 2:27)*

We know from the Old Testament that we are to keep the Sabbath. We know from the New Testament that the Sabbath is for our benefit. Some might want to keep it on Saturday, some might want to keep it on Sunday—the English name assigned to the day of the week isn't important; what's important is that we make the observance. So today we're going to look at three ways we benefit from keeping the Sabbath. First of all, the Sabbath was designed to give us...

- **Rest**

The word Sabbath is taken from the Hebrew Sabat, and means, literally, rest. In the Old Testament—and in Judaism today—the Sabbath begins at sundown on Friday night and lasts until sundown Saturday.

Our Sabbath should be a day we set aside for rest. It should be a day of rest in the true sense of the word: when we sleep a little later, eat a little lighter, move a little slower, and take things a little easier. We need the day to refuel, whether we realize it or not. The commandment reads...*For in six days the Lord made the heavens and the earth, the sea, and all that is in them, but he rested on the seventh day. (Exodus 20:11)*

However, when God "rested" on the seventh day, it wasn't because He was tired and needed to conserve His energy. He rested in celebration of His completed work. Our day of rest should be the same: a chance to revel in the satisfaction of having completed a week of honest, hard work.

When you eat at McDonald's, your intention is usually to get in and get out as quickly as possible. You eat fast food because you're in a hurry, and it's relatively inexpensive. However, when you go to a place like The Captain's Table, and you're spending $150, your attitude towards the meal is different—especially at the end. If, as you took your last bite of food, your waiter brought you the check and your coat and escorted you out the door, you would feel as if you had been cheated out of part of the dining experience. After a great meal you want to relax for a moment and enjoy it. Our Sabbath is like that. Another week is behind us; let's take some time to rest and enjoy it.

Secondly, the Sabbath benefits us because it is a time for...

- **Reflection**

In the book of Psalms, David writes, *"Be still and know that I am God." (Psalm 46:10)* The Sabbath is more than just a day of inactivity. It's more than just a day of nothing. It is an opportunity for us to examine ourselves—our lives, our goals, our priorities. It's a chance for us to think about Last Week: what was good, what was bad; what went right, what went wrong; what you want to repeat, what you want to avoid; and so on. It's also a chance to think about This Week: What do you want to accomplish?...Where do you want to go?...Who do you want to become? It's a chance to give serious consideration to your life—where you've been and where you are going.

Lee Iacocca credits his success as a businessman to his commitment to this principle. As a vice-president of Ford, and CEO of Chrysler, he put in more than his share of long days. But Lee Iacocca made a commitment to be home every weekend, to enjoy his family, to attend church, and to spend time in personal reflection.

I saw a poster once that said *The Main Thing is to Keep the Main Thing the Main Thing.* Spending time each week in reflection enables us to do that. Thirdly, the Sabbath is a time for...

- **Renewal**

Since about the fourth century, the Christian Sabbath has been celebrated on Sunday. The Roman emperor Constantine is given credit for this becoming an official custom. However, in New Testament times it was common for Christians to meet together on Sunday in celebration of the Lord's resurrection. In the early church, Sunday came to symbolize renewal.

Our Sabbath should be a chance for us to experience renewal. Of course, the best way to do this is by attending church. The songs, the prayers, the Scripture, and the message should lead us into closer fellowship with God. People should leave each worship service with their spirits lifted and their hopes renewed. The time spent in church is so brief—less than 1% of your week—but it is often the most important hour in any given seven day period.

An old West Virginia coal-miner worked his mules six days a week, resting them on the seventh. A city visitor teased him about giving them a day off—wondering if the mules attended church with him. The miner said, "I don't work the mules on Sunday because it's for their own good—not mine. After being in those dark mines for six days, the mules need to spend some time in the light of day to prevent them from going blind."

That's what the Sabbath is to us: After a week in darkness, we need to be spend some time in the light of the Son to keep ourselves from becoming blind. It's not so much that the church needs you—it's a matter of you needing the church.

## CONCLUSION

God gave you the Sabbath. It's not a day of oppression, binding you to a bunch of silly rules and regulations. He gave you the Sabbath to help you live a life more focused, more productive, and more centered on him. These three principles—Rest, Reflection, and Renewal—help us keep life in perspective.

*SERIES: HANGING ON THROUGH HARD TIMES*
**DEALING WITH DISCOURAGEMENT**
JOHN 20:1-18

I was eighteen when I got my first job in sales; I was hired to sell memberships to a music club. Since I love music, I thought everyone would want to sign up for this fabulous-yet-affordable program. Along with a half-dozen guys and girls my age, I went through an eight-hour training session, I memorized a lengthy sales presentation, I was given a list of 40 prospects to contact, and I hit the road.

For seven days I called the people on my list. To my surprise, most of them refused to talk to me. Those who did let me in would most often glare at me during my entire presentation. No one bought. Since the job was "straight-commission" I had nothing to show for the hours I had worked that week. By the end of the week I was absolutely despondent, convinced that I was the worst salesman in history.

At Monday's sales meeting, I was surprised to learn that of the six people in our training class, I was the only one who showed up. All the others had quit during the previous week. The sales manager said to me, "Steve, you showed up! That means you've got what it takes to make it in sales." I didn't have the heart to tell him I was there only to turn in my book. He then told me, "Unfortunately, since we have had trouble staffing this office, the district manager has decided to shut it down. They're sending me to Tulsa. If you are interested, you're welcome to come along." I respectfully declined his offer. It would be a long time before I had the courage to try a job in sales again.

One of the biggest obstacles we face is discouragement. Once we get discouraged it's hard to keep going—it's hard to find the will to keep going. When Jesus was arrested and put to death, his disciples were overcome with discouragement. His most vocal follower, the Apostle Peter, denied him, deserted him, and ran for his life. Today we're going to look at how Peter dealt with his discouragement, and how he overcame it. First, let's consider...

- **The cause of discouragement**

Discouragement is caused by unmet expectations. When we don't meet them, or when life doesn't meet them, or when others don't meet them, or when God doesn't meet them, we get discouraged. We act as though we live in a cause-and-effect world, and that things are supposed to turn out a certain way. We believe that if we always do "A", it will always result in "B" — but life simply doesn't work that way.

Parents often become discouraged. Many moms and dads do everything they know to do, yet in spite of their efforts, their children just don't turn out the way they expected. Ministers are also vulnerable to discouragement. Sometimes it seems that our efforts have no impact on the life of the church. We pray, we study, we preach, we visit, we plan...but we don't see any visible results. In fact, a Promise Keepers survey among pastors revealed that 90% of pastors struggle with discouragement! It is hard not to resign ourselves to long term discouragement.

A young man went to see a fortune-teller. She studied his hand and told him, "You will be poor and completely miserable until you are 41 years old." The man said, "Then what will happen? Will I become rich?" "No," said the fortune teller. "You'll always be poor, but you'll become so accustomed to it that it no longer makes you miserable."

Peter experienced discouragement when Jesus died. He was discouraged because the death of Christ destroyed his expectations of how Jesus should establish His earthly kingdom. Peter was also discouraged because during the process he failed to meet his own expectations. Listen to what Peter said to Jesus...
*"Even if all fall away on account of you, I never will."* (Matthew 26:33)

When Peter said this, Jesus told Peter, "This very night...you will disown me three times." And Peter's response was..."*Even if I have to die with you, I will never disown you.*" (Matthew 26:35) Peter put a tremendous amount of faith in himself - too much, in fact. When he failed to meet his own expectations he became discouraged. That's the cause of discouragement; failed expectations. However, if we examine them closely, we'll often find that our expectations are unrealistic. Peter's expectations were unrealistic. Jesus told Peter they were unrealistic, yet Peter refused to listen. Secondly, let's examine...

- **The characteristics of a discouraged person**

When we become discouraged we tend to follow certain predictable behavior patterns in an attempt to overcome our discouragement. First of all...

**a. We compromise.** In the 18th chapter of John, when the soldiers came to arrest Jesus, Peter drew his sword and struck the high priest's servant, cutting off his ear. In doing this Peter compromised the teaching of Christ. Everything that Jesus had said about non-violence and non-resistance was disregarded. Instead, Peter took matters into his own hands. Of course, his plan didn't work. He lowered his standards, but not his expectations. When Peter attacked the high priest's servant, his expectations were still unrealistically high, but his commitment to obedience of the teachings of Christ had dropped several notches. We're the same way. When we become discouraged we cling to unrealistic expectations, and we'll do anything to make them happen — even if we have to sell our standards to do it.

**b. We quit.** Discouragement leads to despair. This is what Peter experienced after he denied knowing Jesus. The Bible says...*Peter went outside and wept bitterly. (Luke 22:62)* The song *He's Alive* by Don Francisco captures the despair that Peter must have experienced that night. It says...

*When at last it came to choices, I denied I knew His name. Even if He was alive, it wouldn't be the same.*

That's despair: The feeling that all hope is lost, and nothing can change things now. Peter experienced it. I've experienced it. You probably have, too.

**c. We withdraw.** *The disciples were together with the doors locked for fear of the Jews. (John 20:19)* When a person is in the depths of despair they stay at home, they become uninvolved, they withdraw into a shell of self-pity. As long as the disciples were hiding behind locked doors they were unable to finish the task that Jesus had given them. When we withdraw we become completely unproductive—and we're not able to accomplish the task that Jesus has given us.

Once when I was an associate pastor, the senior pastor and I went visiting. We stopped at a house that was completely dark. When I said it looked like no one is home, the pastor said, "There's someone here." After several minutes of knocking, Joanne came to the door and invited us inside. We entered a cluttered room lit only by a crack in the drawn curtains. She said, "Sorry it's so dark. I can't bring myself to turn on a light." Joanne's husband had left several weeks before, she spent every day since crying in the dark house. Because of disappointment, she had completely withdrawn from the world.

**d. We escape.** The 12-step term for this is "medicate." We look for something to alleviate the pain of discouragement and despair. For Peter, it was fishing. He just went back to his work.

A successful businessman being interviewed on a morning talk show was asked, "What is the secret to your success?" The man said, "A bad marriage. I couldn't stand to be at home so I stayed at the office until I stumbled onto success." He said it with a laugh, but he gave the impression that he was only half-joking.

How do you escape the pain of discouragement? Some pour themselves into work, some chase a hobby, some overeat, some watch too much TV, some go shopping, some make themselves numb with alcohol. There are many things we can do to cover up the pain of discouragement. The problem is that after we return from our escape, our problems still exist. In fact, they're usually worse.

None of these options—compromising, quitting, withdrawing, or escaping—solve the problem. We only end up cynical, skeptical, bitter, and, like Peter, at rock bottom. What should we do when we become discouraged? Let's examine...

- **The cure for discouragement**

**Consider the empty tomb.** *Then Simon Peter, who was behind him, arrived and went into the tomb. He saw the strips of linen lying there...(John 20:6)* When Peter saw evidence that Jesus had been resurrected, he began to have a glimmer of hope. The gospel of Luke tells us that after Peter examined the empty tomb *he went away to his home, wondering about what had happened.* (Luke 24:12) At this point it may have seemed too good to be true, but there was a spark of hope.

The empty tomb is our spark of hope. It tells us that God has the power to work in our lives today. Karl Barth said "...the resurrection of Christ teaches us that our enemies—sin, the curse, and death—are destroyed. They may still behave as though the game were not decided, but ultimately they can cause no more mischief. We still have to reckon with them; but we need fear them no longer."

The empty tomb reminds us that no situation is hopeless. Peter began winning the battle against discouragement when he encountered the empty tomb. I don't know what the source of your discouragement might be today, but whatever it is, remember the resurrection. Consider the empty tomb. It is proof that Jesus has power over sin and death—and he has power over any challenge we may face. You see, because of the empty tomb, we can...

**Expect the unexpected.** *Early in the morning, Jesus stood on the shore, but the disciples did not realize that it was Jesus. (John 21:4)* Peter and several of the other disciples decided to go fishing together. They spent the night on the water, but caught nothing. Early in the morning, a man standing on the shore called out to them, "Do you have any fish?" They answered, "No." The stranger told them to throw their net on their other side of the boat and they would find some fish. When they did, they were unable to haul the net in because of the large number of fish. John told Peter, "It is the Lord." That was all Peter needed to hear: he jumped out of the boat and swam to shore. Peter had gone to sea that night to fish. He didn't expect to see Jesus. Peter was beginning to learn an important principle: expect the unexpected. You never know when Jesus is going to surprise you with a miracle. You may be on your way to leave flowers at a tomb, you may be out fishing, you may be in a prayer meeting — you never know when he will surprise you with a miracle.

You may be like the man who lay for 38 years beside the pool of Bethesda, who was convinced that it was useless to hope for a miracle. You may be like the man who sat in front of the temple gate day after day begging for money, when what he really wanted was to be healed.

You may be like Lazarus, who died thinking that his closest friend wasn't there to comfort him in his hour of death. You may be like Martha, who thought that God waited too long to show up and now her brother was dead. You may be like the woman at the well, whose search for love led her through a series of failed relationships. You may be like Peter, who, in a moment of weakness, denied and deserted the one whom he loved more than any other. All of these individuals have one thing in common. They each faced the depths of discouragement, and they each had an unexpected encounter with the power of God.

Some of you here today are discouraged beyond description. Maybe it's your job, or your family, or your marriage, or your financial situation. Maybe you're asking yourself "Why should I keep on?...What's the use?...Why don't I just quit?" I can give you a reason. The tomb is empty. Jesus is alive today, and he is at work in our lives. That means we can expect the unexpected. You never know when Jesus is going to surprise you with a miracle. Maybe we can't control the so-called principle of cause-and-effect. Maybe we can't get the results we want when we want them. But we can be faithful. We can keep on. Things won't always be the way they are today. And because the tomb is empty, we have a right to expect the unexpected.

SERIES: HANGING ON THROUGH HARD TIMES
**CRISIS MANAGEMENT**
1 SAMUEL 17

Everybody likes to cheer for the underdog, don't they? Whether it's Indiana Jones taking on the Nazis, or George Bailey taking on greedy Mr. Potter, people love to see the little guy win. That's why the '69 Mets, the '68 Jets, and the USA Hockey team in the '72 Olympics have become American legends. Maybe this is because America's own success is an underdog story. It doesn't seem likely that 13 tiny colonies living on limited resources in an undeveloped country could establish independence from the world's most powerful military force, yet we were able to do it.

From a human point of view, the early Christian church had an underdog's chance of succeeding. Think about it. The leader was dead, and 12 uneducated men were expected to carry on his work. In just a few years 10 of the men had been put to death and another had been exiled. The religious and political powers of the early centuries fought hard to put an end to the Church. Yet, this underdog movement continued to spread at a phenomenal rate—in spite of persecution and oppression.

Everybody likes to cheer for the underdog, but not many of us really enjoy being the underdog. We like to watch people overcome tremendous obstacles, we just don't like to face the obstacles ourselves. Yet, it is inevitable that we will find ourselves in underdog situations, with no way to beat the odds.

No doubt some of you are in this very situation—the challenges are too great, the opposition is too strong, your resources are too limited, and there's seemingly no way to win. There's a Bible story about a young man who found himself here. You know the story of David and Goliath—the ultimate underdog story. You already know how it ends, but today we'll examine three elements of this story—the Crisis, the Critics, and the Contest—and David's response to each one. As we look at how David responded to each situation, we can learn much about how to deal with challenges in our own lives. First, notice...

- **The crisis**

The army of Israel faced a crisis. They were at war with the Philistines. They had come to a standoff, and now Goliath challenged any Israelite to fight him. Not a single man believed he could do it. This was a challenge that they could not win. Their crisis was, in many ways, like the crises we face in our lives. Let's consider the characteristics of the crisis. First of all...

**a. The crisis was larger than life.** *(v. 4) A champion named Goliath, who was from Gath, came out of the Philistine camp. He was over nine feet tall. He had a bronze helmet on his head and wore a coat of scale armor of bronze weighing five thousand shekels; on his legs he wore bronze greaves, and a bronze javelin was slung on his back. His spear shaft was like a weaver's rod, and its iron point weighed six hundred shekels.*

Talk about indestructible! As far as the Israelite soldiers were concerned, Goliath was too big to be defeated. This is what we think about the giants we face. Whether the giant is health problem, or a failing marriage, or financial worries, it's always bigger than we are.

For many years the USSR was considered to be the greatest threat to our national security. During this time there was a certain Soviet mystique that fanned the flame of our paranoia. Alarmists warned that their military was more powerful and more prepared than ours, their people more committed to Communism than ours to freedom, their children better educated than our children, their society more intellectual than ours, and on and on. Even though we eventually discovered otherwise, for a time the Soviets seemed larger than life. Do you remember how afraid we were? Secondly...

**b. The crisis defies our power.** *(v. 8) Goliath stood and shouted to the ranks of Israel, "Why do you come out and line up for battle? Am I not a Philistine, and are you not the servants of Saul? Choose a man and have him come down to me. If he is able to fight and kill me, we will* *become your subjects; but if I overcome him and kill him, you will become our subjects and serve us!" Then the Philistine said, "This day I defy the ranks of Israel! Give me a man and let us fight each other." On hearing the Philistine's words, Saul and all the Israelites were dismayed and terrified.*

This is what giants do. We try to control every detail of our lives, and then a crisis comes along to remind us of how helpless we really are. The crisis doesn't have to be major; it can be a problem at work, or a problem at home, or the inability to defeat some bad habit, or any number of things—but it is always there to remind us that we are powerless. Thirdly...

**c. The crisis will not go away.** *(v. 16) For forty days the Philistine came forward every morning and evening and took his stand.* The problem with a crisis is that it won't go away. If you don't deal with it, it deals with you. You can't ignore it, you can't pretend it isn't there. It will haunt you until you face it. The problem is that most crises are easy to ignore in the early stages. It is rare that a situation goes from "good" to "crisis level" overnight.

Usually there is a process of deterioration... There is a breakdown in communication for months—maybe years—before a marriage deteriorates. Financial problems are just an "inconvenience" for many months until they mushroom into unmanageability. There are often telltale warnings of health problems long before we face the zero hour and yet, as much as we try to turn our back on the situation, it just won't go away.

***David's Response to the Crisis...***So, in the midst of the crisis, David arrives at the scene. He sees Goliath make his challenge and he sees the Israelite army overcome with fear. And what is David's response? He says...*(v. 26) "Who is this uncircumcised Philistine that he should defy the armies of the living God?"*

In these few words David put the crisis into proper perspective. We can learn from his example. *The best response to a crisis is to acknowledge that God is bigger than any problem I will ever face.* Secondly, notice...

- **The critics**

If you attempt anything worthwhile, you will endure criticism. If David had adopted the fearful attitude of the Israelite soldiers—if he had been willing to do nothing about the crisis—he would have been left alone. But as soon as he began to talk about the possibility of defeating the giant, he was met with a barrage of criticism.

David was not the only dreamer in the Bible to be criticized for wanting to do God's will. Noah, Moses, Joseph, Nehemiah, Paul, Peter, (and, of course, Jesus) were all criticized for attempting to do something great for God's glory. Criticism won't come as a surprise to the goal-oriented, but that doesn't change the fact that criticism is painful. However, it's a little easier to endure if you recognize some characteristics of critical people. First of all...

**a. Critics are obsessed with the trivial.***(v. 28) When Eliab, David's oldest brother heard him speaking with the men, he burned with anger at him and asked, "Why have you come down here? And with whom did you leave those few sheep in the desert?"*

Here's a typical critic. David is about to destroy a major threat to Israel's national security, and Eliab is worried about the sheep. Critics have an amazing ability to focus on the trivial and neglect the crucial. Secondly...

**b. Critics believe the worst about people.***(v. 28) "...I know how conceited you are and how wicked your heart is; you came down only to watch the battle."* George Bernard Shaw wrote that "hatred is the coward's revenge for being intimidated." The criticism of others serves as a smoke-screen to make it less obvious that those who criticize aren't accomplishing anything with their own lives.

Francis Asbury, an 18th century bishop in the Methodist movement, was once criticized by a woman for being unsophisticated in his method of evangelism. Asbury politely asked the lady how many she had led to Christ in her life. The lady answered that she had not personally led anyone to faith in Christ. Asbury's response was, "Ma'am, I like my way doing it better than your way of not doing it."

***David's Response to the Critics...***David's brother criticized him for wanting to defeat Goliath. He accused David of neglecting his responsibilities, he questioned David's motives, and he assaulted David's character. But David's brother never did anything about Goliath! Notice David's response to the criticism: *(v. 30) He then turned away to someone else and brought up the same matter.*

David refused to be swayed by criticism. He recognized that the critics didn't know what they were talking about, and so he chose to disregard the criticism, but he wouldn't give up his dream of defeating Goliath.

You can be sure that when you try to accomplish something great for God, you will be criticized by those who do nothing. *The best response is to disregard the critics, but don't disregard your dream.* Next, please notice...

- **The contest**

Until David stepped on the battle field, he could be regarded as just a little kid with big ideas. But once he lined up against Goliath, it became obvious that he was a man to be taken seriously. Even if he lost the battle, David proved that he had more character, more integrity, and more faith than any soldier in the king's army—including the king himself. David *won* the contest just by his willingness to *enter* the contest. Let's look at his strategy.

**a. David established the terms of battle.***(v. 40) Then he took his staff in his hand, chose five smooth stones from the stream, put them in the pouch of his shepherd's bag and, with his sling in his hand, approached the Philistine.*

Notice that Goliath was forced to fight David on David's terms—not with a sword and spear, but with five smooth stones. Even the king tried to get David to wear cumbersome battle armor, but David refused. He knew the only way to meet this challenge was by doing what he did best. It is said that the reason Muhammad Ali was almost unbeatable during his prime was that he made his opponent fight his fight. He knew how to set the pace for a match. Beneath all the self-adoration and corny poetry lay a great boxer who knew what he could do best and stuck to it. No wonder many fighters far more powerful than Ali came to believe that he was "the greatest." Secondly...

**b. David refused to be intimidated.** Finally, David stood face to face with Goliath, with nothing but his slingshot and five smooth stones. As David approached, Goliath tried to intimidate him. *(v. 44) "Come here,"* he said, *"and I'll give your flesh to the birds of the air and the beasts of the field!"*

David responded by saying, *(v. 45) "You come against me with sword and spear and javelin, but I come against you in the name of the Lord Almighty, the God of the armies of Israel, who you have defied. This day the Lord will hand you over to me, and I'll strike you down and cut off your head. Today I will give the carcasses of the Philistine army to the birds of the air and the beasts of the earth, and the whole world will know that there is a God in Israel."*

Can you imagine a young boy speaking with such boldness to an enemy warrior twice his size? David refused to be intimidated by Goliath, and he refused to run from the contest. Instead, he approached the battle with boldness. How do you speak to your giant? What is your attitude toward the contest? Are you intimidated, or do you dare to defy your giant with a bold assertion: "I'm going to cut off your head!"

***David's response to the contest...***Our tendency is to be timid in the face of battle, but that is not what we see in David. Instead, David approached Goliath with reckless abandon, because he knew that the result of the battle was not in his hands. Notice his words to Goliath: *(v. 47) "...for the battle is the Lord's, and he will give all of you into our hands."*

David's response to the contest can be summarized in the statement *"The battle is the Lord's."* Imagine how our attitude toward life's challenges would change if we would believe (and act on) those words. We need fear the contest no longer. In fact, we can now approach challenges with abandon. We can laugh in the face of the intimidator—because we know the battle is the Lord's.

## CONCLUSION

In this story one question comes to mind. What did David have that the soldiers of Israel didn't? Why was he able to defeat an enemy that older, more experienced warriors were afraid to face?

David could face Goliath because he had faith in God's goodness. Since God is good, the crisis cannot last, the critics can't be right, and the contest cannot be lost. Since God is good, the victory is ours.

When you face a Goliath, remember David's response to the crisis: *God is bigger than my problems.* Remember David's response to the critics: *He disregarded the critics, but he didn't disregard his dream.* Remember David's response to the contest: *The battle is the Lord's.* David faced Goliath because he believed in God's goodness. Believing in God's goodness will give you the strength to slay giants, too.

SERIES: HANGING ON THROUGH HARD TIMES
**WHEN YOU'VE GOT PROBLEMS THAT CAN'T BE SOLVED**
1 PETER 1:3-9

I took my family to a major league baseball game a couple of years ago. We went to see the Detroit Tigers play the Texas Rangers. In about the third inning the sky turned dark and it began to sprinkle. However, the game wasn't called off. We were just put on "rain delay." For almost an hour, about 15,000 people were held in limbo while we waited to see how long and how hard it was going to rain. It was interesting to watch how different people reacted to the weather. Some left as soon as the first drops fell from the sky. Others sat through the rain for awhile, but eventually got tired of waiting and went home.

However, we weren't willing to give up that easily; we had driven hundreds of miles to see the game, and we were determined to wait out the storm. Finally, the clouds rolled by and after the grounds crew did their job, the players took the field. Even though the game was far from over, I felt like we had already won: we had outlasted the storm.

At different times in your life you will find yourself in this kind of situation. You will be in the midst of a storm that you didn't cause and that you can't control, and you will have no choice but to wait it out. These kinds of problems are often the most difficult to face, because they make us feel so helpless.

1 Peter was written for people in this predicament. 1 Peter 1:6 says, *you have been distressed by various trials.* The word that's translated *various* means literally *many-colored.* In the NIV it is translated as *"all kinds of trials."* The word that's translated trials means literally *adversity* or *problem.* Peter is saying, in effect, "I realize that you are going through all kinds of problems,"...and he's not just talking about persecution and threat of death, but he also means health problems, money problems, family problems, work problems, and any other kind of difficulty we might face.

Scripture is clear that we will face problems. When Jesus told the story of the wise and foolish men who built their houses, do you remember what common experience both men shared? They both experienced storms that challenged the foundation of their lives.

Today we will look at 1 Peter 1:3-9. As we examine these verses, Peter reminds us of three principles that will help us endure problems that we cannot solve. First of all, we need to remember that....

- **This problem is only temporary.**

Notice that when Peter makes reference to going through all kinds of trials he includes this qualifying phrase *...for a little while.(v.6)* Our problems aren't going to last forever, and we need to remember that they are, by their very nature, only temporary.

Actually, this should be our attitude to all of life. We shouldn't become too attached to this world's pleasures or its problems. We need to keep in mind that we are, as Peter mentions in verse one, only strangers here. As St. John Chrysostrom said, "I have only contempt for this world's threats; I find its blessing laughable." There's an old hymn that says...

> *This world is not my home, I'm just passing through*
> *My home is far away somewhere beyond the blue*
> *The angels beckon me from heaven's distant shore*
> *And I can't feel at home in this world anymore.*

These words reflect the attitude that we need to have in life—especially to our problems. They're only temporary. I'm sure you have heard this two-step formula for dealing with them: *1.) Don't sweat the small stuff. 2.) Remember it's all small stuff.*

Unfortunately, when we look at our problems, they don't seem small. They seem HUGE. When we look at our problems they don't seem temporary, they seem permanent. But the truth is, it is only a matter of perspective.

When you compare the size of quarter to the size of the sun, the difference in diameter is that of less than one inch and millions and millions of miles. Yet you can place that tiny quarter so close to your eye that you cannot see the sun. It works the same way with our problems. When we look too closely at them, we lose perspective and they begin to seem larger than they really are. Our problems are temporary. When we forget that, we lose perspective and do something foolish, or desperate, or both.

A man caught a cold, so he went to see the doctor and asked for a cure. The doctor said, "We can't cure a cold. All I can recommend is for you to take some aspirin, drink plenty of fluid, get some rest, and wait it out. You'll feel better in a few days." The man didn't like what he heard; he wanted to be cured immediately but he had no choice, so he went home. When he woke up the next day, he didn't feel any better. In fact, he felt worse. Still barefoot and in his pajamas, he told his wife, "I can't stand this any longer. I'm going outside, and I'm going to take a long walk." His wife said, "Are you crazy? It's freezing out there! It's raining and sleeting! You'll catch pneumonia!" The man said, "Exactly! And then I'll get well in no time, because I know that doctor can cure pneumonia!"

We need to remember that our problems are only temporary. This applies especially to temptation. Temptation cannot last forever—it's not that strong. If we wait, it will go away.
*Resist the devil, and he will flee from you. (James 4:7)*

Think of the biggest problem you're facing right now. Remind yourself that this problem will not last forever. You can endure anything if you know that it will not last forever. Peter reminds us that when you are going through problems that can't be solved, you should remember that they're only temporary.

- **This problem doesn't have to make me miserable.**

*(v. 6) In this you greatly rejoice, though now for a little while you may have had to suffer grief...* Peter is making reference to all the good things God has given us. In verses 3-5 he lists them.

> *We have received God's mercy.*
> *We have been given new birth, and new life.*
> *We can live this life with a sense of hope and optimism.*
> *We need not be afraid of death, because Jesus conquered death.*

*We have an eternal inheritance that can never be destroyed.*
*We are protected by God's power until the end of time.*

If all these things are true, then we don't need to allow a few temporary problems to rob us of our happiness. The things are that are most important can never be taken away: God's mercy, God's power, and eternal life.

During World War II, Dr. Victor Frankl was imprisoned by the Nazis because he was a Jew. His wife, children and parents were killed in the holocaust. At one point, the prison guards cut his wedding band off his finger. At this time, Frankl said to himself, "You can take away my family, you can strip me of my clothes and my freedom, but there is one thing no person can ever take away from me — my freedom to choose how I will react to what happens to me!" Whenever we face problems, we may not be able to do anything about the problem, but we don't have to let it make us miserable.

Abraham Lincoln said, "A person is as happy as he makes up his mind to be." It is our choice how we react to trials and tribulations. Peter says even though we suffer grief, we have every reason to rejoice because of God's goodness towards us. If we remember this, then no problem we face has the power to take away our joy. Also, Peter encourages us to remember that...

- **This problem will help me grow.**

There is a principle in scripture that many of us have tried to resist all of our lives, but it cannot be sidestepped or avoided. That principle is...*Pain precedes growth*. You cannot have growth without pain. I sometimes wish this weren't true. I wish that pleasure caused growth, but it seldom does. Weight lifters have a slogan: *No Pain — No Gain*. That slogan isn't just catchy — it's scriptural. There is no gain without the pain of discipline, perseverance, and self-denial. Just like every workout makes an athlete a little stronger, so every problem or temptation we endure makes us a little stronger. Peter says...*(v. 7) These [problems] have come so that your faith...may be proved genuine and may result in praise, glory and honor when Jesus Christ is revealed.*

As we face various trials, we need to remember ...

**a. We have the power to overcome any test or temptation.** *God is faithful; He will not let you be tempted beyond what you can bear. (1 Corinthians 10:13)* I saw a rerun of the TV show *thirtysomething* recently, and this subject came up. A character's mother had died, and the priest told her that God would not give her anything she wasn't strong enough to handle. Her response was, "Does that mean if I were a weaker person my mother would still be alive?" That's not the right way to look at a problem. It is not that God gives us problems to match our strength—He gives us strength to match our problems. And He promises that His strength is available whenever we need it.

**b. Every problem can work out for our best.** There are more examples of this in scripture than we have time to mention. But let's consider two. Think of Joseph, sold by his own brothers as a slave, then unjustly accused of misconduct in Potiphar's household, he ended up alone and in prison in a foreign land. But it was these very events that led to his eventually becoming a ruler in Egypt. His life at one point seemed to be a tragedy in the making, yet it turned out to be one of the most inspiring stories in scripture.

About two thousand years later, the Apostle Paul was also unjustly imprisoned. His only crime was preaching the gospel of Jesus Christ. His enemies tried to silence him, but Paul's imprisonment became an opportunity to write letters to the churches he couldn't visit—and, of course, those letters became scripture.

No matter how bad things look, remember that God takes great pleasure in turning the tide in the course of our lives. Listen to His promises in scripture...

- (Nehemiah 13:2)*Our God turned the curse into a blessing.*
- Deuteronomy 23:5 says, *The Lord your God...turned the curse into a blessing for you, because the Lord your God loves you.*
- Romans 8:28 says, *And we know that God causes all things to work together for good, to those who love God...*

## CONCLUSION

Many of you here today are facing storms in your life, and they are just too strong for you to weather on your own. Whether or not you caused the storm is irrelevant. What is relevant though, is how you react to the storm. Remember that because you are a child of God, the storm is really nothing more than a rain delay—and God's promise is that eventually you will win the game.

Yes, you have problems that you can't solve. We all do. But those problems are temporary. And most of all, remember that the problems we face are not meant to take the strength out of us, but to put strength into us. Let's use these tough times as an opportunity to grow closer to Jesus.

*THANKSGIVING MESSAGE*
**BECOMING A GIVER**
2 CORINTHIANS 9:6-15

> *Don't it always seem to go*
> *That you don't know what you've got till it's gone...*

Do you remember that song? *Big Yellow Taxi*. Joni Mitchell. 1969. This song summarizes the plight of so many: too often we don't appreciate what we have until it's too late. Lack of gratitude prevents people from feeling good about their lives; instead of being thankful, they spend their energy focusing on what's missing.

A survey was done in Orange County, California — one of the most affluent areas of our nation. The question was asked, "What do you need most?" and the number one response was "More money." These people already have more money than anyone else on the planet, but they feel they need more. Now, I'm not pointing fingers at them, because I tend to be the same way. So are many of us.

In this land of plenty, too often we live our lives with a sense of lack. "I don't have enough money. I don't have enough time. I don't have enough success. I don't have enough happiness." As a result, our lives become defined by what we don't have, and we fail to appreciate what we do have until it's too late.

I can't count the times I've heard, "I didn't realize how good my job was until I lost it...I didn't realize how precious my spouse was until he or she died...I didn't realize how important my children were to me until they left home..." The more successful, the more affluent, the more blessed we become, our biggest challenge is learning to appreciate — to be truly thankful for — all the good things we have.

In 2 Corinthians Paul teaches a principle of gratitude that I want to share it with you. Every Thanksgiving sermon you've ever heard has probably said that we shouldn't be thankful just one day a year—that we should be thankful all year long. In fact, I contend that if you're not thankful all year long, you can't be truly thankful on Thanksgiving day. We need to learn to develop a spirit of gratitude 365 days a year; Paul teaches us how.

We all know that we should be thankful—in our heads we know that—but in our hearts we don't always feel thankful. So, how does one develop a thankful heart? Learn to give. There is an unbreakable connection between gratitude and generosity; the more you give, the more grateful you'll become.

Some of the skeptics here today will probably think, "How convenient for you, you're telling me that if I give more money to the church I'll be happier." I want to make this clear: I'm not just talking about writing a check to the church every payday. I'm talking about developing the habit of giving to those people you interact with every day. And I'm talking about more than giving your money. I'm talking about giving yourself: sharing your time, your wisdom, and your words of encouragement.

I know a successful businessman who likes to help those who are struggling financially. He doesn't always give them money, except in emergencies, because he knows that handouts won't help them learn to stand on their own two feet. He gives them something much more valuable: he gives them his time and his expertise. He helps them make business decisions, financial decisions, and budgeting decisions that they often don't have the skills to make on their own.

This man is wealthy so it would be much easier for him to just cut a check and be done with them—then he could spend his evenings watching TV. Instead, he gives his time to those who need him, going over their checkbook, their budget, their bills, spending hour after hour helping them establish financial independence. Yes, he's generous financially, but he's also generous in every area of his life—and he's also one of the happiest, most grateful people I know.

There is an unbreakable connection between gratitude and generosity. In order to be truly thankful, we need to cultivate the discipline of giving. Now, I'm not going to tell you how to give.

I think you already know how to do that. Today I'm going to talk about WHY to give; 2 Corinthians 9 shows us three good things that happen when you give. First of all...

- **Cheerful giving pleases God.**

*(v. 7) Each man should give what he has decided in his heart to give, not reluctantly or under compulsion, for God loves a cheerful giver.* Have you ever noticed that sometimes you give and sometimes you're taken from? There's a difference, isn't there? Sometimes we surrender our resources not because we want to, but because we feel obligated. When the hat is passed for the boss's birthday gift, we've got to contribute whether we want to or not, don't we?

Paul says when it comes to giving, don't do it out of compulsion. Don't give reluctantly, and don't fight the opportunity to give. When you see a chance to share your resources with others, do it cheerfully. When you give with that attitude, you make God happy.

Why does the Bible say that God loves a cheerful giver? Because giving cheerfully reflects a proper attitude toward all that you have. A cheerful giver isn't selfish. A cheerful giver doesn't give with strings attached. A cheerful giver doesn't give merely to get something back. God loves a cheerful giver, because when we give cheerfully, we give like God gives. Probably the best verse in all of scripture that sums up how God gives to us is Romans 5:8.*But God demonstrates his own love for us in this: While we were still sinners, Christ died for us. (Romans 5:8)*

Another verse that stands out is John 3:16. *For God so loved the world that he gave his only begotten Son, that whosoever believeth in him should not perish but have everlasting life.*

God gave the gift even though we didn't deserve it. He didn't wait until we proved ourselves worthy. He knew that in giving this precious gift to the world, many people would never appreciate it, many would never accept it, and none of us would ever deserve it...and yet he gave anyway because we needed it. That's cheerful giving. When we give cheerfully, we're giving like God gives, so cheerful giving pleases him. When you're presented with the opportunity to give, respond cheerfully.

Several years ago I had car trouble in the middle of nowhere. I walked to a gas station and called to ask a friend to come pick me up. He heaved a big sigh and said, "You know, I was watching a tennis match." I said, "That's OK, I can walk home," and he said, "No, I'll do it if no one else will." He picked me up and drove me home in silence. As I was getting out of the car I thanked him for his help and he said, "You can thank me by getting your car fixed." I was hurt by his attitude, and needless to say, I never troubled him again.

As I tell that story, I shudder to think of all the times I behaved the same way to those who needed my help—and I was too self-absorbed to notice. All the times I gave begrudgingly and condescendingly. I don't want to be like that, and I don't think you do either. Whenever we have the opportunity to help someone, let's give cheerfully, because cheerful giving pleases God. That's the first principle I want you to remember. The second is...

- **Big giving gets big results.**

*(v. 6) Remember this: Whoever sows sparingly will also reap sparingly, and whoever sows generously will also reap generously.* Paul is saying that little giving gets little results; big giving gets big results. As the saying goes, You can't out-give God. The more you give to him, the more he gives back to you.

I want to clear something up right now—this idea about giving to get. If your only motive in giving is to get something back, like some kind of supernatural investment scheme, you're wasting your time. That kind of giving won't work because it violates the first principle we just talked about. You can't give cheerfully and give selfishly at the same time. You can't be motivated by compassion and greed. It just doesn't work.

The Bible plainly teaches—and this passage specifically teaches—that when you give to God he blesses you abundantly. When you give to him, he gives back to you. But the return isn't always apples-to-apples. When you give financially, he may bless you with financial abundance, or he may bless you in other ways. But there are certain things you can be sure of.

*a. He'll meet your needs.* When you are generous financially, God will take care of you financially. You might not be rich, but won't starve.

I believe this principle works in other areas, too. When you are generous with your time, God will bless your schedule so that you have time to do all that you need to do. When you are generous with your wisdom and knowledge, God will bless you in that area. When you are generous with your family, God will bless you in that area, and on an on. He'll meet your needs. Also, when you give big...

*b. He'll overwhelm you with his grace.* Do you know what grace is? It is God's unlimited mercy when you fail, and his unlimited strength to keep you from failing again. People who live generously receive generously from God—all of his mercy, all of his forgiveness, all of his strength to get through the challenges of life. Do you ever go through times when it seems like God is far away and his strength is unavailable to you? Look for ways to give big—it opens the floodgates of heaven. Also...

*c. Your work will be more productive.* Have you ever seen two people do basically the same thing and get completely different results? Two sets of parents spend 18 years raising their children; one set produces good kids and the other produces spoiled brats? Or, two guys do basically the same job; one guy thrives and the other barely gets by? What's the difference? In the successes and failures, I would venture to say the biggest difference is in an attitude of generosity.

Some people approach their job, or their marriage, or their money, with the attitude, "I've got to stand up for my rights, I've got to protect what's mine, I've got to make sure no one takes advantage of me." Obviously, this isn't a generous attitude.

Others approach things in life with an attitude that says, "I'm going to give and give and give because there's plenty more where that came from." It's these people who thrive relationally;

it's these people who succeed at work; it's these people who have more happiness than they know what to do with. Because when you give big, you get big results. You'll find that your needs are being met, you'll find that you have an abundance of mercy and strength to face your problems, you'll find that you accomplish more at work. This is exactly what God promises in this passage of scripture....*(v. 8) And God is able to make all grace abound to you, so that in all things at all times, having all that you need, you will abound in every good work.*

Your needs are met. You receive an abundance of grace. You abound in every good work. When you give big, you get big results.

- **Generous giving creates a chain reaction.**

In the movie *Pay It Forward* a junior high student gets the idea of helping 3 people, who each in turn pay it forward by helping 3 other people, who help 3 more, and on and on. It's a great idea—and it works. Paul was the first one to introduce the Pay It Forward concept...*(v. 12-14) This service that you perform is not only supplying the needs of God's people but is also overflowing in many expressions of thanks to God. Because of the service by which you have proved yourselves, men will praise God for the obedience that that accompanies your confession of the gospel of Christ, and for your generosity in sharing with them and with everyone else. And in their prayers for you their hearts will go out to you, because of the surpassing grace God has given you.*

Paul is saying when you help others, you're paying it forward—you're creating a chain reaction that will spread the love of God to many other people. He says not only are you doing the obvious—meeting their physical needs—but you're also building them up spiritually, you're teaching them to be thankful to God. And as a result of them being built up spiritually, others will also come to praise God because of your obedience and generosity.

When you help someone else, you create a chain reaction that helps them connect with God, and helps others connect with

God. A teacher who spends extra time with a disadvantaged child isn't just doing her job, she's changing the future. A coach who spends extra time to help a player develop discipline isn't just building a winning team, he's changing the future. A father who teaches his son to pray and walk with Christ isn't just being a good father, he's changing the world for generations to come. There's a chain reaction to generosity. When you give to others, not only does God bless you, but through you he blesses the world.

**CONCLUSION**

Do you want something to be thankful for this Thanksgiving—and every day for the rest of your life? Be thankful that he has given the chance to make a huge difference. Don't wait till it has passed you by before you do something about it. Take advantage of it now. Become a giver.

You may be tempted to focus on the things you don't have, and you may be tempted to focus on the problems that you do have. I challenge you to attack it head-on. Do you want to become truly thankful? Do you want to go from Thanksgiving to Thanks-living? Then become a giver. Give cheerfully, give big, give generously. God will take care of you, and he'll use you to take care of others. I'll close with Paul's words, *(v. 11) You will be made rich in every way so that you can be generous on every occasion, and through your generosity will result in thanksgiving to God.*

*SERIES: A SIMPLE CHRISTMAS*
**A CHRISTMAS LIST FOR FAMILY AND FRIENDS**
1 THESSALONIANS 3:9-13

For as long as I can remember, I've heard people complain that Christmas is too commercial. Even in the movie *Miracle on 34th Street*, filmed more than 60 years ago, a character complains that people are too caught up in the material aspect of the holiday. It has probably always been this way. As long as Christmas has been celebrated, there have been people warning us about the dangers of commercialism.

This year we'll try to get past that. Today we're beginning a four part series called *A Simple Christmas*. For the next few weeks we'll look at ways to make this a Christ-centered Christmas — one in which we grow closer to him and connect with our loved ones on a deeper level; one in which we learn to avoid the craziness that often plagues our lives in December, and in which we discover, in the process, what Christmas is really all about.

Today we'll talk specifically about connecting with our family and friends. If you want to get the most out of this Christmas, then forget (for awhile) what you need to buy and what you need to do, and spend some time focusing on the people you will see during the holidays. The first step in celebrating a simple Christmas is to connect on a deeper level with these people.

There's a passage of scripture that offers some suggestions on how to do that. It's from a letter written by Paul to the church in Thessalonica — a group of believers whom Paul loved very much. In this letter, he pours out his heart to them. The same way that he shares his heart with them is the way we need to share our hearts with our loved ones. Four verses in 1 Thessalonians 3 show us a Christmas list (three lists, actually) that we can make for family and friends. Let's take a look. First of all, to begin the process of experiencing a simple Christmas...

- **Make a list of the people you appreciate the most.**

Your wife, your husband, your children, your parents, your brothers and sisters, your friends, and on and on. Sometime during the week, take the time to make a list of them. And then, before the holidays are over, do two things:

*1.) Thank God for bringing them into your life, and*
*2.) Tell them how much they mean to you.*

This is what Paul did. In verse 9, Paul says...(v. 9) *How can we thank God enough for you in return for all the joy we have in the presence of God because of you?*

Paul was grateful for his relationship to the believers in Thessalonica; he expressed his gratitude to God and expressed his appreciation to them. He took the time to say "Thank you...I appreciate you...You fill my life with joy." This seems like such a simple thing, but I dare say that most of us don't do it nearly enough. I'm not an overly sentimental person, and it seems like the closer I get to someone, the more difficult it is for me to get mushy. Most men are this way — most real men, anyway. (Haha) But keep in mind, there's no way people will know how you feel about them unless you make an effort to tell them.

There's an old joke about the woman who complained to her husband, "You never tell me you love me," and he said, "Look, I said it when I married you. Until I take it back, it's still in effect." That kind of attitude may work for some of us, but it doesn't work for most people. If you want to establish a deeper connection with others, express your appreciation.

If you're an adult, chances are it's been a long time since you've told your brothers or sisters or mom or dad how much you love and appreciate them. And if you've been married more than a decade, chances are it's been awhile since you've told your spouse. So, tell them now. This Christmas is a good time to make up for lost time. You don't have to be melodramatic; it doesn't have to be like a scene from *Touched By An Angel*. Just tell them how you feel. In fact, you can use Paul's words: How can I ever thank God enough for all the joy you have brought into my life? Make a list of the people you love and tell them that you do.

- **Make a list of intangible gifts you can give to each one.**

*(v. 10) Night and day we pray most earnestly that we may see you again and supply what is lacking in your faith.* He wanted to meet with his friends in Thessalonica to build up their faith. He knew, at that particular time, it was what they needed most. As you think of all the people you love, take some time to think about something you can give to each one—something they really need. I'm not talking about action figures or neckties or potholders—I'm talking about something more personal. Something non-material. Something intangible. There is something you can give to each one on your list—a word of encouragement, a smile, a hug, a pep-talk, an apology, a compliment. Ask yourself, "What does this person need most? What can I say to them? What can I do for them? How can I give them a lift?"

I have a friend who saves up jokes for me. He knows I like to laugh, so every time I see him, he gives me something to laugh about. And he nearly always begins by saying, "When I heard this, I thought of you." The fact is, I appreciate that part more than I do the joke.

There's a story about a missionary school teacher in Africa who had been teaching her students about Christmas, and she told them how we give gifts to one another at Christmas time. A few days later one of her students brought her a gift—a beautiful sea shell. She asked him where he got it and he said, "I walked to the beach and picked it out for you." The school was several miles from the ocean, so she knew it had been a long walk for him. She said, "You shouldn't have gone so far to get a gift for me." The student said, "The long walk was part of the gift."

This year, in addition to the gifts that you buy for the people you love, make an effort to give each one something intangible—something that tells them how special they are to you. Thirdly...

- **Make a wish list for each one; share it with them and God.**

I use the term "wish list" because it is, after all, Christmas. What I really mean is a prayer list. This is what Paul did for the Thessalonians. He said...*(v. 12-13) May the Lord make your love increase and overflow for each other and for everyone else, just as ours does for you. May he strengthen your hearts so that you will be blameless and holy in the presence of our God and Father when our Lord Jesus comes with all his holy ones.*

Paul is saying, "What I want for you, dear friends, is that you grow in love, and strength, and holiness." Think of the people on your list. What do you want for each one? Obviously, you want what is best for them. Just by telling them this, you will strengthen their hearts and encourage them.

My young cousin auditioned for a part in a play. His mother knew the competition was intense for this part, and that her son's chances of getting it were rather slim. Each time he talked about the audition, she would try to temper his optimism with some motherly realism, saying something like, "Well, you know there are a lot of people who want that part...some of the people who auditioned have been in professional productions...Even if you don't get the part you want, being in the play will be a good experience..." and on and on. Finally, he said to her, "Mom, can't you just say, 'I hope you get the part.'?"

There are few things as pleasant as hearing someone say they wish the best for you. This season I encourage you to tell each one on your list what your prayer is for them. And say it in an uplifting way. Don't say, "My prayer is that you'll stop being a lazy bum." There's a better way to phrase it, such as: "My prayer is that you'll discover God's mission for your life, and begin to fulfill it."

The greatest gift you can give anyone is to pray for them — for a number of reasons. One reason is that it works. When you pray for someone, God begins to move in that person's life. Another reason is that people find strength in knowing that others are praying for them.

A few years ago I shared a prayer request with a friend in Oklahoma. He said, "Is it ok if I share this request with my prayer group?" I said, "Sure." Over the course of the next several weeks I received about a half-dozen cards in the mail from people who wanted me to know they were praying for me. That meant more than I can say. If you'll take the time to pray for the people in your life, two things will happen.

*1.) You'll strengthen that person.*

*2.) You'll strengthen your relationship to that person.*

## CONCLUSION

Think of those God has placed in your life—those you love the most, those who bring you the most joy. They will be an integral part of your Christmas this year. How you relate to them will determine what kind of Christmas you have.

If you want a great Christmas—if you want to get past the holiday hype and discover the joy of a simple Christmas—then connect on a deeper level with the people you love. Tell them what they mean to you, and give thanks to God for them. In addition to toys and trinkets, give them something intangible and meaningful. And most of all, create a prayer list especially for them, and share it with them and with God.

One of the greatest gifts God has given us is each other—our family and friends. Let's enjoy these gifts; let's celebrate Christmas together.

SERIES: A SIMPLE CHRISTMAS
**HOW TO BEAT THE HOLIDAY BLUES**
LUKE 1:68-79

There's a myth that suicides increase during the Christmas holiday season. It's not true; the Mayo Clinic reports that a recent 35-year long study found no increase in suicides during the period between Thanksgiving and New Year's Day. The Mayo Clinic also reports that even though people aren't more inclined to become clinically depressed during this time of year, many are inclined to get the holiday blues. There's even a medical term for it: SAD—*Seasonal Affective Disorder*.

Emotions that we keep at bay during other times of the year tend to surface during this season. For many people, the Christmas holidays aren't a celebration, they're a time of tension, disappointment, loneliness, and frustration. No doubt most of you have experienced this once or twice. For some of you, it's an annual event. Today we'll look at *How To Beat the Holiday Blues*. First, let's take a quick look at the cause.

**What causes the blues?**

*Unrealistic Expectations.* During Christmas we want everything to be perfect, and, of course, it never is. One mom told me, "At Christmas I want to be able to at least pretend I have a normal home." She expected the dysfunction of her family life to disappear just because it was cold outside, but it never did. Each year she became a little more disappointed.

*Financial Pressure.* Each year we want to give the kids their "best Christmas ever." In addition to our kids' gifts, we have a zillion other gifts to buy for extended family members, friends, co-workers, employers, and on and on. Plus we spend more on food and travel and decorations.

*Busy Schedule.* Even the most sedentary people—people who socialize only once or twice a month during the rest of the year—have a packed calendar during the month of December.

There are parties and programs to attend, and we have to squeeze in time to do our shopping and baking and visiting and all the other activities that come with the season. We get too busy, and we feel like we're in such a hurry we don't have time to enjoy Christmas.

*Family Conflict.* Some people you see only once a year for a good reason: you don't get along. There are relational conflicts that date back decades, and every year these wounds are re-opened. One young father said, "The part I most dread is visiting my parents. We travel 500 miles just to endure 3 days of criticism about every detail of our lives—from how we raise our children to the kind of church we attend. But if we ever decided not to go home for the holidays, we would never hear the end of it."

These are some of the things that cause the holiday blues—there are probably others—and today we will look at some way we can avoid these pitfalls. Christmas doesn't have to be stressful. It can be a time of experiencing God's presence and connecting with our loved ones on a deeper level. But those things cannot happen if we spend too much, do too much, and expect too much from everyone else around us.

Paul said, *Do not conform any longer to the pattern of this world, but be transformed by the renewing of your mind. (Romans 12:2)* Today we'll look at three ways to rethink your attitude about Christmas. You'll learn how to beat the holiday blues, and see show this season can be transformed into a simple, Christ-filled Christmas. These ideas come from Luke 1:68-79. This is the song that Zechariah sang when his son, John the Baptist, was born. The song isn't so much about the birth of his own son as it is about the coming of the new Messiah. Here are three things...

- **Rethink your expectations.**

People who struggle with disappointment often approach the holidays with the wrong kind of focus—they try too hard to make it a perfect Christmas for themselves. They mentally script out how everything should be and what everyone should do. Not only do they end up disappointed, everyone else ends up exhausted. People who expect too much are emotionally draining. So give yourself and everyone in your family a break: expect less. Don't demand perfection from yourself, or your kids, or your siblings, or anyone else.

Remember, your family is not on TV, and you are not June or Ward Cleaver. Some things won't happen as planned. You'll run out of wrapping paper, or you'll forget to buy batteries, or you won't be able to assemble the bike, or the turkey will be dry, or someone will show up late for the family meal, or the kids will get into a squabble, or the adults will get into a squabble, or all of the above.

Rethink your expectations about this holiday season. Instead of asking "What will this Christmas be like for me?" ask, "What will I be like this Christmas?" Instead of thinking about what you can get out of it, think about what you can give. Isn't that what we're trying to teach our children to do? Maybe we should try it, too. Approach Christmas with the attitude of a servant; see each event as an opportunity for ministry.

This is exactly what Zechariah prophesied for his son. He said his son ministry would be...*(v. 77, 79) to give [God's] people the knowledge of salvation through the forgiveness of sins...to shine on those living in darkness...to guide our feet into the path of peace.* In the next few weeks you'll see many people—including some you don't see very often—and you'll have a chance to minister to them...to be merciful, to be forgiving, to be a peacemaker.

Imagine the kind of Christmas everyone would have if your attitude became: Christmas doesn't have to be perfect for me this year; I just want to spread love and joy to everyone else. Sounds like something Pollyanna would say, doesn't it? Well, maybe, but people will sure appreciate it. Rethink your expectations this year; minister God's love to everyone. Secondly...

- **Rethink your obligations.**

In December you can easily find yourself with something to do every night of the week. At our house, in the next ten days we have 3 ballet performances, 2 band concerts (and special rehearsals for each one), a Christmas party to attend, and relatives coming in to visit—and Christmas is still weeks away! We haven't picked out our tree yet, or trimmed it; we haven't taken the kids to do their shopping (or finished all of ours), and what's more, we have relatives coming in. We haven't decorated the front of the house; we have a big, tangled ball of lights in the attic that needs to be unraveled; we haven't yet addressed our Christmas cards—in fact, I'm not even sure we've bought them yet—and did I mention that we have relatives coming in?

It's easy to get overwhelmed. There's all this stuff to do, and your schedule spins in circles until you finally admit there's no way you can do it all. Save yourself some trouble; realize it now. Remind yourself: "I can't do everything I want to do, or that everyone wants me to do, or all that I think I should do. I have to re-think my schedule and make sure I do those things that are most important."

It would be a shame to make it to a half-dozen parties but never have time to serve others. It would be a shame to see all the lovely decorations on the houses in the best neighborhoods, but to never notice the people this community who are in desperate need during this time. It would be a shame if Christmas became just a flurry of activity, preventing you from finding the opportunity to share Christ with someone else.

This Christmas season I'm challenging you to rethink your obligations. All those things you think you have to do in order to make this a perfect Christmas, well, maybe some of them aren't really all that important. Think about what really matters. In today's text, Zechariah gives us a clue. He's talking about why God is sending the Messiah to earth, and he says one reason is...
*(v. 74-75) ...to enable us to serve him out without fear, in holiness and righteousness before him all our days.*

Jesus came into this world in order to give us a whole new perspective on life. He came so that we could learn how to spend our days not serving ourselves, but serving him.

We serve him by serving others, so look for opportunities to do it. When you help someone, you offer your service not only to them, but to God. Rethink your obligations. Restructure your priorities. Give yourself a chance to do something for someone else this holiday season.

Some may ask, "What does this have to do with beating the blues?" Everything. It's hard to be depressed when you're helping others. It's how we are made. Helping others doesn't just benefit them, it benefits us, too. Solomon said...*A generous man will prosper. He who refreshes others will himself be refreshed.* (Proverbs 11:25)

Rethink your obligations. Instead of filling your schedule with activities that please only you, look for ways to serve others. And take joy in knowing that you are doing something to benefit someone else. Thirdly...

- **Rethink your celebrations.**

It's amazing how some celebrate Christmas—rocking around the Christmas tree, drinking too much at the office party, or judging how well it went by the gifts you get. Even Christians sometimes make the mistake of putting too much emphasis on the externals of the holiday—family time, big meals, unwrapping presents. There's nothing wrong with these things, but there's much, much more to celebrate at Christmas.

During my first year of ministry, Christmas fell on a Sunday. I was pastoring a church of about 50 people. On the Sunday before Christmas, one of the leaders came to me and said, "We've decided not to have church next Sunday." I thought he was joking, so I laughed. He said, "No...I'm serious. We all want to be with our families on Christmas day, and it's too much trouble to get out and come to church." I had already expected the Christmas Day turnout to be lower than usual, but I didn't expect that we would shut the doors of God's house on his Son's birthday! Later, I made this announcement: "Here's the deal. We're having church on Christmas Day. It will be a different kind of service. You don't have to dress up—in fact, you can bring the kids in their pajamas if you want. I'll bring my guitar and we'll sing Christmas carols, and we'll read the Christmas story, and we'll have communion."

I thought my family might be the only ones there, but as it turned out, almost everyone showed up. We had a simple service with singing and scripture reading. We held hands and prayed. We shared communion. Afterward, one lady in the church, (who never was my biggest fan) said to me, "That was one of the loveliest services I've ever been to." Of course, that might have been because I didn't preach. I think, however, it was because the service was a simple celebration of God's love shown to us through the gift of his Son.

I'm saying this: In addition to the family celebrations and parties, let's not forget to celebrate Jesus. Without him, our lives would be nothing. Without him, this world would be in total chaos. (You think things are bad now? Imagine what the world would be like if Jesus had never come.) Take some time this year to worship Christ as our Lord and Savior. It's a cliché, but it's true: Jesus is the reason for the season. Let's all celebrate him this Christmas. This is what Zechariah encouraged us to do...(v. 68) *Praise be to the Lord, the God of Israel, because he has come and redeemed his people. He has raised up a horn of salvation of for us...(v. 72)...to show mercy to our fathers, and to remember his holy covenant.*

## CONCLUSION

As we read in the book of Romans earlier, we are transformed by the renewing of our minds. Paul is saying: "Change your thoughts and you can change your life." I'm saying the same thing about Christmas: Change your thoughts, and you can change your Christmas.

You don't have to be on edge all month. You don't have to dread the hectic pace. You don't have to miss out on God's blessings. Rethink the way you approach Christmas. Rethink your expectations and your obligations—and look for ways to minister to and serve others. Rethink your celebrations—remember to focus your attention on Jesus: worship him and celebrate the wonder of love. This will help you beat the holidays, and will give you the best Christmas ever.

SERIES: A SIMPLE CHRISTMAS
**HOW TO GIVE CHRISTMAS GIFTS ALL YEAR LONG**
MATTHEW 2:1-12

Everyone agrees that we should be compassionate at Christmas, and it's a sociological fact that we are. People tend to give more and help others more during December than any other time. This is partly because we have more opportunities. For example, most of you have probably given money to the Salvation Army already, simply because someone was standing conveniently at the mall's entrance, ringing a bell. If the bell ringer was there in July, you would probably give then, too.

It's good that we're so willing to show kindness during the holidays, but we all know that our acts of compassion shouldn't be limited to the few weeks between Thanksgiving and Christmas. We should live and give with compassion year round. The story of the three wise men teaches us how to do that. These principles work 12 months a year. So, as you buy gifts this Christmas you can use these ideas, and you can also apply them in January, February, March, and so on. This story offers three principles on giving. Let's take a look at each one. First of all, when you give...

• **Give more than you expect to receive.**

When the wise men came to see Jesus, they knew they weren't going to a gift exchange. They were going to see a child, a newborn baby. They were visiting a child who was, quite literally, born in a barn. His parents were poor; the possibility of reciprocation didn't exist. Of course, the wise men didn't care. They came to give, not receive.

It's not that way with us, sometimes. Hard feelings have developed in families when someone didn't get back as much as they put in; they felt cheated. Understand: when it comes to giving, you can't be cheated. The objective in giving is to give more than you get back.

One of my co-workers suggested this to her family: "Let's give each other the same gift this year—$20 cash. When it comes time to open the presents, we'll take the $20 bill we brought, hand it to the person next to us. They'll take the $20 bill they brought and hand it to the person next to them, all the way around the room. That way, we all get a fair deal. Everyone walks in with $20 and walks out with $20, and no one is unhappy." She was joking, of course, but there are probably some people who liked the idea. That's not what giving is about.

James Hewitt tells a story of a college friend named Paul who received a car from his brother for Christmas. A kid on the street saw the new car and said, "Hey mister, is that yours?" Paul said, "Yes, my brother gave it to me for Christmas." The kid was amazed and said, "Your brother gave it to you and it didn't cost you nothing? Boy I wish..." Paul thought he was going to say, "I wish I had a brother like that." But the street kid surprised him. He said, "Boy, I wish I could be a brother like that." There is a tremendous reward in giving. Give more than you expect to get.

- **Give out of love, not out of obligation.**

*(v. 11) They saw the child with his mother Mary, and they bowed down and worshipped him.* Have you ever received a gift from someone with the impression that the gift was given more out of duty than desire? As if they really had a choice, they wouldn't have given you anything at all? Have you ever given a gift with that attitude? That's not giving a gift, it's paying a bill. When you give with that attitude, people can tell.

The Bible teaches us to give out of love. Paul said...*Each man should give what he has decided in his heart to give, not reluctantly or under compulsion, for God loves a cheerful giver. (2 Corinthians 9:7)*

My friend had a fight with her sister two years ago. They're still not on speaking terms—but each Christmas they still exchange gifts. When I asked why she said, "Because I give gifts to everyone in my family." Obviously, this gift has little meaning and little value. The gift she really needs to give is the gift of reconciliation.

It's a simple as this: if your gift isn't motivated by love, it doesn't matter what the gift costs—it's worthless. The wise men's gifts were special, not because they were valuable, but because they were given with a heart full of love for Jesus.

A few years ago when Homeland Security Director Tom Ridge was governor of Pennsylvania, he sent out $100 rebates on school-district property taxes. This happened just before the election, so naturally he was accused of trying to buy votes. However, hundreds of tax-payers responded in an unexpected way: they returned the money to the school district. The Philadelphia school district received more than $40,000 in rebate gifts. The most interesting part is that the majority of gifts came from people outside the Philadelphia school district, who felt the under-funded city schools needed the money more than their suburban schools. These people had nothing to gain by sending their money to another school district. They did it because they cared. (*Newsweek*, Dec.11, 2000, p.64) Give out of love, not obligation. The third principle for giving is...

- **Give gifts that tell people what they're worth.**

*(v. 11) They opened their treasures and presented him with gifts of gold, and of incense, and of myrrh.* Interesting gifts for a child, aren't they? What did they mean? According to custom, gold was the gift for a king, incense was for a priest, and myrrh was used to embalm the bodies of the dead. When the wise men brought their gifts to Jesus, they didn't come bearing trinkets for a child. They brought gifts that indicated who he truly was—the king of kings, the great high priest, the one who would die for the sins of the world.

When you give, give a gift that says "I believe in you. You're worth something." I think it was in Los Angeles that a drive began a few years ago to give new shopping carts to the homeless, since many of them were using old, beat-up carts. Now, we have an obligation to help the homeless. However, I don't think the solution can be found in giving them new shopping carts. It's a gift that seems to say, "You're homeless and that's all you'll ever be, so here's a new buggy. Now leave us alone." A much better gift, obviously, would be to give the homeless a place to sleep, or job training, or substance abuse counseling, or whatever it is they need to become the person God created them to be. We need, as a society, as a church, and as individuals, to look for ways to give gifts that affirm the value of the person receiving the gift. We can't give with an attitude that says, "I give because I'm generous." We must give with an attitude that says, "I give because you're worth it."

The Talmud says, "He who gives a coin to a poor man obtains six blessings, but he who addresses him with words of comfort obtains eleven blessings." What does it mean? It means that we should give in such a way that builds up the recipient.

Too often we give condescendingly, with strings attached. We try to use our gifts to manipulate people into doing what we want them to do. The gift comes with a subtle message: "Now you owe me." This isn't giving, it's bribery. It doesn't build up the one who receives the gift. Neither does it glorify God.

The wise men brought valuable gifts to Jesus because they recognized his value. When you give, give a gift that says, "You're worth something to me."

## CONCLUSION

In this series we've been talking about how to re-discover the simplicity of Christmas. Two weeks ago we talked about finding ways to give intangible gifts to those you love. Last week we talked about beating the holiday blues by being a servant to others. And this week, again, we see how giving plays a crucial role in experiencing Christ's presence during Christmas—and throughout the rest of the year.

The key is found in giving. Give more than you hope to get; give out of love, not obligation; give in a way that says, "You are worth something to me."

*SERIES: A SIMPLE CHRISTMAS*
**WHAT CHRISTMAS IS ALL ABOUT**
MICAH 5:4-5

This year we should keep a list of all the things people say Christmas is supposed to be about—because each year it seems the descriptions get a little crazier. You hear it on talk shows, in Christmas specials, in office conversations, in political speeches, and on and on. You know what I mean. Things like, "Giving—isn't that what Christmas is all about?" Or, "Helping the unfortunate—isn't that what Christmas is all about?" Or, "Being with family—isn't that what Christmas is all about?"

The best one I've heard (or the worst, depending on your perspective) was found in Jay Leno's *Book of Headlines*. An advertisement placed by The Center for Dental Implants says, "The Gift of Chewing Is What the Holidays Are All About." That solves the mystery, doesn't it? You wonder why we put up trees, decorate our houses, wrap presents, take time off work, and travel great distances to see relatives? It's so people can chew.

This might come as a surprise, but the Bible has a different idea regarding the meaning of the Christmas season. That's what we'll look at today. The prophet Micah foretold Bethlehem as the birth place of the Messiah. He said...*(v. 2-3) But you, Bethlehem Ephrathah, though you are small among the clans of Judah, out of you will come for me one who will be ruler over Israel.*

This is a reference to Christmas. He's saying that Christ would be born in Bethlehem. He goes on to say...*(v. 4-5) He will stand and shepherd his flock in the strength of the Lord, in the majesty of the name of the Lord his God. And they will live securely, for then his greatness will reach to the ends of the earth. And he will be their peace.*

These two simple verses teach us what Christmas is all about. They tell us why Jesus came into the world, and what he expected to accomplish here. Micah says that Jesus came to be a shepherd to his flock. He came to take care of us. To lead us. To protect us. To save us. He came to be our shepherd. What does that mean — that Jesus is our shepherd? Today we'll look at three ways he wants to be your shepherd. First of all…

- **He gives you strength.**

(v. 4) *He will stand and shepherd in the strength of the Lord.* What Christmas is all about is that you don't have to live life in your own strength. You don't have to handle it on your own. You have help. You can turn to God for strength, and he will give it to you.

While attempting to rescue a fellow soldier, Bob Wieland lost both his legs in Vietnam. He had dreamed of being a professional baseball player after the war, but that dream was gone forever. Many men in this situation are overcome with bitterness, but Bob wasn't. He said, "I lost my legs, not my heart", and he continued his quest for athletic achievement. He walks on his hands now, and has completed a three year Walk Across America. He has participated in the Race Across America on a custom-made bicycle, and in the Hawaii Ironman Triathlon. He can bench press an amazing 507 pounds. How does he do it? He said that he learned to cast all his cares on Jesus [1 Peter 5:7], and he learned how *the weakness of God is stronger than man's strength. (1 Corinthians 1:25)* In his words, "I do the best I can to apply the Word of God to my life, because I know it works."

That's the kind of strength Jesus offers. No matter what happens, we can depend on him to get us through. Our lives don't have to be characterized by failure, or bitterness, or missed opportunities. He will give you the strength to face whatever comes your way.

That's what Christmas is all about. It means you are not alone. You are not a victim of the circumstances life throws your way. You have a shepherd, and you can live in his strength. Are you facing challenges right now that are bigger than you are? Are you in a battle that you don't have the strength to win on your own? You don't have to face it alone. God will be your strength. In fact, trying to live in your own strength, without

God's help, is a recipe for disaster. Isaiah says...*But see here, you who live in your own light and warm yourselves from your own fires and not from God's; you will live among sorrows. (Isaiah 50:11)*

This kind of living leads only to sorrow. Jesus came to save us from such futility. He came to give us strength for daily living. That's what he wants to do. Secondly...

- **He gives you security.**

Let's face it: We live in an insecure world. Neither certainty nor safety exist, even though we spend our lives trying to find both. We look to the government, or our employer, or our investments, or our relationships—and none of them can give the security we need.

Like Bob Wieland learned in Vietnam, at any moment life can come crashing down around us. One simple word can change everything—a word like "divorce" ...or "cancer" ...or "downsizing." We hear that word and suddenly the world doesn't seem so safe anymore. The fact is, we don't know what will happen tomorrow; we don't even know what will happen later today. We can't depend on the world to offer security, because it doesn't have it to give. There's only one place we can find security. Micah said...*(v. 4) And they [his flock] will live securely, for then his greatness will reach to the ends of the earth.*

Jesus offers the security of knowing that he is in control, and he has the power and ability to take care of us. That's what a shepherd does, and that is what he wants to do for you. Listen to these words from Ezekiel. *I myself will tend my sheep and have them lie down, declares the Sovereign Lord. I will search for the lost and bring back the strays. I will bind up the injured and strengthen the weak...(Ezekiel 34:15-16)*

What's he saying? He's saying "I will take care of you. You are safe with me. I will tend to you. If you're lost, I will find you. If you stray, I will bring you back. If you're injured I will strengthen you. I am your shepherd. I will take care of you." God made this promise..."*Never will I leave you, never will I forsake you.*" *(Hebrews 13:5)* Jesus also said..."*My sheep listen to my voice. I know* them, and they follow me. I give them eternal life, and they shall never perish; no one can snatch them out of my hand." (John 10:27-28)

You want security? Jesus offers it to you. That's why he came into the world...that's what Christmas is all about. He offers the kind of security the world cannot—security based not on things and circumstances, but on his never-ending love for you. And his greatness, Micah says, reaches to the ends of the earth. There is no place you can go, or nothing that can happen, that extends beyond the power of God to take care of you.

Sheep find no safety in themselves. They can't protect themselves from the enemy, and they can't take care of themselves on their own. They need a shepherd, and so do we. We need protection from the world. We need protection from the enemy. We need protection in the midst of disaster, and only Jesus can give it to us. That's why he came: to give you security.

- **He gives you serenity.**

Have you seen the Seinfeld where George's dad, Frank Costanza, learns the relaxation technique of saying "Serenity Now"? When his blood pressure starts to rise, his doctor told him to say, "Serenity Now." Only Frank doesn't say it, he screams it. And it doesn't work. No matter how loudly he bellows "Serenity Now", it never comes. George's friend who was in a mental hospital tells him, "Serenity Now doesn't work. That's what put me in the institution. It's 'Serenity Now', insanity later."

It is just a little insane to think we can find peace by shouting "Serenity Now"—and that's about how foolish some of our other attempts at finding peace are. We try to find peace by drinking alcohol, or over-eating, or working day and night, or jumping from relationship to relationship, and it simply doesn't work.

We don't live in a peaceful world. Most people don't have inner peace, and you only have to glance at the headlines to remind yourself that external peace doesn't exist either. Jesus came to bring peace to all who follow him. His birth was foretold by Micah with the words...*(v. 5) And he will be their peace.* His birth was announced by the angels, who said..."*Glory to God in the highest, and on earth peace to men..."* (Luke 2:14) And as Jesus was approaching death, he said to his disciples..."*Peace I leave with you; my peace I give you....Do not let your hearts be troubled and do not be afraid".* (John 14:27) Jesus came to give us peace. Even when we can't experience peace in the world around us, we can experience his peace in our inner world.

Jesus came to take away all the things that destroy our peace. He wants to carry your burdens; he wants to lift your anxieties, he wants to take away your sins. Those things that tend to make you miserable are the very things Jesus came to fix. That's what he wants to do. He wants to be your shepherd. He wants to give you peace.

**CONCLUSION**

It's humbling to admit we can't take care of ourselves, but that's what we must do. In the Bible, we're compared to sheep, and it's not exactly a flattering comparison. Sheep aren't industrious; they don't work for you. They don't protect the family; no one ever has a "guard sheep." Neither are they particularly bright; you never see sheep in a circus act. The one thing sheep can do, by nature, is follow the shepherd. They're good at following. They're good at trusting. And that's what God wants you to do: he wants you to follow him...he wants you to trust him.

He sent Jesus to be a shepherd to all who would follow him. He will take care of you. You can cast all your cares and concerns, all your worries and anxieties, all your sin and unbelief on him, and he will take them all away. That's what Jesus came to do. Remember the words from Ezekiel...*I will search for the lost and bring back the strays. I will bind up the injured and strengthen the weak...(Ezekiel 34:16)*

Jesus came to be a shepherd, to help you live each day in his strength, to give you the kind of security this world simply cannot offer, and to fill you with peace. He came to seek and save the lost, so that all who follow him may experience life in all its fullness. That's what Christmas is about.

| | | | |
|---|---|---|---|
| Genesis 2:18-24 | 109 | John 2:1-11 | 117 |
| Genesis 45:1-15 | 187 | John 10:22-30 | 91 |
| Exodus 20:9-11 | 327 | John 14:23-24 | 97 |
| Numbers 11:4-34 | 245 | John 15:1-8 | 239 |
| Joshua 3:7-17 | 337 | John 20:1-18 | 332 |
| 1 Samuel 17 | 317 | John 20:19-31 | 257 |
| Isaiah 43:1-7 | 11 | Acts 16:16-34 | 103 |
| Psalm 4 | 205 | Romans 6:1-23 | 53 |
| Psalm 5 | 35 | Romans 8:1-17 | 61 |
| Psalm 13 | 47 | Romans 8:26-39 | 67 |
| Psalm 19 | 23 | 1 Cor. 9:24-27 | 253 |
| Psalm 31 | 209 | 1 Cor. 12:1-7 | 17 |
| Psalm 37 | 197 | 2 Cor. 9:6-15 | 351 |
| Psalm 51 | 73 | Ephesians 3:1-12 | 5 |
| Psalm 55 | 41 | Ephesians 4:2 | 231 |
| Psalm 107:23-32 | 165 | Philippians 1:3-11 | 305 |
| Psalm 127 | 31 | Philippians 4:4-7 | 211 |
| Isaiah 6:1-8 | 157 | 1 Thess. 3:9-13 | 359 |
| Isaiah 43:1-7 | 11 | 1 Thess. 5:17 | 281 |
| Isaiah 55:1-5 | 223 | 2 Thess. 1:11-12 | 133 |
| Jeremiah 17:9-10 | 273 | 1 Timothy 1:12-14 | 85 |
| Ezekiel 37:1-14 | 149 | 1 John 5:9-13 | 141 |
| Micah 5:4-5 | 375 | 1 Peter 1:3-9 | 345 |
| Matthew 2:1-12 | 371 | Timothy 1:12-14 | 85 |
| Mark 10:46-52 | 313 | | |
| Mark 16:1-8 | 79 | | |
| Luke 1:68-79 | 365 | | |
| Luke 7:36-50 | 173 | | |
| Luke 12:13-21 | 265 | | |
| Luke 12:57-59 | 181 | | |
| Luke 15:11-24 | 125 | | |
| Luke 18:1-8 | 319 | | |

www.ingramcontent.com/pod-product-compliance
Lightning Source LLC
Chambersburg PA
CBHW020347170426
43200CB00005B/75